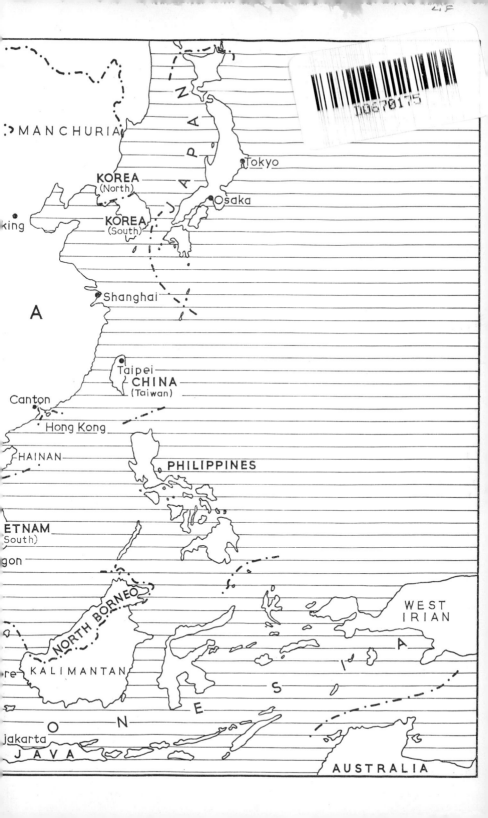

ECONOMIC DEVELOPMENT
IN EAST ASIA

ECONOMIC DEVELOPMENT IN EAST ASIA

By

E. STUART KIRBY

FREDERICK A. PRAEGER, *Publishers*

NEW YORK · WASHINGTON

BOOKS THAT MATTER

*Published in the United States of America in 1967 by
Frederick A. Praeger, Inc., Publishers, 111 Fourth
Avenue, New York, N.Y. 10003.*

© George Allen & Unwin Ltd., 1967

Library of Congress Catalog Card Number: 67-26565

PRINTED IN GREAT BRITAIN

TO
PROFESSOR G. C. ALLEN

*who guided me and many others
in this field*

*on the occasion of his retirement from
the Chair of Political Economy
at Universtiy College, London*

Contents

INTRODUCTION

Subject	15
ECAFE	15
Communist Asia	17
Developing countries	17
Diversity and separateness	18
Sources and footnoting	19

1. ASIAN PERSPECTIVES

Diffuse development	21
Economic dependence on the West	22
Colonialism	23
Asia among the underdeveloped Regions	24
War and liberation	25
Nationalism and development	27
Technology and pragmatism	29

2. POPULATION PRESSURE

The lot of Esau	32
Distribution of the population	33
Labour power	35
The exponential curve	35
Population policy	37

3. FOOD SHORTAGE

The Malthusian problem	42
Cereals	42
Rising demand and imports of foodstuffs	45
Staple foods: area and yield	46
Basic diet changes	48
Irrigation	50
Fisheries	52
Meat	54
Other food products	55
Malnutrition	56
The farm-food balance	57

4. FOREIGN TRADE

(a) Total trade relationships	61
The growth of trade	61
Total exports	64
Total imports	65
The overall balance of trade	67
Shares of the countries	67
(b) Interregional comparisons	67
Regional distribution of world trade: destinations of exports	67

Regional distribution of world trade: sources of
imports   70
Regional distribution of the balance of trade   71
(c) Geographical structure of the Region's trade   72
Distribution of the Region's exports   72
Distribution of the Region's imports   74
Origins of imports   74
(d) The instability of trade   76
Instability in the total trade   76
Variability in import-sources   77
Variability in export-destinations   78
The irregular balance of trade   80
Variations in the size of the deficit   82
Depletion of exchange assets   84
(e) The terms of trade   85
Value shares   85
Prices and terms of trade   87
(f) Development goods and consumption goods   88
The weight of primary products   96

5. THE RAW MATERIAL BASE
Minerals   98
(a) fuels: coal, natural gas, petroleum   98
(b) metals: iron, manganese, chrome, vanadium, cobalt,
molybdenum, tin, nickel, tungsten, copper, zinc, lead,
antimony, mercury, bauxite, magnesite, asbestos   101
(c) chemicals and others: sulphur, potash, phosphate, rock,
salt   113
(d) diamonds, gold and silver   114

6. INDUSTRIALIZATION
The scale of world progress   116
Rates of production-increase   121
Measuring the progress of industrialization   125
Electricity   136
Textiles   139
Inception of a synthetic rubber industry in Japan   147
Iron and steel   148
Miscellaneous industries   151
The industrial structure of East Asia   155

7. TRANSPORT AND COMMUNICATIONS
Shipping   159
Railways   166
Motor vehicles   168
Telephones   168
Inland telegrams   170
Foreign telegrams   172

Inland letter mail 173
Foreign letter mail 174
Proportion of domestic to foreign mail 177

8. NATIONAL BUDGETS
Deficit budgeting 188
The public debt 192
The burden of armaments 196
Welfare items 197
Economic development heads 197
Taxation 199

9. ECONOMIC PLANNING
Partial planning: Cambodia, South Vietnam, Indonesia,
Philippines, Burma, Ceylon 203
Large-scale national democratic plans: India, Pakistan 207
Some planning difficulties exemplified by the case of India 212
Planning in a developed capitalist country: Japan 215
Communist planning 216
No planning: Hong Kong 217
A varied pattern 218

10. INTERNATIONAL AID
America and Western aid 219
Communist aid 225

11. THE RESULTS FOR THE ASIANS
The welfare of the individual 227
Medical facilities 227
Housing 228
National Income 230
Inflation 233
Productivity 237
Industrialization: a conclusion 240

INDEX

List of Tables

INTRODUCTION
0.1 Countries included in this study 15
0.2 Membership of ECAFE 16

CHAPTER 1
1.1 The East Asian developing region's ranking in the underdeveloped world 24

CHAPTER 2
2.1 Area and population 33
2.2 Density of population 34
2.3 Crude rates of live births and deaths: per annum 36
2.4 Population projection: East Asia 38
2.5 Urbanization 39

CHAPTER 3
3.1 Indices of agricultural production 43
3.2 Population increase and production of basic cereals 44
3.3 World fisheries 53
3.4 Asian and world fisheries 53
3.5 Production of meat 55
3.6 Calories and protein, *per capita* 56
3.7 Production, exports and imports of cereals 58
3.8 Total imports of food 58

CHAPTER 4
4.1 East Asia and world trade 62-63
4.2 Balance of visible trade 66
4.3 Trade of the ECAFE Region: distribution between its countries 67
4.4 Direction of the exports of the ECAFE Region 73
4.5 East Asian and world imports 74
4.6 Sources of imports by the ECAFE Region 75
4.7 Distribution of the Region's total trade 77
4.8 Distribution of the Region's total imports 78
4.9 Distribution of the Region's total exports 78
4.10 Indices of the Region's trade, by main areas 80
4.11 Quantum index and unit value index of trade 80
4.12 Balance of trade, ECAFE Region 82
4.13 Deficit on the balance of trade as a percentage of total trade 83
4.14 Balance of visible trade: East Asian and world trends 84
4.15 Trade deficits and exchange reserves: developing ECAFE countries 85
4.16 World index of export prices of food and raw materials 87

4.17 World price-indices of some basic-resource commodities   87
4.18 Imports, consumption goods and capital goods: developing countries of the Region   88
4.19 Changes in the percentage shares of consumption goods and capital goods in total imports; developing countries of the Region   90
4.20 Japan's imports, consumption goods and capital goods   93
4.21 Changes in the percentage shares of consumption goods and capital goods: Japan   94
4.22 Percentage distribution of imports, capital goods and consumption goods   95
4.23 Quantity of exports of primary products from the Region   96
4.24 Percentage distribution of exports, capital goods and consumption goods   97

CHAPTER 5
5.1   Production of coal   99
5.2   Production of natural gas   100
5.3   Production of crude petroleum   100
5.4   Production of iron ore   101
5.5   Production of manganese ore   104
5.6   Production of chrome ore   104
5.7   Production of molybdenum ore   105
5.8   Production of tin concentrates   105
5.9   Non-ferrous metals: world consumption and prices   106
5.10 Consumption of tin in various countries   106
5.11 International Tin Council's Buffer Stock and market price   107
5.12 Reserves of tin, 1960-70   108
5.13 East-West trade in tin   108
5.14 Production of nickel ore   109
5.15 Production of tungsten ore   109
5.16 Production of copper ore   110
5.17 Production of zinc ore   111
5.18 Production of lead ore   112
5.19 Production of bauxite   113
5.20 Production of salt   114
5.21 Production of gold   115

CHAPTER 6
6.1   General index of industrial production   117
6.2   Index of production: all manufactures   118
6.3   Production indices: heavy industry and light industry   118
6.4   Changes in industrial production in various periods   120
6.5   Distribution of the working population   126
6.6   Share of industry in gross national product   133
6.7   Increase in the total production of energy   134

6.8 Total and *per capita* consumption of energy, East Asia 135
6.9 Electricity: installed capacity in the region 136
6.10 *Per capita* total consumption of energy: by Regions 137
6.11 *Per capita* consumption of energy, East Asia 138
6.12 Cotton spindles: number of ring spindles installed 139
6.13 Production of cotton yarn 140
6.14 Cotton looms installed in factories 141
6.15 Production of woven cotton fabrics 143
6.16 Iron and steel production, East Asia and the world 149
6.17 Production of metallurgical coke, East Asia 151
6.18 Miscellaneous items of industrial production 153-154
6.19 Percentage distribution of value added in mining and manufactures 155
6.20a Index numbers of industrial production, world and East Asia 156
6.20b Index numbers of industrial production, non-Communist world and East Asia 156
6.21 Shares of Japan and India in the total value added in industry in East Asia 157
6.22 Indices of non-agricultural employment 157

CHAPTER 7

7.1 Merchant fleets of the world and the Region 161
7.2 Shipping in East Asia: vessels entered 162
7.3 Goods loaded and unloaded by international shipping 163
7.4 Cargo balance, Asia and the world 163
7.5 Goods loaded and unloaded, East Asia 164-165
7.6 Railway freight: East Asia and the world 166
7.7 Railway traffic: East Asia 167
7.8 Motor vehicles in use: East Asia 168
7.9 Number of telephones in use: Asia and the world 169
7.10 Telephones in use: Asian Region 169
7.11 Number of domestic telegrams sent and received 170
7.12 Foreign telegrams sent and received 171
7.13 Domestic letter mail 173
7.14 Foreign letter mail 174
7.15 Ratio of domestic to foreign letter mail 176

CHAPTER 8

8.1 National budgets: heads of expenditure and receipts 178-189
8.2 Growth of expenditures, revenues and deficits 192-193
8.3 Public debt, East Asian countries 195-196

CHAPTER 9

9.1   Investments in India's Second and Third
      Five Year Plans   209
9.2   Investments in India's proposed Fourth Five
      Year Plan   211
9.3   Numbers of senior officials, India   212

CHAPTER 10

10.1 International aid received by East Asian
      countries from Western countries and UN
      agencies   221
10.2 International aid received by East Asian
      countries per head of population   221
10.3 International aid to East Asian countries,
      1958-60   222
10.4 Aid to Asia by the Communist countries   226

CHAPTER 11

11.1 Housing (densities)   228
11.2 Gross domestic product, by Regions   230
11.3 Index of total and *per capita* product, Asian
      Region   231
11.4 Annual growth in total and *per capita* GDP   232
11.5 Price indices   233
11.6 Parity rates for international income-com-
      parisons   234
11.7 GDP, total, at parity rates   235
11.8 GDP, *per capita,* at parity rates   237
11.9 The *per capita* income gap: Asian countries
      and others   238
11.10 Value of output per worker in certain
      countries   239
11.11 Value of output per worker, in sectors—
      agricultural and other   240
11.12 *Per capita* consumption of energy   241

INTRODUCTION

This book reviews the economic development from 1945 to 1965 of the following fifteen countries of East Asia:

Table 0.1. Countries included in this study

Burma	Japan
Cambodia	Korea: South
Ceylon	Malaya[a]
China: Mainland	Pakistan
China: Taiwan	Philippines
Hong Kong	Thailand
India	Vietnam: South[b]
Indonesia	

Notes: [a] 'Malaya' includes Singapore and former British North Borneo Territories, where relevant. 'Malaysia' always includes these; 'Malaya: Federation' is used where they are excluded.
[b] 'Indochina' is used in overall reference to the former French Indochina, i.e. Cambodia, Laos, Vietnam/Annam and Cochin China.

All these appellations are used here only in a geographical sense for ease of reference, without political *parti-pris*. These fifteen countries will be referred to collectively below as 'East Asia' or 'the region' (with a small 'r').

ECAFE

Where the Region is mentioned – with a capital 'R' – reference is to the area covered by ECAFE (the United Nations Economic Commission for Asia and the Far East). After the war the Economic and Social Council of the UN recognized these Regions as special crisis-areas and established ECAFE (in 1947) and the Economic Commissions for Europe (ECE 1948 – pre-existing however under the League of Nations) Latin America (ECLA 1948) and latterly Africa (ECA 1958).

The area of ECAFE is less well defined than that of the other Commissions. The insertion in the title of the word 'and' between 'Asia' and 'the Far East' is semantically most curious. The Far East is certainly very much in and of Asia. This fumbling formulation betrays the initial uncertainty about the territories and problems to be covered, which has since been greatly clarified, but the illogical title remains. The scope of ECAFE has been extended as follows.

Table 0.2. Membership of ECAFE

Governments of:

Foundation members (1947)	Added later	
Australia	Afghanistan	1953
	Brunei (Associate)	
	Burma	1948
	Cambodia	1954
	Ceylon	1954
China		(Taiwan)
France		
Hong Kong (Associate)		
India		
	Indonesia	1951
	Iran	1958
	Japan	1953
	Korea	1954 (South)
	Laos	1954
	Malaya (Federation of)	1957
	Mongolia	1961
	Nepal	1954
Netherlands		
	New Zealand	1948
	North Borneo (Associate)	
Pakistan		
Philippines		
	Singapore (Associate)	
Thailand		
UK		
USA		
USSR		
	Vietnam	1954 (South)

The *geographical scope* of ECAFE – the area of its study, reporting and concern – related initially to the *Asian* countries in Table 0.2 other than Iran which was added later. Most recently the *Oceanic* countries (Australia, New Zealand and Western Samoa) were added.

ECAFE's foundation *terms of reference* were to promote measures to 'raise the level of economic activity' and strengthen economic relations intra-Regionally (within the Region) and inter-Regionally (with other Regions and their countries) to make studies, collect, evaluate and disseminate information, perform advisory services and assist ECOSOC – in all the economic aspects, but including technical assistance. To these were added in 1959 to 'deal as appropriate with the social aspects of economic development and the inter-relationship of economic and social factors'.

ECAFE made prodigious progress in many respects in its first two decades, producing increasingly adequate informational and analytical work.

Certain non-Asian nations (France, the Netherlands, UK, USA and USSR) are important members, though their actual holding of territory in the area is significantly a thing of the past. Apart from Portuguese Timor and Macao the only colonial unit with no self-government or State sovereignty is now Britain's Crown Colony of Hong Kong; but the non-Asian member-countries of ECAFE are weighty and welcome participants, colleagues in its development. Hong Kong is now the only Associate Member of ECAFE; but participates fittingly as a place of startling industrialization, development and good government.

Thus the 'ECAFE Region' includes, besides the fifteen countries studied in this book, the West Asian or Middle-Eastern, North-Central Asian and (since 1964) Oceanic countries which were in ECAFE at the dates in question.[1]

COMMUNIST ASIA

Of the Asian communist states only Mongolia is a member of ECAFE, though their areas are within its geographical and subject scope. Obviously China looms gigantically in any consideration of the Region's – or the world's – problems. To omit Mainland China would be to leave at least half the canvas void and in many respects falsify the perspectives of what remained of the picture. Information on Communist China is by no means so scanty or so little analysed as is widely believed, but the difficulties of full or direct comparisons are evidently great.[2] Mainland China is dealt with as fully as possible in this book.

DEVELOPING COUNTRIES

After Japan's admission to ECAFE (later also to OECD) and particularly since the phenomenal recovery and expansion of Japan's economy from the mid-1950s, the term 'developing countries of the Region' is used to denote the rest of the Region, other than Japan (and, from 1964, Australia and New Zealand). In general, and in United Nations usage, Japan has since 1963 been classed among the advanced developed or industrialized countries.

'Developing countries' came to be the standard designation only at the end of the 1950s. Before the war the expression 'backward countries' was often used. After the war its pejorative tone was wholly unacceptable to newly independent countries with a much longer and more illustrious cultural and general history than some 'developed' countries. The term 'underdeveloped' tended to be substituted, but soon appeared to be subject to the same disapproval. 'Emergent', the epithet coined in the Bandung group, has been little used elsewhere. The Russians have not adopted it either. In its turn it, too, might be considered to be after all too slighting, as suggesting a fledgling status.

The separateness of Japan's economic or technical advancement is very clear. Japan figures as a 'workshop of the world'. To obtain truly Asian comparisons on a common denominator of stage of development Japan should often be excluded from the averaging. Until the extent of Japan's pre-eminence and its implications are fully realized there will be no full objectivity in judgments about the economy of the region. It is for example a brute fact that, despite the much propagandized efforts towards industrialization in Mainland China, the *addition* to industrial capacity occurring in Japan every two years since 1951 has represented the equivalent of the *whole* modern industrial capacity of China.

DIVERSITY AND SEPARATENESS

It is thus very misleading if 'the Region' is thought of as close-knit or integrated with a common or cohesive trend or policy of development in any such sense or manner as West Europe, North America, or even the British Commonwealth or EFTA. In the case of Asia the entry in Webster's Dictionary for 'Region' appears only too apt. Its attempt at definition concludes: '. . . hence, in general, an indefinite area'.

There is in Asia powerful 'negative unity': a sense of common problems, resistance and antipathy to 'colonialism'. Nevertheless Regionalism has not developed in any more positive sense, organizationally, functionally or in practice; despite substantial efforts in that direction which will be duly considered below.

First, the background must be considered more generally. Various further demarcations are in question. 'Asia' in general is an imprecise concept. To quote a most useful Western commentator:[3] 'Asian Asia' is that part of the world's largest landmass which is 'not fundamentally European or Mediterranean in its civilization'. Siberia is thus excluded, but not Soviet Central Asia. 'Asian Asia' is nevertheless 'a positive concept'; and particularly the area dealt with in this book, 'the Asiatic Triangle . . . the southern and eastern margins of the great continent'. This is South and South-East Asia; these further designations are necessarily employed. Together these areas constitute the great Fertile Crescent of the Eastern Hemisphere.

Geographers subdivide the Asiatic Triangle more specially into three 'realms' (which are also triangular on the map) namely: (a) South Asia: India, Pakistan and Ceylon. Population (c. 1960) 560 million. (But South Asia is generally used more loosely to refer to the whole southern half of Asia.)

(b) South-East Asia: Burma, Thailand, Indochina, Malaysia, Indonesia and the Philippines. Population 220 million.

(c) East Asia: China, Korea and Japan. Population 860 million. But East Asia is often used to include (b) above, as well as (c). Or to include all these three 'realms'; as it does in this book, with the exclusion of some peripheral areas which, in the period concerned, were not integral to the Regional development.

SOURCES AND FOOTNOTING

Except where otherwise specified, all figures and statements are from official sources; though inferences, comments, views and qualifications are the author's own. Among the large (and in the circumstances very creditable) statistical and general work of ECAFE which has been extensively drawn upon, particularly valuable items are ECAFE's *Annual Surveys* and *Bulletins*.[4]

Footnotes are used in this book only to indicate sources of information, titles and other details of publications: all substantive matter and comments are in the text. The notes are assembled, by chapters, at the end of the book; and preceded

by a list of abbreviations used in references. Finally there is a
full index; and maps of East Asia.

Chapter 1

ASIAN PERSPECTIVES

DIFFUSE DEVELOPMENT

Asian development involves one half of the world's population, and all the problems on which the future of the human race may depend. Generalizations and theories must be regarded with extreme caution; the countries are so different that aggregation is usually difficult and often misleading.

Civilization is older in Asia than in Europe; yet the Asian countries and regions have developed much more separately than the European, with far less of a common basis. In Europe there were continuous juxtapositions, fusions or overlaps – besides positive movements, even deliberate efforts at comprehensive acculturation – which have brought its twenty-odd nations so closely together that their combination in one political, social and economic unit now has its advocates.

Our fifteen Asian countries have not been subject – until very recently – to any such consolidating influences or pressures. They have developed along their own paths, with no cultural or economic fusion. This is not only because they differ much more strikingly than do the Western countries in soil, climate, race, religion, culture, resources and other parameters; it is due also to physical features creating objective as well as subjective barriers, not only between one Asian country and another but between parts of a single country. The separation may be by great deserts (such as those east of India and northwest of China), gigantic mountains (such as those of the Himalayas, Tibet or North Korea), impenetrable jungles (as between Burma, India, Thailand, Indochina and Malaysia), great rivers (such as the Mekong), or wide and stormy waters (such as the China Seas).

Some strong movements overswept these barriers: the military Pan-Asian conquests of the Mongols, the eastwards expansion of Buddhism from India, the persistent caravan trade across north-central Asia, the seafaring of the Arabs and others. Nevertheless, regionally-unifying influences came only recently, with the incursion of the Westerners. An Ancient Greek maxim is fulfilled most powerfully in Asia. The land has divided, more drastically than in the Mediterranean area; while the sea has united, it has done so only sporadically. Through long ages the East Asian countries communicated and traded relatively little with each other; at present they still traffic distinctly less among themselves than with other countries and regions of the world.[1]

ECONOMIC DEPENDENCE ON THE WEST

World maps illustrating the flow of goods or shipping – or of funds, persons, ideas or any other factor in human development – would show extremely heavy concentration in and around the North Atlantic, with less density in the Mediterranean, dwindling increasingly East of Suez; reviving only as Japan is approached, but thinning again over the Pacific. Off this main artery, the subsidiary inter-Asian links are very slender. Even the feeder-lines are not heavy; South and South-East Asian countries deal for the most part directly with industrialized countries.[2]

Moreover, the unevenness is distinctly increasing; though world trade and Asian trade have greatly expanded in recent times, the proportions between these flow-lines have become more divergent. East Asia's trade and shipping relations with the developed countries multiply and thicken distinctly more than do those within East Asia itself, especially those between its underdeveloped countries.

The first law of economic development in East Asia has from the outset been that water transport is cheaper (and usually easier) than land transport. This was vividly instanced in 1945-6 by the case of UNRRA supplies to China. The net cost of transporting these a mere 20-200 miles overland for the last stage of their journey in China was – quite apart from bribery and malfeasances – much higher than that of some 7,000 miles of sea carriage from the ports in the USA.

The distances involved are prodigious; for example, Tokyo is about as far from Shanghai as London from Gibraltar, Peking is roughly the same distance from Canton, the length and breadth of India about the same expanse. The distance from Singapore to Tokyo is about the width of the Atlantic from England to Canada. The distance from Singapore to Bombay is less; it is about the length of the whole Mediterranean. China is roughly the size of the United States, India and Pakistan similar in extent to Western Europe.

While 'colonialism' has largely disappeared in the first two post-war decades, in the economic aspects especially there is increasingly real dependence on the developed countries. Material and ideological considerations, subjective and objective reactions are widely mixed; they must be discussed together.

COLONIALISM

The basis for the direly needed and ardently desired economic development was formed in the era of Western colonialism; with lasting influence, though the colonial period was really short (in East Asia relevantly about 1845-1945). It is as necessary as it is difficult to judge objectively how far the outcome was affected by the scale, extent and depth of penetration of Western Colonialism on the one hand – which may easily be exaggerated in some propagandistic or emotive responses – and what was on the other hand inevitable for geographical, intrinsic or endogenous reasons.

The classic Marxist-Leninist formulation saw the colonialists' aim as securing raw materials and markets for their own manufactures: as an offshoot and extension of the Industrial Revolution. Philanthropic, intellectual or adventurist motivations were minor, from the point of view of economic development. Political or social changes were not pressed by the colonialists; rather they patronized and confirmed in power native rulers, feudal monopolists, indigenous vested interests, even Oriental despots, using rather than recasting the societies they found, they 'froze' the basic social structures and economic arrangements at some pre-modern stage of the latters' evolution.

The original and proper sense of 'colony' is a settlement abroad of populations from a homeland. In Asia, Western settlers were relatively few and did not form considerable groups. Certain 'enclaves' were sharply noticeable: mining or plantation areas, reproducing microcosmically the homeland conditions for the 'expatriates', were equipped from the metropolitan country, returned dividends and senior staff there. They were strikingly separate from the economy of the colony, being rather extensions of the home country. Less blatantly 'apart' were the white communities in the capital, port and market cities – economically at least – though they persisted in their social or caste barriers.

ASIA AMONG THE UNDERDEVELOPED REGIONS

Many comparisons are drawn between the developing Asian countries and the developed countries. Comparisons with the non-Asian underdeveloped areas are, however, also instructive. Table 1.1 shows broadly the share the developing countries of East Asia have in the total, not of the world's, but of all the

Table 1.1. *The East Asian developing region's ranking in the underdeveloped world*[3]

Percentage of total (Non-Communist) developing countries':

	1	2	3	4	5	6
	Population (1961)	Area (1961)	Gross Domestic Product (1958)	Exports (1963)	Imports (1963)	US Aid (1945-63)
Burma	1.59	1.02	.61	.81	.65	.00
Cambodia	.41	.27	.24	.27	.30	.70
Ceylon	.72	.10	.68	1.09	.88	.22
China: Taiwan	.81	.05	.67	.99	1.00	2.83
Hong Kong	.29	.00	.44	2.63	3.61	.12
India	31.55	4.89	16.45	4.96	6.56	20.07
Indonesia	6.82	2.85	3.67	2.10	1.43	1.68
Korea: South	1.86	.14	1.45	.26	1.56	6.10
Malaysia	.71	.49	1.37	6.72	6.28	.02
Pakistan	6.88	1.42	2.84	1.26	2.48	8.00
Philippines	2.12	0.44	2.99	2.19	2.03	1.45
Thailand	2.00	.77	1.12	1.41	1.66	.89
Vietnam: South	1.04	.25	.68	.23	.80	4.27
Total	56.80	8.69	33.21	24.92	29.24	46.35
Other Asia	3.58	8.76	2.76	2.89	4.00	3.99
Mediterranean —Near East	11.37	12.99	18.95	26.14	27.05	22.73
Tropical Africa	12.48	38.74	10.17	13.59	12.12	5.57
Latin America	15.77	30.82	34.91	32.46	27.58	21.36
Total (all underdeveloped countries in the non-Communist world)	100	100	100	100	100	100

underdeveloped countries' population, area, national income, international trade and American aid, in comparison with those in the other regions.

It is seen that these thirteen countries have just over half the total population of all developing countries in the world, only one-twelfth of their area, one-third of their income, a little over a quarter of their trade and nearly half of the American aid.

Per person the region as a whole has distinctly the least share of land area, income and trade of any underdeveloped area, and the least share of American aid (except tropical Africa) among the five regions. The differences are striking; e.g. the high position of Malaya and Hong Kong in trade and income and the comparatively high *per capita* incidence of aid in certain countries (though the absolute amounts per person, spread over the large total populations concerned, are, of course, relatively small). On the *per capita* basis the East Asian developing countries are in fact the world's poorest region.

WAR AND LIBERATION

Nineteenth-century colonialism inscribed on its banners 'Law and Order'. It introduced the world economy and the modern age to an East Asia little prepared for or inclined to such a development. Only in Japan was there a national, wide, purposeful and prompt response to this challenge. Elsewhere fatalism, apathy or quietism were widely and generally the characteristic Asian moods, often with some disdain of foreign materialism. Colonialism spread over the surface of this hemisphere, seizing its key points, but remained an external mould; it did not largely reshape or replace the inner foundations of the local social and economic structures. Modern nationalism did not become strong in Asia until the 1930s – and not strong enough to take power until 1945-50, when the framework of the older order lay shattered, mainly by forces quite other than internal nationalistic pressures.

It was the Second World War that disintegrated the old order, ravaging the economies, societies and policies of this whole Region so widely and deeply as to inaugurate a diametrically different era. Diverse and complex nationalisms, avidity for modernization, an intense and immediate desire for economic and technical progress, are the present traits.

The war was made by the Japanese militarists, paralleling the motives and methods of their allies the German Nazis and Italian Fascists. The Japanese had harried China since 1894. In 1931 they occupied Manchuria; and in 1937-8 all but the remote interior of China. At the end of 1941 and early in 1942, they swiftly occupied the Philippines, Indonesia, Indochina, Malaysia, Thailand and Burma. This whole Japanese-occupied area was declared to be the 'Greater East Asia Co-prosperity Sphere': with, for the first (and so far the only) time, a grandiose and comprehensive scheme for the integral economic development of the whole Region. Like the greater Nazi Reich, the development was to be on neo-pan-colonial or supracolonial lines, with Japan as the great industrial centre, supplied from this empire and finding its markets there.

Japan's economic warfare failed, almost as rapidly as its military Blitzkrieg had succeeded. The Coprosphere (as it was at once dubbed by Western propagandists with a classical education) immediately fell into two parts; an Inner Zone (Japan, Korea, East and South China, Formosa) and an Outer Zone (the rest). In 1942-3 Allied counter-attacks by sea, air and land brought transport in the Outer Zone very largely to a standstill; beginning the process of attrition whereby industrial Japan was very effectively blockaded. In 1944-5, the process was inexorably pushed into the Inner Zone, right up to Japan itself. Virtually all Japanese shipping was sunk. The twenty-four main cities of Japan and innumerable other targets were heavily bombed, with effects fully comparable to those in Germany, before the atomic bombs were released.

In the whole Region economic life was severely vitiated and extremely fragmented. Not merely each country but every district and locality had to fall back on the simplest and most dire self-sufficiency. People raised vegetables or inferior subsistence foods such as cassava. Wooden boats were built for the limited fishing or transportation. Hundreds of millions of Asians led improvised existences. The Japanese largely removed domestic and general stocks and fittings, as well as industrial equipment and supplies, to Japan. Hardly any replacements or maintenance were possible. The whole area fell into such dilapidation and decrepitude as was not seen in Occupied West Europe.

India, Pakistan and Ceylon on the Allied side were not overrun and not subject to these conditions. Their trade and industrialization in fact developed substantially during the war, but under various strains, especially the overloading of transport, organization and other facilities and the lack of normal peacetime maintenance.

In 1946-7 rationing and improvisation generally continued. Nowhere in the world were normal supplies available except in America. Overall shipping and feeding arrangements were made by the Allied Reoccupation authorities.

The Japanese fostered Asian nationalist groups or movements, by their own lights and for their own purposes, in their occupied territories (including an Indian movement). Broader Asian nationalist parties and organizations sprang up everywhere in strength. The days of foreign rule were numbered. Political clashes, civil and race strife followed in the whole Region.

Post-war East Asia was in extreme distress, penury and dislocation. It is necessary to note the nadir from which East Asia is now – parlously but substantively – rising into full development. The present resurgence started in large part from zero levels, at a time of abnormal difficulties. Indices based on the immediate post-war years may be misleading if this is not considered. In the extreme instance Communist China emitted abundant propaganda in terms of very large percentage increases over 1949; which is in perspective only if it is realized that 1949 did not represent 'par', but the conditions of extreme depression, standstill and disorder.

NATIONALISM AND DEVELOPMENT

The subsequent course has been nationalist, with the following salient aspects. The economic and social focus has been on industrialization. The political focus has been on a midway course, professing neutrality between systems. Blaming 'colonialism' for all difficulties is probably no more – but no less – significant than the ascription by naïve socialists of all evils on 'capitalism'. The state has however been the means, and planning the method, of evolution in the desired direction. This was inevitable. There was no other group able to undertake the tasks. Moreover, only the state could be ostensibly above the conflicts of interest which are necessarily involved.

The universal drive for industrialization was conditioned in

Asia by the circumstances of the epoch of the Second World War. Iron and steel appeared to be the solid basis of the affluent society; guns, tanks, shells and battleships the means of national security and power. Heavy industry was given all priority, in the belief that its development would underlie and bring forward every other kind of development. This was the reasoning of non-Marxists, as well as Marxists; but the influence of Soviet Russia was important in this connection. Russia had achieved a significant industrialization and modernization, from a similar state of backwardness, by putting heavy industry first. The fact that it had dealt ruthlessly, both in this and in the agrarian sector, tended at first to be somewhat overlooked.

During the 1950s however, the real and social costs of Russia's industrialization came to be widely realized. Critical and general books on contemporary totalitarianism were certainly more widely read in Asia than such works as Engels' *Condition of the Working Class in England in 1844*. At the same time the USSR's development took a new high road, joining the post-industrialized advanced countries, displaying a certain *embourgeoisement* and placing itself in the higher category of nuclear and space technology.

China has taken over the banner of Asian-style Communist development which the Russians raised in the 1920s; but its success and its relevance as a model for Asian development are uncertain, while its military and political initiatives in and against developing countries such as India, Indonesia, Korea and those of S.E. Asia have not given it the image of an Asian partner.

The political vicissitudes may in the long run be of minor and transient importance compared to the technological evolution and realization of its implications. Advanced modern techniques are now the real focus of interest. It is understood that 'resources' are entirely relative to techniques; even if the resources are limited, continued rapid technical progress makes even constant resources more extensively and efficiently usable.

Politically the Maoist call to Asians to 'struggle', to pursue a guerrilla ethos and glory in a penurious way of life seems to parallel the appeal of some nineteenth-century agitators to the *Lumpenproletariat*, which Marx so deeply scorned; however influential in certain areas at times, it does not appear to be in the main stream of development in the Region.

In the technological aspect also, Maoism does not compete with the means and models of development offered by the West and Russia. Nor do the Asians need to look solely to distant places. Development under capitalism in Japan has made its society now 'affluent' by Asian standards; the obviously superior material levels in such regional centres, port cities and business communities as Hong Kong, Singapore or Taiwan have a far greater 'demonstration effect' than claimed results in Communist China. Modern nationalism must thus be considered in terms of the confrontation between underdeveloped countries and highly developed techniques.

There is another aspect. Nationalism would seem to imply each country pursuing its own path with its peculiar methods and forms. Modern nationalisms move strongly in a common direction, all adopting the standardized equipment, methods and ways of living which industrialization has made universal. The ideology of nationalism nowadays rests hardly at all on advocating the superiority of indigenous ideas and methods, but much more on postulating an absolute common denominator – progress, particularly industrial progress – in terms of which each rising nation can and will first match, then outstrip, any others. The theme-song might have been taken from a film of the post-war period: 'anything you can do, I can do better.'

TECHNOLOGY AND PRAGMATISM

The progress of technology is, however, double-edged to the developing world. The 'technological gap' between the advanced countries and the underdeveloped countries vastly increased in the first two post-war decades; it threatens to become a gulf in the next period. The initial threat to the underdeveloped countries has been to their position as primary producers, acutely dependent on marketing the raw materials which they provide. Technical progress has meant constant economizing by producers in raw materials, also their replacement by substitutes like artificial fibres and synthetic rubber.

Dependence on primary or extractive industries is deemed to be largely an aspect of colonialism. To break with this, to enhance national security and for other reasons, national self-sufficiency was much desired in the earlier part of this period. It had perforce to be largely cultivated in any case, in the era of general post-war shortage. The desire for industrialization sometimes embraces these motivations also. With the end of post-war shortage, the resumption of normal manufacturing output in the West and Japan and the disappearance of the 'seller's market' in the mid-1950s, the situation radically changed. Meanwhile Asia's continuing agrarian crisis persistently and powerfully claimed attention. By the 1960s a more balanced view of industrialization supervened, with more equal attention to agriculture and to factory industry. Even Chairman Mao finally proclaimed the need to 'walk on two legs', developing agriculture as well as industry.

Here again technological considerations are vital. The mechanization of agriculture, for instance, presents quite different problems in monsoon Asia from those which were solved in America or Russia or Europe. In industrialization, the model to be emulated appeared at the beginning of the period to be naturally the 'black' Industrial Revolution based on iron and coal, the successful form in the West and in Russia, with special emphasis on heavy industry. Few indeed stopped even to consider that this sort of industrialization might not be suited to Asia, where the conditions might call rather for varying emphasis on light rural labour-intensive industries, with other methods of organization.

In this context also, by the 1960s, more cautious judgments had to be attempted. Meanwhile industry, especially heavy industry, had made startling progress in the advanced countries. Developing countries were setting their aims at targets which – qualitatively as well as quantitatively – were receding rapidly from their range. For example Communist China proclaimed the aim of catching up in certain respects with Great Britain in fifteen years; but the British economy did not stand still, and no date is now attached to this Chinese aspiration.

In economic history, it is in principle an advantage to be a latecomer: avoiding the mistakes of precursors, the very latest methods are adopted. This may unhappily not apply if 'the latest' is measured in months rather than years; when a forbiddingly high and rapid rate of obsolescence has to be faced, the necessity is to be able not only to acquire the new equipment but to apply the modifications which will very quickly follow.

Consciousness of the 'technological gap' has thus increased in Asia, with these varied implications. It would be inaccurate and small-minded to say that these developing countries have 'missed the bus' or are pursuing a 'bandwagon' that has passed. There has been a great increase in international understanding and collaboration, in practical sophistication, with a sober – but by no means passive or unpurposeful – standard of judgment in such matters.

This chapter has briefly reviewed the subjectivity of the matter. In the background and the perspectives of the Asian problem subjectivity has played only too great a part in this period. The objective conditions and results are more amply examined below on the basis of the statistical evidence, which grew prodigiously in quantity and significantly in quality in the two post-war decades.

Chapter 2

POPULATION PRESSURE

THE LOT OF ESAU

Consideration of East Asia's development problem begins and ends with the question of overpopulation. The region does not have a large part of the world's land area, but does have a heavy share of its population. Its area (less than 18 million sq. kilometres) is 13 per cent of the world's land area. But it carried just over 1,000 million people in 1948, or about 45 per cent of the human race; rising to over 1,600 million in 1963, or over 50 per cent of mankind.

The region's numbers and density of population thus increased 60 per cent in that period. The other underdeveloped Regions also increased their populations but their numbers are far less and their shares of the world's land greater, so that their problems of man: land ratios are much less acute. Latin America has almost twice East Asia's area; it more than doubled its population in the period, but had only about 10 per cent of East Asia's population in 1948 and about 14 per cent in 1963. Africa has nearly three times East Asia's area. It increased its population about 50 per cent in the period, but its peoples numbered about 18 per cent of those in East Asia, throughout this time.

Taking in contrast the more developed Regions, Europe has 3.6 per cent of the world's land surface, with about 16 per cent of the global population in 1948 and 14 per cent in 1963, its population increasing about 12 per cent in the period. North America has almost double East Asia's area, with about 9 per cent of the world's inhabitants. Oceania has about 0.5 per cent of the world's population (though its population increased about 25 per cent in the period) on 6 per cent of the land area. The USSR's vast territory is similar in area to that of North America, its population slightly larger.

The human question is most easily visualized in terms of density (Table 2.2). In overall perspective the number of persons per square kilometre increased in the world in 1948-63 by about one-third, in the Americas and the Soviet Union by about a

Table 2.1. *Area and population*[1]

	Area: million km² (%)		Population (millions)			
			1948	(%)	1963	(%)
World	135.8	(100%)	2,349	(100%)	3.160	(100%)
Region:						
Burma	.68		18		23	
Cambodia	.18		2		6	
Ceylon	.07		7		11	
China: Mainland	9.56	(7%)	463	(20%)	720	(23%)
Taiwan	.04		6		12	
Hong Kong	.00		2		3.6	
India	3.05	(2%)	342	(15%)	460	(15%)
Indonesia	1.49		70		100	
Japan	.37		80		96	
Korea: South	.10		20		27	
Malaysia: Fed'n	.13					
Singapore	.00		5		8	
Sabah	.08		1		1.8	
Sarawak	.13⎱		1		1.3	
Brunei	.00⎰					
Pakistan	.95		73		99	
Philippines	.30		20		30	
Thailand	.51		18		29	
Vietnam: South	.17		7		15	
Total	17.81	(13%)	1,117	(47%)	1,642	(52%)

quarter, in Africa by about two-thirds, in Europe by about one-seventh; in East Asia by about one half.

DISTRIBUTION OF THE POPULATION

These are, of course, overall regional figures of total areas, regardless of arable quality, etc.; including, for instance, the northern wastelands of North America. The region as a whole, and even China, ostensibly has about the same density as Europe. The United Kingdom and Belgium are more crowded than Japan. In Sinkiang, of course, the density was only two and in Tibet one, even in Manchuria thirty-eight in 1945 and fifty in 1961; but in China Proper the corresponding figures are ninety-nine and 170. In Java, Madura and Sumatra the figures were 130 and 170, in the eastern islands fourteen and sixteen, in Kalimantan (Indonesian Borneo) five and six; and there are great variations elsewhere. These underdeveloped countries contain great infra-developed sub-regions.

The high pressure of population has nevertheless caused relatively little centrifugal movement of people, or decentralization of development, within these countries. The difficulties to

B

Table 2.2. *Density of population*[2]
(persons per sq. kilometre)

	1948	1963		1948	1963
World	17	23	Malaysia:		
			Federation	38	58
Africa	6	10	Brunei	7	16
N. America	8	10	Sabah	4	6
L. America	8	11	Sarawak	5	6
Europe	78	89	Singapore	1,100	3,055
Oceania	2	2	Pakistan	77	104
USSR	8	10	Philippines	67	101
			Thailand	34	56
East Asia			Vietnam	60	90
Burma	27	35			
Cambodia	13	33	All East Asia	59	91
Ceylon	108	162			
China: Mainland	48	75			
Taiwan	170	325			
Hong Kong	1,777	3,481			
India	110	157			
Indonesia	50	67			
Japan	218	259			
Korea: South	216	273			

internal migration are great, as experience increasingly proves. Totalitarian methods are applied only in China. The infrastructural expenditure is large and represents a high ratio of capital to output, which may largely be not the kind of output most desired, i.e. industrial capacity. Some hundreds of dollars (equivalent) are required for transportation, housing, roads, schools and other facilities, even on a comparatively local scale of movement.

This applies *a fortiori* to international or intercontinental movements. There is less and less thought as time goes on of the 'empty lands' elsewhere accommodating the 'hungry people' of Asia. Emigration from the Region remains a very important question, but the sheer weight of numbers renders it no longer capable of being considered a complete solution: even if, for example, Australia and Canada doubled their population by accepting Asian immigrants, this would now 'look after' the increase in population in India and China for no more than one year.

Within Asia there is relatively little international movement of people. (Though it is to be noted that some hundreds of thousands of people went from Mainland China to Hong Kong in 1949-50, and the flow has continued at 50,000 a year. Three million Japanese were repatriated after the war. In more horrible circumstances five million refugees went from Pakistan to India and three million from India to Pakistan, at the Partition.) Peaceful voluntary migration has been limited; xenophobia, in this respect as in others, must be said to have increased. Various European countries gladly receive a million or more foreign workers, very many of a different race; few doors are even moderately ajar in this respect in Asia.

LABOUR POWER

Obviously there is a general abundance of labour in the Region, relative to employment opportunities. Skilled labour is, however, quite another question. Both the age-distribution and the quality of the population are important in this connection. There is an increasingly high ratio of dependants to total population; a heavy human investment in a relatively large population below working age. A sad proportion of this population still never reaches the economically productive age, while infant and juvenile mortality and the incidence of disease continue – despite notable improvements – to be high, the expectation of life low. Nevertheless, increased survival is in fact the major reason for the population increase.

The population-pyramid of industrialized Western countries is narrow-based and tapers high, as normally depicted by setting out the numbers along the base-line and the ages up the perpendicular; that of the underdeveloped countries is broad-based and squat. The proportion of economically productive persons is relatively large in the former. In developed countries, 20-25 per cent of the population is below working age (fifteen); in underdeveloped countries, about double that proportion, 40-45 per cent.

In Taiwan, to instance one of the fastest-growing populations, for every 100 productive workers there were in 1963 over 130 dependants; compared with eighty-two in Japan, seventy-eight in the US and sixty-nine in England.[3]

THE EXPONENTIAL CURVE

If the present numbers are embarrassingly large, the potential and prospective growth is widely considered to be nothing short of alarming. The curve of population is climbing near to the vertical.

The main factor is a fall in the death rate, which is expected to continue with medical and social progress, rather than a rise in the birth rate (which might rather fall with such progress). Death rates have generally fallen strikingly in the Region since the war, especially in recent years. Birth rates have also declined, but not correspondingly. It is little realized that almost all East Asian countries now have lower crude death rates (per thousand of total population) than the European average (of about eleven per thousand) – owing to the predominance of younger age-groups in their large populations. The indications are summarized in the next Table.

Table 2.3. Crude rates of live births and deaths: per annum,
per 1,000 persons[4]

| | 1945/9 average | | | 1961 | | |
	Births	Deaths	Difference	Births	Deaths	Difference
Burma	36	36	0	38	18	20
Ceylon	38	16	22	36	8	28
Taiwan	40	15	25	38	7	31
Hong Kong	25	9	16	34	6	28
India	26	17	9	28	12	16
Japan	30	17	13	17	7	10
Malaya: Fed.	41	18	23	42	9	33
Philippines	30	13	17	27	7	20
Thailand	25	13	12	33	6	27

Cambodia, Indonesia and South Korea continue to have high death rates, like Burma's in the 1950s; but all are likely to fall significantly in the near future.

According to ECAFE, only four countries in the Region have 'proper' sustained census-series enabling 'reliable' demographic analysis (viz.: Ceylon, Japan, Malaysia and Taiwan). In 1960 and 1961, in response to a strong United Nations resolution, twelve countries of the Region made new census efforts. The result was a shock. It appeared that previous estimates of population growth had been generally too low, particularly in India, Korea, Pakistan, the Philippines and Thailand: countries containing two-thirds of the Region's population outside China, and one-fifth of the world's. India's and Pakistan's population estimates were then revised upwards by 6 per cent (to 432 million and 93 million respectively) the Philippines' by 12 per cent to 28 million and Thailand's by 18 per cent (to 26 million), or by 7 per cent for the whole group.

At the same time the growth-rates has been underestimated much more greatly than the total numbers: India's was raised by 54 per cent over that previously stated (to 2.0 per cent a year), Pakistan's by 36 per cent (to 1.9 per cent), the Philippines' by 23 per cent (to 3.2 per cent) and Thailand's by 58 per cent (to 3.0 per cent); on the average, by 43 per cent (to 2.5 per cent) for the whole Region.

Underestimation appears to have been discovered earlier in Communist China, which then contained more than half the Region's population. The first 'real' census was taken there in 1953; it is believed that the rise in the growth-rate which it showed was somewhat alarming to the Chinese authorities and it is significant that no second census was planned there, the decennial passing without it and with no further announcements being subsequently made. ECAFE, in the studies on the world census in 1960-1, revised its growth estimate for Mainland China downwards (by some 18 per cent, from 2.8 per cent to 2.3 per cent); nevertheless it found the growth of the Region altogether greater, and more accelerating, than had been thought.

Projections of future population figures became correspondingly more alarming. The numbers in East Asia are expected to increase by some 50 per cent between 1960 and 1980, and to double in the last four decades of the twentieth century (Table 2.4). Fears focus primarily on the subsistence and standard of living problems – in powerful conjunction with the possible political implications – but there are other aspects which should be considered. Among these, perhaps, are the organizational and general questions of the internal as well as the external adjustments of China containing 1,000 million people, an India of another 1,000 million, and the rest of Asia with the same number. So far as the economic yardstick is concerned the UN General Assembly designated, at the end of 1962, the 1960s as a 'Development Decade' with the general target of raising the underdeveloped countries' national incomes 5 per cent a year and their food production 4 per cent a year. These percentages are modest in themselves, but in *per capita* terms they are halved, or worse, by the great rise in population.

POPULATION POLICY

Might the population increase be slowed, by deliberate policy or changing circumstances? It is considered that in normal

Table 2.4. Population projection: East Asia[5]

(millions)

	1960	1965	1970	1980	1990	2000
Burma	22	25	28	35	—	—
Cambodia	6	6	7	10	—	—
Ceylon	10	12	13	18	—	—
China (Mainland)	644	688	735	835	931	1,024
China (Taiwan)	11	12	14	17	21	25
Hong Kong	3	4	4	6	7	8
India	433	484	541	661	783	908
Indonesia	94	106	118	153	—	—
Japan	93	98	101	111	118	123
Korea (N. and S.)	35	40	46	59	74	90
Malaysia	10	11	13	18	—	—
Pakistan	93	106	121	154	188	227
Philippines	27	32	38	56	—	—
Thailand	26	31	36	48	—	—
Vietnam	31	34	38	46	—	—
Total	1,538	1,689	1,863	2,237	2,614	3,030

historical evolution the rate of population growth does fall off as
life becomes more modernized in general, and urbanized in
particular. This question has been little investigated in East Asia
(except in Japan) but field experience suggests that the principle
does apply in that country; but distinctly less in the rest of Asia,
owing to the subsistence-level conditions in Asia, and the
strength of traditionalism. Only a comparatively tiny minority
of 'westernized' Asians are thus affected. Though there are some
strikingly populous cities in Asia, urbanization is not really as
well marked – even in its extent, certainly in its demographic
effects – as in the West. The population increase comes over-
whelmingly in the rural areas, from the peasantry. Table 2.5
gives some indications.

However large, 'metropolitan' concentrations in Asia appear
(even in Japan) to be smaller, *relative to the whole population*,
than those in western countries. The smaller and minor cities
are likely to be less 'modernized' than those in the West, though
they are entering on rapid change. Rapid rates of city expansion
in Asia (e.g. the Kansai in Japan, Tientsin) are striking, but are
partly due to the extension of city boundaries, and are not un-
matched in the West (e.g. Los Angeles). Asian society, outlooks
and living standards are not yet changing substantially in directions which make for smaller families.

Heroic efforts have been devoted to birth control, but without

Table 2.5. Urbanization[6]
(a) Population of capital plus three other largest cities (000; %)

		Region				Others	
	Year	Nos.	% of total population		Year	Nos.	% of total population
Ceylon	1963	738	1%	Australia	1963	4,980	46%
China:				France	1963	8,644	18%
Mainland	1958	18,100	3%	UK	1963	11,065	21%
India	1962	12,498	3%	USA	1963	19,440	10%
Japan	1962	19,621	5%	USSR	1963	12,242	5%
Pakistan	1958	3,092	3%				

(b) Growth-rate of some major cities: per annum, % (in period):

China: Mainland			Australia:		
Tientsin	20%	(1953-57)	Canberra	18%	(1958-63)
Mukden	5%	(1956-57)	Sydney	2½%	(1958-63)
India:			Melbourne	3%	(1958-63)
Bombay	4%	(1954-62)	Brisbane	3½%	(1958-63)
Madras	1%	(1954-62)	France:		
Japan:			Paris	5%	(1959-63)
Tokyo	3%	(1958-62)	Marseilles	4%	(1958-63)
Osaka	22%	(1957-62)	Lyons	3%	(1958-63)
Nagoya	27%	(1957-62)	USA:		
(Malaya):			Chicago	4½%	(1957-60)
Singapore	3%	(1959-62)	Los Angeles	18%	(1957-60)
			USSR:		
			Moscow	5%	(1958-63)
			Leningrad	1½%	(1958-63)

(c) Urban population as percentage of total population

	t_1		t_2	
	Year	Urban (%)	Year	Urban (%)[a]
Burma	1921	9.8		
	1931	10.4		
Ceylon	1946	15.4	1963	14.9
China: Mainland	1949	10.6	1956	14.2
China: Taiwan	1947	50.7	1955	56.0
India	1941	12.8		
	1951	17.3	1961	17.9
Japan	1946	30.4	1960	63.4[b]
Korea: South	1949	19.6	1960	28.0
Malaya: Federation	1947	26.5	1957	42.7
Pakistan	1941	7.9		
	1951	10.4	1961	13.1
Philippines	1948	24.1	1956	35.3
Thailand	1947	9.9	1960	11.8

Notes: a Classification may differ between countries, also between censuses in the same country; the figures are to be viewed accordingly.
b In Japan especially (and in other countries to some extent) the limits of many cities have been expanded, giving the 'urban' percentage an upward bias.

marked effect as yet, except in Japan. The Japanese people have shown extreme realism and pragmatism in this as in other matters – under government auspices. The population of Japan was deliberately stabilized in the 1950s to grow by only one million a year, or 1 per cent. Contraception has been widely introduced and practised; but it is well known that the legalization of abortions has been a main point, their number rising to one million a year. The Indian government has given great though far less drastic encouragement to family planning, with considerable foreign aid, which however has not yet had any notable effect on the total figures. Other countries of the Region are now making family planning a part of their policy (e.g. Pakistan, South Korea) or giving substantial government support to private efforts (Hong Kong and Singapore).

Roman Catholicism, opposed to clinical methods of birth control, has some influence in parts of East Asia (such as the Philippines and Vietnam). Elsewhere Buddhism enjoins the sacredness of life. On the political plane, nationalism opposes family planning on 'manpower' grounds. So does Marxism, which holds labour to be the source of value, equating 'the masses' with Society, denouncing Malthusianism as capitalist deception and proclaiming that Socialism means plenty, for any numbers.

Communist China has twice or thrice initiated family planning 'drives' – and once or twice reversed this policy. These movements in any case hardly reached rural masses which form 80 per cent of China's 700 millions. Moreover the handling has been schizophrenic; those who have spoken out of turn have suffered in consequence, like the eminent economist Ma Yin-chü who was dismissed for opining that quality of population was more important than quantity, and stressing that the Soviet Russians intelligently took this view. Present Chinese Communist policy certainly promotes birth control in practice, ostensibly on 'health' grounds; though priority clients also include 'activists' whose time, energy and involvements should be all for the State alone. Moreover, it widely enforces late marriages; but altogether the effects are not yet great, the annual increase continues to be in the order of fifteen millions.[7]

However much these tides may change, the large numbers are already there. Only an actual reduction by a substantial amount would raise *per capita* standards; even if the numbers fell the development needs would remain prodigious, the tasks enormous. The past is long and great in Asia, but it is the future that must haunt its dreams. A tremendous effort of development, requiring a concerted world effort, is necessary merely to secure that the frustration of these vast numbers of people is not to be intensified. To ensure much more, that their situation will not worsen into a desperation that could be fatal, in a time when the means of nuclear annihilation will spread into the hands of all nations, requires an effort more prodigious than has ever yet been even remotely contemplated.

Chapter 3

FOOD SHORTAGE

THE MALTHUSIAN PROBLEM

The greatest and most persistent question is whether the growth of numbers is already outstripping the means of subsistence, with cumulative effect in future prospect.

Until the late 1950s the UN Food and Agriculture Oganization tended to be relatively optimistic on this issue; subsequently it became more pessimistic. FAO found the Region slightly more successful than the world as a whole in raising *overall* agricultural production; as shown in Table 3.1 (i). Because of the population growth this, however, represented no increase in *per capita* terms: the 23 per cent increase in the Region's total agricultural output only matched its increase in population in the same period.

In respect of *food production per capita*, the Region may nevertheless have done percentage-wise as well as the world as a whole, or insignificantly better, slightly more than keeping up with its population increase (Table 3.1 ii). It must at the same time be stressed that the absolute levels of nutrition are distressingly low in Asia; its peoples are keeping barely and unevenly above the starvation line. Moreover the 'par' has only been maintained for the Region as a whole; it will be noted that seven countries were below the average and four of them suffered a slight *per capita* decline.

In view of the still accelerating population growth on a widening base, the difficulties will be intensified in the next few decades.

CEREALS

The basic grains must be considered first as of key significance. The following shows graphically the lag between the rate of increase in their production and the growth of population.

Burma, Thailand and Vietnam were formerly great rice-surplus exporting countries, where the planted area was extensible; but the end of their surplus position appears to be now in sight. Elsewhere it is likely – even apart from political or social

Table 3.1. *Indices of Agricultural Production*[1]
$(1952/3-1956/7=100)$[2]

(i) *All agricultural commodities*

	1953/4	1958/9	1962/3
Whole world	99	110	120
Far East[a]	98	111	123
Countries above Far East average, 1962/3:			
Ceylon	95	110	128
Taiwan	94	126	138
Japan	85	116	131
Malaya: Federation	93	110	127
Philippines	98	114	130
Thailand	105	108	146
Below the average:			
Burma	98	107	121
India	100	110	119
Indonesia	101	107	113
Korea: South	98	121	120
Pakistan	98	102	111

(ii) *Per capita food production*

Whole world	101	103	102
Far East[a]	101	103	104
Countries above Far East average:			
Ceylon	92	95	108
Taiwan	99	109	105
Japan	86	112	123
Thailand	110	94	113
Countries below average:			
Burma	99	105	102
India	103	101	99
Indonesia	104	100	98
Korea: South	100	114	100
Malaya: Federation	92	98	103
Pakistan	103	93	94
Philippines	101	100	99

Note: a The Region, excluding Mainland China.

disruptions – that production deficits will increase alarmingly, in food especially:[3]

Japan, the most successful rice-producing country, has raised yields at just over 1 per cent a year in recent decades. In India, where population is growing at 2.3 per cent a year and where nearly all increases in food production over the next

Table 3.2. *Population increase and production*
of basic cereals
(1935/9 to 1960/2)[2]
Annual compound rate of change in:

	1 yield per acre	2 population	Col. 1 minus col. 2
Rice			
Burma	0.6%	2.1%	−1.6%
India	0.7%	2.2%	−1.5%
Indonesia	0.5%	2.3%	−1.8%
Korea: South	0.7%	2.9%	−2.2%
Taiwan	0.9%	3.7%	−2.8%
Thailand	−0.3%	3.0%	−3.3%
Wheat			
India	0.6%	2.2%	−1.6%
Pakistan	0.5%	2.1%	−1.6%
Maize			
India	0.5%	2.2%	−1.7%
Indonesia	−0.2%	2.3%	−2.5%
Pakistan	0.5%	2.1%	−1.6%
Philippines	0.0%	3.3%	−3.3%

several years must come from rising yields, the failure to substantially improve (*sic*) on the outstanding Japanese performance will result in steadily declining food output per person.

The contrast with advanced countries is lugubrious, even in respect of Asia's own specialist crops:

France, in raising wheat yields at 2.3 per cent per year (and maize yields at 2 per cent) has made substantial progress in raising *per capita* output for its population, which is increasing only one per cent a year. But the French performance . . . would not have been adequate had it faced population growth rates as high as those currently prevailing in many less-developed countries. The United States has raised wheat yields 2.7 per cent per year (also rice yields 1.9 per cent, and maize yields 3.7 per cent). However, given a fixed land base and a population growth rate comparable to (that in the developing countries) output per person would have declined.

The situation was underlined in 1966 by news headlines about food riots in India, where the grain crops were remarkably good in 1964 but fell by some 14 per cent in 1965; the FAO estimated that 100 million people were 'affected' and the Indian Government that 11½ million needed famine relief. A serious lack in the

English language is another term to define shortage less than actual famine; like the French word *disette,* which aptly describes the general Asian situation 'at best'.

Summing up for the underdeveloped region generally, *per capita* food production was certainly low before the war and further deteriorated in the post-war period. Despite subsequent recovery 'recent *per capita* production is still *below the pre-war level'.*

RISING DEMAND AND IMPORTS OF FOODSTUFFS

'At the same time, there has been an increase in income and demand so that net import of cereals into the developing ECAFE Region increased.'[4]

Net import of cereals into the region excluding Japan and Mainland China increased by over 40 per cent (from 4.2 million tons) in the ten years from 1951-2, or by 6 per cent per head of the whole population.

Food imports are obviously at the expense of the ardently desired imports of capital goods and compete with them for the limited foreign exchange.

In addition, Communist China changed at the beginning of the 1960s from being an exporter of cereals to a substantial importer. In 1958, for example, 838,406 tons of cereals were *exported*: or over 1 kg. per head of the population. In 1956 the Food Minister stated that the annual export was 1½-2 million tons of cereals: or nearly 10 kg. per head of its population. Such purchases continued; and are likely to continue in future. In 1965 Mainland China bought abroad about 5 million tons of grain and negotiated for similar or increased imports from 1966 to 1969, plus tenders to as far ahead as 1971.

Much of the past importation of food has been a foreign-aid gift: to the extent of no less than US $5,000 million between 1954 and 1963. Besides saving the lives of recipients, this facilitated the industrialization and development policies of various countries.

Will it be continued on this scale of more than one and one-third million dollars per day, rising by some three-quarters of a million dollars a day to meet the current population increase? Let alone being multiplied many-fold, to meet the real needs of the situation? Or just increased by some $150,000 a day to bring the ECAFE Region's recipient populations (excluding Mainland

China, which represents some 50 per cent of its population!)
up to merely the world's average standard of nutrition?

It seems unlikely. It may even be unreasonable, if the view
is taken that the countries must themselves make the main effort.
Unless domestic production is duly increased, however, the
projection from the present situation is that by no later date
than 1970, the end of the Development Decade proclaimed by
the United Nations, net import of cereals into the Region may
have to be increased to some 18 million tons, or three times the
level at the beginning of the Development Decade. The prodigious increase in output and efficiency of agriculture in the
capitalist developed countries (in startling contrast with the poor
performance of agriculture in Communist countries) can easily
meet the quantitative needs; but it would have to be done largely
on aid, gift and credit terms. The required foreign exchange
expenditure to pay for the import of 19 million tons of cereals
in 1970 would swallow up a large part of the available foreign-
exchange resources of the whole Region; it would be much
beyond the means of the countries which received food-aid to
pay for it themselves.

STAPLE FOODS: AREA AND YIELD

The next steps in the analysis are to trace the progress of the
domestic food supply in the region in terms of sown area and
production. Taken first are the cereals which are the prime basis
of subsistence in this largely vegetarian region:

    (a) cereals:

        1. rice
        2. wheat
        3. maize
        4. millet
        5. sorghum

Next to be considered are the starchy roots which are inferior
alternatives or supplements to the cereals:

    (b) starchy roots:

        6. potatoes
        7. sweet potatoes and yams
        8. cassava

The numbering here shows the order of preference of the
region's people: at the top of the list from 1 are the superior,

most desired or needed basic foods, at the bottom to 8 the despised or makeshift items. The following outlines the developments in respect of these in the region (excluding Mainland China) over the period of abut 1950-63.[5]

(i) area

The total area under all these crops increased from 124 million ha. on the average of 1948-9/1952-3 to over 148 million ha. in 1962-3, i.e. by 20 per cent – apparently less than the increase in population. The proportions of the total area devoted to the different crops hardly varied in the period: mainly rice (53 per cent) then millet and sorghum (about 14 per cent each) wheat (about 12 per cent) sweet potatoes, yams and cassava (about 1 per cent each) and potatoes ($\frac{1}{2}$ per cent).

However, the greatest proportionate expansions in area were largely in the inferior crops. Thus group (b) the roots increased in area 45 per cent; group (a) the cereals 20 per cent. By this criterion the increases were as follows: greatest in cassava (which increased its cultivated area by 58 per cent) then maize (54 per cent), potatoes (40 per cent), wheat and sweet potatoes (33 per cent), sorghum (12 per cent) and millet (6 per cent).

(ii) output

Turning to the production figures, the whole harvest of all these crops increased in the same period by 30 per cent in weight; more clearly keeping up with the population growth, but with no handsome margin of improved subsistence. In these terms the proportions between the crops are different. Rice represented about 58 per cent of the total quantity; wheat, sweet potatoes and cassava about 8 per cent each, maize, millet, sorghum and potatoes about 4 per cent each. The proportion of cereals in the total moved up slightly (from just under to just over 80 per cent).

However the production of the cereals increased by about one quarter (from 133 million metric tons to 165) whereas that of the starchy roots increased by 57 per cent (from about twenty-five to forty). And again the relative increases in output tended to concentrate on the inferior local foodstuffs; rice increase 28 per cent, millet 22 per cent, sweet potatoes 38 per cent, sorghum 43 per cent, wheat 58 per cent, potatoes 62 per cent, cassava 79 per cent, maize 104 per cent.

(iii) yields per unit of area

The yields of all these crops increased. Overall their increase was some 13 per cent; very distinctly less than the increase in population. In the crude terms of the simple weight of these foodstuffs that could be got from one hectare, the starch-roots group figures about eight times as large as the cereals groups. In the rudimentary terms of filling empty stomachs, the contributions by weight of millet and sorghum were only 1 per cent each, wheat and maize 3 per cent each, rice 5 per cent but cassava 25 per cent and the two categories of potatoes 30 per cent each. Because one hectare in 1962-3 yielded only about 400 kg. of millet, 500 of sorghum, 1,000 each of wheat or maize, 1,500 of rice, but 8,000 of cassava and 10,000 in each of the two categories of potatoes.

The pattern of increases is again interestingly different. Per unit yields increased in the period 20 per cent for the cereals as a whole, 12 per cent for the starch-roots taken together; item by item, maize 43 per cent, sorghum 30 per cent, wheat 18 per cent, potatoes 17 per cent, millet 16 per cent, cassava 12 per cent and sweet potatoes 7 per cent.

BASIC DIET CHANGES

Rice and wheat are much preferred. They should nowadays be considered together as staples. The former distinct preference for rice in a large part of the Region (broadly speaking, all but the northern parts of China and of the Indo-Pakistan subcontinent) has been modified in very recent years, with a relative rise in the preference for wheat. This process has been evident in Japan for more than half a century; and marked in such places as the port-cities elsewhere in Asia for about a generation. Looking more closely at the figures used above, the following comparisons emerge. Wheat is produced significantly in only four of the countries of the Region excluding Mainland China – India, Japan, Korea and the Philippines—each of which grows rice also. The ratio of the total areas under rice to those under wheat fell 13 per cent from exactly 3 : 1 at the beginning of the period to 2.7 : 1 at the end. The ratio of production (amount harvested, rice : wheat) in these four countries fell by 17 per cent, from 5.35 : 1 to 4.38 : 1. In terms of yields per hectare the corresponding fall in the ratio was from 2.1 : 1 to 1.96 : 1, or some 7 per cent.

This marginal but qualitatively important shift in the eminently preferred cereals is noteworthy. To the above calculation must be added the large and proportionately rising imports of wheat into the Region. The same preferential shift is presumably a factor in the turn by Mainland China to importing wheat, though the main reasons are (i) net shortage of food against growing population (ii) a system that is disincentive to the producer and (iii) because rice is not available from the agriculturally advanced countries (though there is a large scheme to produce it in Northern Australia).

For the rest the difficulty of maintaining increasing returns in rice and wheat cultivation and the necessity to resort to inferior land under inferior crops are underlying features. Great efforts have been made to intensify further the already labour-intensive production in those items. It is most difficult to do this for rice – for which the Asian methods are already highly perfected, the social implications so involved that it has been well said that 'rice is not a crop but a way of life' and suitable land most scarce. Inferior crops are less palatable, less acceptable; but are resorted to perforce, because of the relative shortage of good foodstuffs, while the inferior ones offer better quantitative returns and take less good land.

The pressure on the land is very largely for these basic food crops. In the region excluding Mainland China and Japan the five cereals and three starch-roots occupied 53 per cent of the arable area on the 1948-53 average, rising to 64 per cent in 1963. In Taiwan and Japan they took virtually 100 per cent of the arable area throughout the period. The other countries may be significantly ranged as follows, according to the relativity of the pressures in them of population on land. In South Vietnam the eight food crops took 72 per cent of the arable area at the beginning of the period, 86 per cent at the end. If this may be rendered for the sake of brevity as '72-86', the other countries' situations are: Philippines 51-79, Cambodia 46-71, Indonesia 51-70, Thailand and South Korea both 52-62, India 47-56, Pakistan 51-56, Ceylon 38-40 and the Malayan Federation 14-18. In the last two countries plantation crops are, however, of prime importance; and the vital importance of cash-crops elsewhere must also be borne in mind, all these being alternatives foregone where the land is laid down to the direct-sustenance food crops.

The proportion of the area under the inferior group (b) crops was doubled in Indonesia (from 6 per cent of the whole arable area to 11 per cent) the Philippines (1.5 to 3 per cent) and India (0.3 to 0.6 per cent); in Taiwan the limits of such shifting are nearer, the percentage being 11 per cent both at the beginning and at the end of the period.

In terms of tonnage the group (b) foodstuffs actually exceed the group (a) ones in Taiwan; where the production was divided between them in the ratio 44 per cent of (a) to 56 per cent of (b), throughout the period. In Burma, Ceylon, the Malayan Federation and Pakistan this ratio was virtually 100 per cent of (a) to 0.0 per cent of (b) throughout the period. The other countries show, however, a greater proportion of (b) in the total – and a significantly rising one. Thailand for example reported 96 per cent of (a) on the 1948-53 average against 4 per cent of (b); sharply changing to 81 per cent of (a) against 19 per cent of (b) in 1962-3.

This particular item certainly contains an error – the group (b) items were heavily under-recorded in the former period, so that this statement greatly exaggerates the shift for that country. If, however, we may designate this instance of Thailand as 96 : 4-81 : 19, the other countries' codings are : Pakistan 99 : 1-98 : 2 , India 94 : 6-93 : 7, Cambodia 87 : 13-85 : 15, S. Korea 84 : 16-71 : 29, Philippines 81 : 19-80 : 20, Japan 61 : 39-59 : 41, Indonesia 56 : 44-53 : 47. South Vietnam's ratio was 93.7 for the base period, but corresponding figures are not available for 1962-3. In the regional total the shift was 83 : 17-80 : 20 (in million metric tons, 123 : 25-165 : 40); this may be expressed as a 14 per cent rise in the second term of the ratio, the inferior foodstuffs, relative to the first.

IRRIGATION

All these farinaceous food supplies depend particularly upon irrigation. So do other crops; notably vegetables, which should be mentioned next as an essential part of Asian feeding. Regrettably, however, the statistical data are lacking on which any specific or aggregative study of them can be attempted in this survey.

For similar reasons irrigation can only be summarily discussed here. Taking again the Region minus Mainland China and Japan, it appears that of the total area (789 million ha.) just over 30 per cent is arable. This arable area holds in the overall average 3.3 persons per ha. but with such variations between countries as: 2-3 in Burma, Cambodia, India, Thailand, 3-4 in Malaya and Pakistan, 4-5 in Ceylon, the Philippines and South Vietnam, 5-6 in Indonesia, leaping to over 12 in Taiwan and South Korea.

Only about 20 per cent of the region's arable area was actually irrigated at the beginning of the 1960s. However, this understates the achievements of individual countries: over half the arable area was irrigated in Taiwan, over one-third in Indonesia, South Korea and Pakistan, South Vietnam 21 per cent, Thailand 17 per cent, India 15 per cent, Philippines 12 per cent, Federation of Malaya 10 per cent, but Burma 6 per cent, Cambodia 3 per cent and Ceylon only 2 per cent.

Irrigation should nevertheless be extensible throughout, to roughly the proportion realized in Taiwan. That country had in fact closely approached the irrigable limit by the mid-1960s; its leadership in this respect became even more marked in the first half of the Development Decade. In 1961, 56 per cent of its arable area was irrigated; plans to irrigate a further 34 per cent by 1964 were largely realized. Ceylon also substantially realized plans to increase by 11 per cent in the early 1960s. South Vietnam planned a corresponding increase of 37 per cent, but this obviously remains on paper. Other countries in contrast planned only significant increases by 1966 over 1957-60 – India, South Korea and Thailand 5 per cent, Indonesia and Malaya 3 per cent, Burma 1 per cent. In the regional total the result is an extension of irrigation over only an additional 5 per cent of the arable area. Even this remained on paper for the most part; the plans were in many cases not fulfilled.[6]

In these calculations the large countries swell the total figures; if India and Pakistan are excluded the total area is 389 million ha., of which only about 14 per cent is arable, instead of 19 per cent. I.e. India has some 38 per cent of the total area of these countries but nearly 60 per cent of its arable area, Pakistan about 12 per cent of the total and 12 per cent of the arable, whereas Indonesia shows nearly 20 per cent of the total but about 7 per cent of the arable. Some of the small countries have led percentagewise in irrigation; whereas the largest quantitative scope is in some of the large countries.

Obviously the quality of the actual and planned irrigation works should be considered as well as their quantity. Reference should be made particularly on the one hand to the virtues of multipurpose projects combining irrigation, flood-control, electricity-generation and social growth-points, and on the other hand to those of small-scale works dispersed and directed to the individual-peasant basis of village or household societies and economies. This reverts also to the debate about 'balanced' or 'unbalanced' growth. However, irrigation is in any case most vital to the expansion of the greatly preferred food crops, such as rice and wheat, and for the diversification of agriculture in other respects.

FISHERIES

Marine products are a very important item of Asian diets. Naturally consumption is heavily concentrated in the insular and coastal areas. The inland populations at greater distances consume relatively little fish, transport being inadequate, refrigeration and storage facilities little developed. The latter factor is most important in the case of fish, but must be borne in mind for all other foodstuffs also: the incidence of losses in storage or transit (spoiling, insects, etc.) is very high throughout; its reduction would mean a great increase in effective supply.

Inland, great progress has, however, been made in raising fish in fresh or brackish waters; this is now making a considerable contribution to the diet. There has also been striking improvement in fisheries organization, motorization of craft, modernization of equipment, preservation of products (salting, drying, curing, canning), transport, storage, distribution, refrigeration.

Nevertheless, much remains to be done in this vast field of activity, many problems are still to be solved and the progress is very uneven. Asia is not maintaining its share of the world's total catch of fish – which is falling distinctly behind its share of the world's population.

Japan's successful development in ocean fishing is well known. Total catch was $3\frac{1}{2}$ million m.t. live weight in 1938, reduced to less than $2\frac{1}{2}$ in 1958 in consequence of the war, rising to 4.3 in 1953, $5\frac{1}{2}$ in 1958 and nearly 7 (double the pre-war) in

Table 3.3. World fisheries: percentage distribution
between continents, of the total catch (million m.t., live weight)[7]

	Per cent		(index, 1938=100)			
	1938	1948	1953	1958	1963	(Index)
Africa	2.5	4.3	6.3	6.3	6.0	(240)
N. America	15.0	18.6	14.7	12.3	9.3	(62)
S. America	1.2	2.3	2.3	4.9	18.3	(1525)
Asia	46.3	34.9	40.7	44.4	38.4	(83)
Europe	27.2	31.8	27.9	23.7	19.1	(70)
Oceania	0.4	0.5	0.4	0.4	0.4	(100)
USSR	7.4	7.6	7.7	8.0	8.6	(116)

1963. This not only contributes largely to the Japanese food supply but sustains a very large export. Might the other regional countries emulate this success story? Or that of Peru, which increased spectacularly (from 0.2 million tons in 1953-5) to vie with Japan in 1962 for the position of the world's greatest producer? The record for Asia as a whole is summarized in Table 3.4.

Table 3.4. Asian and world fisheries[8]

Total catch (million tons live weight)	1938	1948	1953	1958	1963
World	21.00	19.50	25.70	32.60	46.40
Asia	9.70	6.81	10.44	14.48	17.00
(Asia as % of world	46%	35%	41%	45%	39%)
Indices (1958=100)					
World	64	60	79	100	142
Asia	67	47	76	100	123

Individual countries have made great efforts, with varying results. Taiwan produced 350,000 tons in 1963 (four times pre-war). Mainland China approached Japan's production at some 3 million tons before the war, but did not recover that level till 1958. Hong Kong roughly quadrupled its catch, to 75,000 tons. India doubled (1948-63) to 1 million tons, South Korea's figures for the same period are 285-444,000, Malaya's 139-243,000, Pakistan's increase more striking at 23-345, the Philippines' 195-565, Thailand's 161-419, Indonesia's 420 in 1959 and 705 in 1963.

The development of freshwater fisheries and fish-cultivation (an old art in E. and S.E. Asia) is notable. It is credited with some two-thirds of the total catch in the case of Pakistan, up to one-third in both the Chinas and in Indonesia and Hong Kong, a quarter in Thailand, less elsewhere; all of which may be under-statements excluding much of the subsistence-farming. The Indian Ocean is one of the world's main areas for the extension of fisheries. The possibilities of further development in inland waters are also very large.

With zoological exactitude, whaling has been excluded above; but it should be mentioned here with reference especially to Japan as the sole entrepreneur in the region. There were nearly 44,000 whales killed in the world in 1948-9, nearly 10 per cent of which were slaughtered by Japanese whalers; over 63,600 in 1962-3 (an increase of 45 per cent) of which the Japanese whaling industry accounted for 38 per cent, increasing its catch by more than 700 per cent. The British Commonwealth's catch declined in the same period from some 14,800 to 2,974 (i.e. by some 80 per cent): the Soviet Union's, starting from about the same level as Japan's in 1948-9, rose by over 300 per cent.[9]

MEAT

The production and consumption of meat in the Region remain low, in *per capita* terms especially; though there have been significant developments both in domestic production and some growth of imports (of particular interest to Australia and New Zealand).

The lack of attention to *upland* activities in general, and pastoral production in particular, remains a striking feature of South and East Asian development. Professor Pierre Gourou has effectively sounded this topic. The development of dairying and livestock in Japan is highly remarkable. The sacredness of the cow in India is proverbial – but its quality there is pathetic. Elsewhere pastoralization is not a strong trend in the Region. What are the possibilities of great changes which might greatly improve the food situation in that respect?

Full analysis of the present progress is difficult, particularly because of the lack of information on one major item in this category, poultry, and one major country, India. For the rest of this food group some striking progress may, however, be recorded: production more than doubled in beef, veal, pork, mutton and lamb between 1952 and 1962. Japan and Taiwan were outstanding in this respect, each having quadrupled its production (largely in pork).[10]

The quality has outstandingly risen in these countries; for example Japanese ('Kobe') beef is now definitely in the gourmet's dictionary. Published figures are as in Table 3.5.

Table 3.5. *Production of meat* (000 m.t.)[11]

	Beef and veal 48/9-52/3	62	Pork 48/9-52/3	62	Mutton and lamb 48/9-52/3	62	Total 48/9-52/3	62
Burma (commercial)	1	11	9	12	3	3	13	26
Cambodia (inspected)	4	3a	13	18a	—	—	17	21
Ceylon (inspected)	16	15	—	—	1	2	17	17
China:								
Taiwan (total)	2	6	54	217	1b	1	57	224
Japan (commercial)	61	147	46	325	4b	3	111	475
Korea: South	15	17	6	45c	—	—	21	62
Malaya: Singapore	2	—	9	18	1	—	12	18
Pakistan (commercial)	205	258	—	—	65	81	270	339
Philippines (commercial)	38	39d	78	161	1	3	117	203
Vietnam: South	10	14	23	58	—	—	33	72
Total	354	510	238	854	76	93	668	1,457
(Index	100	144	100	359	100	122	100	218)
cf:								
Australia	628	804e	89	122	332	596	1,049	1,522
Japan as % of Australia	10%	18%	52%	266%	1%	0%	10%	31%
New Zealand	186	286	40	40	324	472	550	798
Japan as % of New Zealand	33%	51%	115%	813%	1%	0%	20%	60%

Notes: a1961. b1959. c1961; but 1959 and 1960 were 69 and 67 respectively. d But 52 is recorded for 1960. e Excluding live exports.

OTHER FOOD PRODUCTS

Production and consumption of dairy produce of all kinds has accordingly increased phenomenally in Japan – which is nowadays at European level in this respect as in others – and in major cities elsewhere. Butter (ghee) is an important item in India. Elsewhere butter is not statistically important; nor is cheese. Milk is certainly important; but the increase in milk production has not made any major contribution to increasing Asia's domestic food supply, particularly in *per capita* terms. Vegetable oils and oilseeds are very important to the Region, both in domestic feeding and for export; they are considered elsewhere in this book.[12]

MALNUTRITION

The next sections discuss the region's imports of food and comment further on the farm-food balance. Even before doing this it is necessary to present the state of food shortage also in terms of dietary deficiency; as it is particularly essential to bear in mind what types of food are required, and which are being supplied.

ECAFE's conclusion in 1965 was that total food supply in the Region – including the significant imports – not only remains at a low level (at marginal subsistence) but is actually falling. In dietary terms, in the ECAFE Region *per capita consumption* remained in 1964 still below the pre-war level and *per capita protein consumption* was also below the pre-war level. While both were well below the world average; *per capita* calorie consumption being 85 per cent of the world average, *per capita* protein consumption 82 per cent. Table 3.6 gives particulars.

Table 3.6. Calories and protein, per capita[12]
(a) *In total: versus requirements. Per person, per day*

		Calories		Protein	
		Actual	% of requirement[b]	Actual (grammes)	Of which, animal
Ceylon	t_1	1,998	87%	43	8
	t_2	2,080	90%	44	8
China: Taiwan	t_1	2,140	91%	43	8
	t_2	2,350	99%	58	15
India	t_1	1,740	76%	46	5
	t_2	2,000	87%	52	6
Japan	t_1	1,960	83%	49	9
	t_2	2,290	97%	70	20
Pakistan	t_1	2,000	87%	48	8
	t_2	1,980	86%	45	7
Philippines	t_1	1,690	74%	—	—
	t_2	1,810	80%	43	14
cf:					
Australia	t_1	3,170	—	97	66
	t_2	3,140	—	90	60
New Zealand	t_1	3,350	—	100	67
	t_2	3,500	—	110	76

Notes:

a $t_1 =$ $t_2 =$

For		$t_1 =$	$t_2 =$
	Ceylon	1952-53	1960-2
	China: Taiwan	1951-53	1960-2
	India	1951-1953/4	1957/8-58/59 and 1961/2
	Japan	1951-53	1960-2
	Pakistan	1951/2-53/4	1957/8-59/60 and 1961/2
	Philippines	1953	1960-2

b The requirement specified rose very slightly in the period, in the following cases:

	From	To	
China: Taiwan	2,350	2,370	i.e. by 0.8 per cent
Japan	2,350	2,370	i.e. by 0.8 per cent

In other cases it was constant at:

Ceylon	2,300	Pakistan	2,300
India	2,300	Philippines	2,270

(b) *Composition of the calorie intake in* (a) *above:* (%)

		Cereals	Pulses and nuts	Meat and fish	Milk and eggs	Fats and oils	Others
Ceylon	t_1	58.2	17.6	2.5	1.7	4.7	14.9
	t_2	60.1	15.1	2.3	1.7	4.2	16.2
China: Taiwan	t_1	67.0	3.8	9.1	0.5	3.8	15.6
	t_2	67.4	4.2	8.7	0.7	4.8	14.0
India	t_1	67.3	12.0	—	6.1	4.2	9.7
	t_2	67.3	10.5	—	5.5	4.6	11.3
Japan	t_1	70.5	6.0	3.6	1.1	2.2	16.4
	t_2	61.0	7.1	4.9	2.9	5.0	18.8
Pakistan	t_1	74.6	3.3	1.3	5.4	4.5	10.4
	t_2	76.5	2.5	1.1	4.5	4.8	10.3
Philippines	t_1	66.6	2.0	7.1	1.4	2.6	20.0
	t_2	64.3	3.3	8.5	2.0	3.3	18.3
cf:							
Australia	t_1	29.5	1.7	20.0	11.1	12.6	24.8
	t_2	26.4	1.8	22.6	12.5	11.3	25.2
New Zealand	t_1	26.0	1.5	19.6	17.2	14.2	21.2
	t_2	24.6	1.5	19.8	18.4	14.1	21.4

Notes: t_1 and t_2 as in (a) above.
'Others'=starchy roots, sugar, fruits and vegetables.

The diet is thus poor; and improving very slightly if at all. It is especially poor in protective foods. Attention focuses on the supply position in terms of the farm-food balance and primarily of the cereals; though it should be borne in mind that there is a very large consumption of vegetables which is statistically unknown.

THE FARM-FOOD BALANCE

The countries in Table 3.7 (ii) thus had to get about half their food imports from outside the Region, the exports from the surplus countries in Table 3.7 (i) representing only about half their requirements. And their total import requirements rose by nearly 25 per cent in the period.

Table 3.7 does not include Japan, which imports large quan-

Table 3.7. *Production, exports and imports of cereals*[13]
(in 000 tons)

(i) *Net exporters*

	1951/2-1953/4			1960/1-1962/3		
	Production	Net Exports		Production	Net Exports	
		Quantity	(% of production)		Quantity	(% of production)
Burma	5,791	1,717	(30%)	7,099	2,465	(35%)
China: Taiwan	2,041	28	(1%)	......net import......		
Thailand	7,435	2,212	(30%)	8,754	2,535	(29%)
Vietnam: South	4,678a	364a	(80%)a	4,955b	140b	(3%)b
Totals	19,945	4,321	(22%)	20,808	5,140	(25%)

Notes: a Indochina: i.e. Cambodia, Laos and Vietnam.
b Vietnam: South, only.

(ii) *Net importers*

	1951/2-1953/4			1960/1-1962/3		
	Production	Net Imports		Production	Net Imports	
		Quantity	(% of total supply)		Quantity	(% of total supply)
Ceylon	533	914	(63%)	956	910	(49%)
China. Taiwan	......net export......			2,586	258	(9%)
India	62,214	3,972	(6%)	84,465	4,428	(5%)
Indonesia	11,389	997	(8%)	15,689	1,792	(8%)
Korea: South	3,594	703	(16%)	4,439	401	(8%)
Malaya: Fed.	640	960	(60%)	924	1,277	(42%)
Pakistan	17,025	652	(4%)	20,881	1,236	(6%)
Philippines	3,805	367	(9%)	5,086	355	(7%)
Totals	100,200	8,565	(8%)	135,026	10,657	(8%)

tities of food. The next Table (3.8) gives some particulars. (Note that it refers to all foodstuffs, not only to cereals as in the preceding Table.) Japan's food imports are only fractionally from the Region; on this it is not necessary to go into details here, the question at present being to identify the perspectives of the overall balance.

Table 3.8. *Total imports of food*[14]
(by value: million us $)

	1952	(Index)	1962	(Index)
Developing ECAFE countries	1,596	(100)	1,483	(93)
Japan	587	(100)	692	(118)
Total	2,183	(100)	2,175	(100)
(Japan as % of total	27%		32%)	

Thus production of cereals increased in the exporting countries in Table 3.7 by over 4 per cent in this period, in the importing countries by nearly 35 per cent; or for all together by nearly 30 per cent. Yet, though the exporting countries in the Region raised their net imports by over 19 per cent, the others increased their net imports by over 24 per cent; so that the import balance for the whole group increased by 21 per cent.

In *per capita* terms, some of the variations are interesting. Among the surplus-countries Burma made the most striking contribution, in that its *per capita* export of cereals rose by 21 per cent in this period; but its *per capita* production rose by only 4 per cent and *per capita* home consumption fell by 4 per cent. In Thailand, on the other hand, all these indicators fell – (*per capita* throughout, in the following) – exports by 12 per cent, production by 10 per cent and home-supplies by 9 per cent. In Ceylon production increased by no less than 43 per cent; imports were reduced by 20 per cent yet home-availabilities increased by 3 per cent. In Taiwan also home-availabilities rose by 3 per cent though production fell 7 per cent; and the country changed from being a small net exporter (1 per cent) to a distinct net importer (9 per cent). India also achieved a notable production increase (by 13 per cent) and raised the availabilities by 12 per cent, despite a 7 per cent increase in imports. Indonesia similarly increased production (by 14 per cent) but increased imports greatly – by 48 per cent – to raise the supply per person by 16 per cent. In Korea on the other hand imports were drastically reduced – by 53 per cent. With only a very slight rise in production (1 per cent) to offset this, availabilities were reduced by 8 per cent. In Malaya an 8 per cent increase in production, with imports hardly changed, resulted in only a 3 per cent rise in the supply per person. In Pakistan production rose 3 per cent and imports were greatly increased – even more than in Indonesia, namely by 59 per cent – yet supplies per head rose only 5 per cent. In the Philippines there was a 1 per cent rise in production and a 27 per cent reduction in imports, resulting in a 1 per cent fall in availabilities. (All the figures in this paragraph are *per capita*.)

The masses of people in all these lands are at a low subsistence level. Increases of such a low order, even in countries which achieved them, therefore cannot be considered much cause for satisfaction: while the general and increasing dependence on imports is a very serious matter. Moreover there are extreme variations from year to year and between countries, localities and classes or groups of people; hence it must be stressed that the issue is fraught with uncertainty, indeed with fear, for the hundreds of millions of people to whom these figures refer.

What is needed is not increases of 3 per cent, of 16 per cent, or even 50 per cent, but – as ECAFE asserted in 1965 – a 'more than doubling' of food production in the Asian Region. The Commission's staff noted that this might be possible, given some very large inputs indeed: improving methods of cultivation, supplying enough fertilizer and adequate irrigation. 'More than doubling' would mean raising food supply to a level approaching European standards. A lower aim is more immediately postulated – to raise the levels to those of the most advanced country in the Region, Japan. ECAFE considered that this would require a doubling of regional food production:[15]

> In order to raise and improve dietary levels throughout the developing ECAFE Region so as to reach, by 1975, those now (1963) prevailing in Japan, food production would have to be doubled, even if there were no acceleration of population growth.

All discussions of economic development in Asia must close by reverting to the subject with which they had to begin: the growth of population. Population is doubling in little more than one generation, birth-rates remaining high and death-rates falling swiftly; while the parlous lot of the average East Asian improves, despite great efforts, only very marginally and uncertainly. After fifteen years of hopeful concentration on industrial development the crux is still in agriculture, the real issue is the hunger of 1,000 million people.

Chapter 4

FOREIGN TRADE

Hitherto the condition and prospects of the Region have depended primarily on its foreign trade. This chapter considers – in the following order as far as possible – the interlocking problems of total trade relationships, exports, imports, the balance of trade and terms of trade.

The overall trade account is considered first.

(A) TOTAL TRADE RELATIONSHIPS

The growth of trade

Considering total trade first – imports plus exports – there has been a very large increase in Asia's overall trade. The trade of the Region as a whole increased by 217 per cent in 1948-64 (Table 4.1); distinctly more than the trade of the world as a whole (172 per cent). This would seem very satisfactory, but the underlying realities are highly disquieting. In the first place the Region's post-war share in world trade (at around 10 per cent) was nevertheless smaller than pre-war (over 16 per cent in 1937).

In the second place the gains were very unevenly shared. The above figures exclude Mainland China (considered separately later). They do however include Japan, which greatly biases the comparison with the rest of the world in favour of the Region, since Japan's condition was extremely depressed in 1948 and its growth from 1950 onwards was spectacular. Excluding Japan, the other countries in Table 4.1 increased their total trade, not by 217 per cent, which is the figure for the Region as a whole, but by only 104 per cent; and their share in the total trade of the world fell from 9 per cent in 1948 (which was similar to their pre-war percentage) to 6.7 per cent in 1964. Japan had 4 per cent of world trade in 1937, less than 1 per cent in 1948 and 4.7 per cent in 1964. India and Pakistan together had 2.6 per cent of world trade in 1937, rising to 3.3 per cent in 1948 but falling to 2.2 per cent in 1964. The individual shares of the remaining countries of the Region in the world market are consequently very small, though some of them have in-

Table 4.1. EAST ASIA AND WORLD TRADE[1]

	(i) Imports (c.i.f., in million US $)					Index 1948=100 (except Korea and Taiwan for which 1954=100)			
	1937	1948	1954	1959	1964	1937	1954	1959	1964
Burma	91	176	204	223	256	52	116	127	145
Ceylon	90	301	293	421	415	33	97	140	138
Hong Kong	278	523	601	866	1,496	53	115	166	286
India	(a)	1,616	1,297	1,975	2,435	(b)	80	122	151
Indochina	64	188	351	309	422(c)	34	187	164	224(c)
Indonesia	283	464	629	459	650(c)	61	136	99	140(c)
Japan	1,138	684	2,399	3,600	7,938	166	351	526	1,161
Korea	—	—	243	283	404	—	100	116	166
Malaya	388	842	1,419	1,845	2,238	46	169	219	226
Pakistan	(a)	312	334	353	998	(b)	107	113	320
Philippines	125	655	536	601	868	52	82	92	133
China : Taiwan	—	—	211	231	428	—	100	109	203
Thailand	49	144	312	426	667	34	217	296	463
Total, East Asia	3,190	6,051	8,959	11,740	20,096	53	148	194	332
Total, World	27,622	60,106	79,780	106,480	158,900	46	133	177	264

(a) The 1937 figure for India and Pakistan combined is 671.
(b) The 1937 index for India and Pakistan combined is 29, with 1948=100.
(c) 1963.

Table 4.1. EAST ASIA AND WORLD TRADE[1]
(ii) Exports (f.o.b.)
(million US $)

	1937	1948	1954	1959	1964	Index 1948=100 (Korea and Taiwan: 1954=100)			
						1937	1954	1959	1964
Burma	193	229	251	224	235	80	110	98	100
Ceylon	124	306	380	368	394	41	124	120	129
Hong Kong	253	404	423	574	1,012	63	105	142	250
India	(a)	1,363	1,182	1,304	1,749	—	87	96	171
Indochina	107	92	97	136	157(b)	116	105	148	130
Indonesia	548	394	867	872	696(b)	139	220	221	176
Japan	956	258	1,629	3,457	6,674	371	631	1,340	2,586
Korea	81	—	24	19	119	338	100	79	496
Malaya	520	829	1,408	1,932	1,809	63	170	233	217
Pakistan	(a)	494	359	321	427	—	73	65	86
Philippines	153	318	401	520	737	48	126	164	232
China: Taiwan	—	—	93	157	332	—	100	169	357
Thailand	73	223	283	358	599	33	127	161	269
Total, East Asia	3,720	5,168	7,770	10,730	15,500	72	150	208	300
Total, World	24,454	54,000	77,670	101,800	151,800	45	144	188	281

(a) Exports of India and Pakistan together in 1937 were 712 (index 26, with 1948 as 100).
(b) 1963.

creased their trade greatly. Moreover, the qualitative composition and *per capita* value of their trade have to be considered.

Total exports

The war affected Asia's exports more than those of other Regions. World exports in 1948 were 122 per cent greater than in 1937, in value terms; East Asia's only 39 per cent greater. In the post-war period until 1959, Asian exports fared better. In the six years 1948 to 1954, East Asia's exports increased more than the world's (50 per cent against 44 per cent). In the following five years to 1959 East Asia's exports similarly fared better than those of the world as a whole (39 per cent increase against 31 per cent). In the following period, however, the comparison turned to Asia's disfavour: the exports of East Asia increased only 44 per cent between 1959 and 1964, while those of the world as a whole increased nearly 50 per cent.

The Region's share in world exports fell accordingly. In 1937 the Region had over 15 per cent of the world's exports; throughout the post-war years, around 10 per cent. This includes Japan with nearly 4 per cent in 1937, 0.5 per cent only in 1948, 2 per cent in 1954, 3.3 per cent in 1959 and 4.4 per cent in 1964. There is a false impression that Japan's exports loomed larger in the 1960s, in their share of the world market as a whole, than before the war; though their quality and impact have certainly changed. The shares of the various countries are small, and mostly declining. India and Pakistan together contributed 3 per cent of all world exports in 1937, in value; in 1948 their joint percentage was only slightly higher (3.4 per cent), in 1954 it had declined to 2 per cent, in 1959 to just half their 1937 share and in 1964 even slightly less. During the 1950s and onwards Malaya (with Singapore) earned more from exports than these two great nations together; in 1964 still more than India and four and a half times as much as Pakistan. While Hong Kong's export earnings, already more than a third of the former British India's in 1937, were about a quarter in 1948-54-59 and rose to nearly a half in 1964. The remainder of the region (excluding Mainland China, Japan, India, Pakistan, Malaysia and Hong Kong) thus accounted generally for only 1 per cent or less of world exports throughout all the years specified, except in 1948, when they had about 2 per cent.

Within this general perspective the export performance of the different countries may be further evaluated from the index figures in Table 4.1 (ii). As export prices rose greatly from 1937, and again from 1948 – it is safe to say four or fivefold altogether for the more lucrative items – in real terms many of these countries became worse off in export earnings as time passed. Burma and Pakistan were especially poor in export performance. Even at current values, compared with 1948 or even 1937 their exports were stagnant or stationary.

Ceylon, Indochina, India and Indonesia did only moderately; their exports have increased by distinctly less than 100 per cent since 1948; in the case of these countries, owing to the population growth, *per capita* exports did not significantly increase, even in terms of current prices. A third group of countries recorded great increases: South Korea increased its exports to five times the 1948 figure, Taiwan to three and a half times, Malaya to over three times. The rest of the underdeveloped countries show various increases, by between 100 per cent and 170 per cent, significantly greater than the population divisor, but sadly below the trend of prices. Japan in contrast reached over seven times its 1937 export figure and nearly twenty times its 1948 level.

Total imports

In imports also, the war affected East Asia more than other regions. World imports in 1948 were 118 per cent greater in value (at current prices) than in 1937; East Asia's 90 per cent greater. The world expanded its exports in this wartime period slightly more than its imports. In the post-war period, on the other hand, East Asia increased its imports more than did the world as a whole. In the six years 1948 to 1954 the world's imports increased 33 per cent, but the region's rose 48 per cent; and again in the next five years to 1959 world imports rose 31 per cent, the region's 44 per cent. In the subsequent five years to 1964, the comparison changes. The region's imports continued to rise – by 49 per cent – but the expansion in total world imports was this time much greater, at 71 per cent.

Thus the post-war East Asia of 1948 had been able to raise its exports only about one-third as much as the world in general; but had raised its imports about three-quarters of the extent to which the world at large had done. To this extent the region fell during the war behind the world average in trade development.

C

In 1948-54 the proportion by which East Asia raised its import spending was 50 per cent greater than that for the world as a whole; whereas it raised its export earnings only 14 per cent more than did the world as a whole. In 1954-9 East Asia raised its expenditure on imports by about 31 per cent more than did the world as a whole; whereas it raised its export earnings only about 25 per cent more than did the world as a whole. There was thus some improvement – in the following sense. The region was still importing beyond its earnings through visible exports, but the gap between the respective rates of growth was slightly narrowing. In 1959-64 this gap narrowed much further, as the world indulged in a greater increase in imports, but the region did so to a much smaller extent, expanding its imports 31 per cent less than did the world as a whole; however, the region expanded its exports 14 per cent less than did the world as a whole.

The same qualifications apply as in the case of exports; prices and population rose greatly throughout this period, rendering the progress in 'real' and *per capita* terms correspondingly slight. Again the variations between the countries are marked. Japan's imports, reduced in 1948 to little over half those of 1937, proceeded to increase over tenfold by 1964. Hong Kong's in 1948 were nearly double those of 1937 and nearly trebled by

Table 4.2. Balance of visible trade[2]
(million US $)

	1937	1948	1954	1959	1964
Burma	+102	+53	+47	+1	-21
Ceylon	+34	+5	+87	-53	-21
Hong Kong	-25	-119	-178	-282	-484
India	..	-253	-115	-671	-686
Indochina	+43	-86	-254	-173	-265
Indonesia	+265	-70	+238	+412	+46
Japan	-182	-426	-770	-143	-1,264
Korea	..	..	-219	-264	-285
Malaya	+132	-87	-11	+87	-429
Pakistan	..	+182	+25	-30	-571
Philippines	+28	-337	-135	-81	-131
China. Taiwan	..	..	-18	-74	-96
Thailand	+24	+79	-29	-68	-68
Total, East Asia	+530	-883	-1,189	-1,010	-4,596
Total, World	-3,168	-6,051	-2,110	-4,700	-7,100

1964. Thailand's in 1948 were treble the pre-war and further quadrupled by 1964; Pakistan's trebled, Indonesia's, Taiwan's, Indochina's and Malaysia's more than doubled in the post-war period. The variations in India's, Korea's, Burma's, Ceylon's and the Philippines' imports were more moderate.

The overall balance of trade

The balances on the merchandise account are consequently as shown in Table 4.2.

Shares of the countries

It is interesting, therefore, to note the distribution of the region's total trade among its countries. Main features are the relative rise of Japan and the decline of the shares of India and other countries (Table 4.3).

Table 4.3. *Trade of the ECAFE Region: distribution between its countries[3] (percentage of total imports plus exports, value)*

	1948	1951	1953	1963
Burma	4%	2%	3%	2%
Cambodia	..	..	..	1%
Ceylon	5%	4%	4%	2%
China: Taiwan	..	1%	2%	2%
Hong Kong	8%	9%	8%	8%
India	31%	19%	15%	13%
Indonesia	8%	12%	10.5%	6%
Japan	9%	18%	24%	42%
Korea: South	..	0%	2%	2%
Malaya:				
Federation	5%	5.5%	4%	4%
Singapore	10%	14%	9.5%	7%
Pakistan	9%	7%	7%	4%
Philippines	8%	5%	6%	4%
Thailand	3%	4%	4%	4%
Vietnam: South	..	..	..	1%
	100%	100%	100%	100%

(B) INTERREGIONAL COMPARISONS

The perspectives are further clarified by comparing Asian trade development with that of other areas.

Regional distribution of world trade: destinations of exports

The regional pattern of world trade underwent significant changes during the quarter-century from 1938-63. Total world exports in 1963 were just over six and a half times their 1938 value; the index at current prices f.o.b. with 1938 = 100 was 653 ($23,500 million in 1938, 153,500 million in 1963). We may consider first the world import pattern – the destination of these exports – by broad Regions. The increased exports went much more to the developed countries than to the underdeveloped countries, the United Nations index for the former being 680, for the latter over one-third lower (534).

(i) *Imports by the developed countries*

In this United Nations definition 'developed countries' includes the USA, Canada, Western Europe, Australia, New Zealand, Japan and South Africa. Their respective value indices were:

Developed countries: index of imports
(1938 = 100)

	1963
World	653
North America	749
Western Europe	685
Australia and New Zealand	498
Japan	492
South Africa	852

The developed countries of the Western Hemisphere, and South Africa, took a larger percentage of the world's exports in 1963 than in 1938; Japan, Australia and New Zealand received a smaller percentage in 1963 than in 1938:

Percentage of world exports
going to
(*developed countries*)   *in*

	1938	1963
North America	17%	19%
Western Europe	39%	41%
Australia and New Zealand	3.2%	2.4%
Japan	4.7%	3.5%
South Africa	0.7%	0.9%
Total, developed countries	58%	78%

(ii) *Imports by underdeveloped countries*

The United Nations definition of 'underdeveloped countries', the index for which was used above, includes all the other countries in the world *except all the Communist countries* – i.e. it excludes the USSR, Communist China, North Korea and

North Vietnam. These will be considered separately below. Taking the underdeveloped areas according to this United Nations classification, the situation may be summarized as follows:

	Underdeveloped countries		
	Index of imports, 1963 (1938 = 100)	*Percentage of world exports received, in*	
		1938	1963
Middle East	11,909	2.3%	4.3%
Africa	752	2.8%	3.2%
Latin America	569	7.3%	4.1%
East Asia	331	10.8%	5.5%
Total, underdeveloped countries	23%		17%

The Middle East claims a very large percentage increase in its intake of the rest of the world's exports; but its absolute shares were very small. Africa, excluding the Union of South Africa, also showed a large percentage increase in its intake of world exports; but its absolute shares were also small. The same applies to Latin America.

The East Asian region – excluding Communist China, North Korea and North Vietnam – had an index, as receivers of the world's exports, little over half the index of the rise in total world exports. Our region's expansion of imports (this is in value terms at current prices throughout) was in a proportion only 44 per cent of that of North America, 48 per cent of that of West Europe, 58 per cent of that of Latin America. While East Asia's intake of world exports fell by nearly a half, as a percentage of the total, from 10.8 per cent in 1938 to 5.5 per cent in 1963.

There remain the Communist countries, which have not been included in the above analysis. Of these, only the USSR and East Europe figure very largely in world trade. The index for the USSR and East Europe was 783 in 1963; together they received 10 per cent of all world exports in 1938 and 12 per cent in 1963.

Communist China, North Korea and North Vietnam together (i.e. very largely Communist China, the others contributing comparatively minor amounts) show an index number of 226. Their intake of total world exports was about 2.6 per cent of the world total in 1938, falling to 0.9 per cent in 1963.

It is clear that the East Asian region, despite its vast population and area, is a weak part of the total market for the rising exports of the world; moreover, it is a declining one. Because of the large concentration of the world's population increase in this area, the weakness and the decline in *per capita* terms are very serious.

Regional distribution of world trade: sources of imports

Did the East Asian region do better than other Regions as a supplier of the world's imports? The index of total world imports, at current prices c.i.f. with 1938 = 100, was 634 in 1963; 616 for world imports from the developed countries, 561 for world imports from the underdeveloped countries (defined as before). The absolute figures were (in $ million) total world imports 25,400 in 1938, 161,100 in 1963. The indices for imports by the rest of the world, and their percentage shares, are as follows, for the developed areas:

	Index of exports, 1963 (1938 = 100)	Percentage of world imports furnished, in 1938	Percentage of world imports furnished, in 1963
Developed countries			
North America	807	11%	14%
West Europe	548	52%	45%
Japan	629	4.2%	4.1%
Australia and New Zealand	457	2.9%	2.1%
South Africa	366	1.8%	1.0%
Total, developed countries		72%	66%

The developed countries, other than the United States and Canada, thus somewhat reduced their share in world exports.

The region which most greatly increased its exports to the rest of the world was, by far, the Communist 'bloc' as a whole – with an index of no less than 11,059 and percentages of 6.7 per cent in 1938, 11.7 per cent in 1963. This was largely due to the recent export rise of the USSR, which contributed only 1 per cent of all other countries' imports in 1938 but nearly 4.4 per cent in 1963 – with an index of 438 in 1963. Mainland China's exports to the world outside the Communist Bloc have been extremely small ($4 million in 1948 and 1953, 50 in 1958, 70 in 1963; representing 1 to 2 per cent of the world total at the last two dates).

For the underdeveloped areas, in the UN definition, the position is as follows:

	Underdeveloped countries		
	Index of	Percentage of world	
	exports, 1963	imports furnished, in	
	(1938=100)	1938	1963
Africa	750	2.6%	3.1%
Latin America	568	6.0%	5.4%
East Asia	453	9.3%	6.6%

East Asia's export performance is thus even more unsatisfactory, overall, than its import performance. In the movement of world trade it is a laggard; while it leads in population growth, so that in *per capita* terms its position is particularly unsatisfactory.

Regional distribution of the balance of trade
The world's adverse balance of commodity trade thus grew – subtracting the figures of exports f.o.b. from those of imports c.i.f. – from $2,000 million in 1938 (index 100) to $7,600 million in 1963 (index 380). Now this adverse balance was at both dates ascribable primarily to the developed countries; which ran a deficit on visible trade of $2,700 million in 1938 (over 5.5 per cent of total world trade, exports plus imports), rising to $6,800 million in 1963 (over 2.1 per cent of the total trade). The underdeveloped countries on the other hand had an excess of imports over exports (though it was a comparatively small one: $200 million in 1938, $500 million in 1963). This represented about 1.7 per cent of their total trade in 1938 and 0.8 per cent in 1963.

As the underdeveloped countries do not have the invisible earnings from services of all kinds which the developed countries enjoy, a trade deficit is a more directly serious matter for the latter than for the former. To estimate the progress of the East Asian region in particular, the essential comparison is between that region and the other underdeveloped areas. The developing non-Communist East Asian countries had a trade deficit of $190 million in 1938; which was not very serious, in the sense that it represented less than 0.4 per cent of their total trade. In 1963 their balance of trade position had notably improved, showing a surplus of $2,140 or no less than 11 per cent of their total trade.

Comparison should be made with the following. Latin America's adverse balance greatly increased between 1938 and

1963; it represented over 5 per cent of its total trade in each of those years. Underdeveloped Africa's trade was roughly in balance in 1938 with a surplus representing only about 0.5 per cent of its total trade; in 1963 there was still a small favourable balance (0.1 per cent) though its trade had greatly increased. The Middle East had a favourable balance in 1938, representing over 13 per cent of its total trade, but – in the subsequent prodigious increase in its total international trade by some ten times – it saw this changed in 1963 into a deficit representing nearly 12 per cent of its total trade. From this overall point of view of the balance of payments, the position of East Asia as a whole has therefore eased; and it has done better in this respect than the other underdeveloped areas, even though it has not shared equally with them in the total increase in trade.

(C) GEOGRAPHICAL STRUCTURE OF THE REGION'S TRADE

The layout of the trade of East Asia, between countries and areas, must be considered.

Distribution of the region's exports

Taking the ECAFE figures year by year (Table 4.4) in value terms, about one-third of the exports of ECAFE countries went in the period after 1950 to destinations within the Region. In the first half of the 1950s a quarter went to West Europe. Between 1953 and 1958 this proportion dropped towards one-fifth, but in 1958-63 it rose again above one-quarter. The proportion going to the United States was about one-fifth in 1950, slightly less in both 1953 and 1958, falling to less than one-sixth in 1963.

The rest of the world (other than the ECAFE Region itself, Western Europe and the USA) thus took about one-fifth of the Region's exports in each of those years except 1958, when this proportion fell to about one-sixth. The Region itself remained its own best customer (one-third or slightly over), West Europe the next (one-quarter, with slight variations up and down), and US and the rest of the world remained fairly equal, as recipients of the Region's exports, at about one-fifth each; but the share of the US showing a downward trend. This latter feature is important because exports to the United States are the source of dollar earnings. A greater proportion of the Region's exports goes to the sterling area (slightly over one-third in 1950, falling to one-third in 1953 and 1958, rising slightly again in 1963); much of the rest is sterling-based. The category 'sterling area' of course substantially overlaps with that of the Region, which includes many sterling countries.

The Korean War boom was very moderately sustained (at current prices) in total exports from 1950 to 1953 (which rose by about 3 per cent) and in exports to the ECAFE Region and W. Europe (3 per cent and 4 per cent). Against this there was, however, a fall between 1950 and 1953 of 10 per cent in the exports to the United States and equally 10 per cent in the exports to the sterling area as a whole.

Between 1953 and 1958, on the other hand, there was a much greater growth in total exports (by some 27 per cent) and this was significantly in exports to the USA (32 per cent) and sterling area (28 per cent), while those to West Europe and the ECAFE Region increased in a more moderate ratio (12-13 per cent).

In the third quinquennium 1958-63, in contrast, total exports increased by only 5 per cent; and this was largely to the ECAFE Region itself (30 per cent increase) and to West Europe (equally 30 per cent increase), while exports to the sterling area rose only 10 per cent and those to the USA showed the very significant fall of 17 per cent.

The main perspectives of the export picture are thus as follows. Total exports at current prices increased 38 per cent in fifteen years. This is a considerable rate of growth but is very unsatisfactory in real terms, considering the growth of population and the rise in prices. They were divided as noted above in very rough equality between four broad customer-areas (the Region itself, W. Europe, the USA, the rest of the world) and in relation also to the sterling area. The growth in exports was, however, concentrated distinctly on the Region itself and West

Table 4.4. *Direction of the exports of the ECAFE Region*[4]
(million US $)

	ECAFE countries	West Europe	USA	Sterling area	Total exports
1950	2,432	1,690	1,392	2,574	6,725
1953	2,502	1,795	1,238	2,339	6,940
1958	2,814	1,993	1,630	2,998	8,829
1963	3,699	2,569	1,361	3,304	9,289

Table 4.5. *East Asian and world imports*[5]
(a) *Value (c.i.f., in million in US $)*

	1937	1948	1954	1959	1964
Burma	91	176	204	223	256
Ceylon	90	301	293	421	415
China: Taiwan	—	—	211	231	428
Hong Kong	278	523	601	866	1,496
India	(a)	1,616	1,297	1,975	2,435
Indochina	64	188	351	309	422(c)
Indonesia	283	464	629	459	650(c)
Japan	1,138	684	2,399	3,600	7,938
Korea	—	—	243	283	404
Malaya	388	842	1,419	1,845	2,238
Pakistan	(a)	312	334	353	998
Philippines	125	655	536	601	868
Thailand	49	144	312	426	667
Total, East Asia	3,190	6,051	8,959	11,740	20,096
Total, World	27,622	60,106	79,780	106,480	158,900
Total, East Asia, excluding Japan	2,052	5,367	6,560	8,140	12,158

(b) *Index* (1948 = 100: except Korea and Taiwan,
for which 1954 = 100)

	1937	1954	1959	1964
Burma	52	116	127	145
Ceylon	33	97	140	138
China: Taiwan	—	100	109	203
Hong Kong	53	115	166	286
India	(b)	80	122	151
Indochina	34	187	164	224(c)
Indonesia	61	136	99	140(c)
Japan	166	351	526	1,161
Korea	—	100	116	166
Malaya	46	169	219	226
Pakistan	(b)	107	113	320
Philippines	52	82	92	133
Thailand	34	217	296	463
Total, East Asia	53	148	194	332
Total, World	46	133	177	264
Total, East Asia, excluding Japan	38	122	152	226

Notes: (a) The 1937 figure for India and Pakistan combined is 671.
(b) The 1937 index for India and Pakistan combined is 29, with 1948 = 100.
(c) 1963.

Europe, for each of which there was a 50 per cent increase. The increase in exports to the sterling area was about half as marked (28 per cent); while exports to the USA declined slightly (2 per cent).

Distribution of the region's imports

The course of the region's total import trade and of world imports as a whole is summarized in Table 4.5 on page 74.

Examination of the value of the imports from each area gives another perspective. The value of imports from within the Region increased by 26 per cent in 1950-3 and 41 per cent in 1953-8 but only 5 per cent in 1958-63. Imports from West Europe increased in value by no less than 60 per cent in 1950-3, but only 9 per cent in 1953-8 and 19 per cent in 1958-63. Imports from the USA rose 45 per cent in 1950-3 and 43 per cent in 1953-8 but declined 2 per cent in 1958-63. Imports from the sterling area increased 25 per cent in 1950-3 but only 7 per cent in 1953-8 and declined 7 per cent in 1958-63, being about the same in 1963 as they had been ten years earlier. Taking the whole period overall, imports from West Europe and the United States showed very large increases (by 109 per cent and 105 per cent respectively) while imports from the ECAFE Region increased 87 per cent (rather more than the increase in total imports from all sources, which was 83 per cent); while the imports from the sterling area increased only 25 per cent.

Table 4.6. *Sources of imports by the ECAFE Region*
(million US $)

	ECAFE countries	West Europe	USA	Sterling area	Total imports
1950	2,217	1,384	1,243	2,140	6,058
1953	2,794	2,221	1,800	2,682	8,882
1958	3,928	2,419	2,572	2,866	10,568
1963	4,140	2,886	2,524	2,671	11,097

Origins of imports

Total imports by the Region increased between 1950 and 1960 by over 80 per cent; at prices which were rising more than the prices obtained for its exports, which rose only in the order of 40 per cent in the same period. The imports from the five main areas of the world which were distinguished above were in broadly the same proportion as the Region's exports to them. The countries of the ECAFE Region drew rather more than one-third of their imports from within the Region itself, about one-quarter from Western Europe, one-fifth (rising in this case to about one-quarter) from the USA. The rest of the world thus provided some 20 per cent in 1950, 25 per cent in 1953, falling to 15 per cent in 1958 but rising greatly to 35 per cent in 1963. The sterling area furnished one-quarter in 1950, rising to 30 per cent in 1953 and 27 per cent in 1958, but falling back to 25 per cent in 1963.

The magnitude and seriousness of the fluctuations must again be stressed; also the balance of payments problem, which is considered below. The rise in imports was strikingly out of phase with the progress of exports. A closer study of the sequence enables a much more optimistic view to be taken: in that the great percentage rise in imports occurred in the first quinquennial period, 1950-3, when total imports rose nearly 50 per cent. This 'import spending spree', prompted by the earlier gains in the Korean War boom, subsequently subsided; imports rose 20 per cent in 1953-8 and only 5 per cent in 1958-63.

In 1950 the Region supplied 37 per cent of the imports, 31 per cent in 1953, 37 per cent again in 1958, but 41 per cent in 1963. The development of intra-Regional trade was thus late, the Region's share falling in the first quinquennium and accelerating in the two later ones. Imports from West Europe were, for the same years, respectively 23-25-23-26 per cent; so that the share of West Europe remained rather constant. The share of the United States rose only slightly, and also later: the figures being 20-20-24-23 per cent. The imports from the sterling area, as a percentage of the total, moved on a distinctly and fairly evenly falling trend: 35-30-27-24 per cent.

(D) THE INSTABILITY OF TRADE

Instability in the total trade

It is important to identify closely the respects in which the Region's trade basis is uncertain or unstable and the extent of the variables in it. If we take *total trade* (imports plus exports: Table 4.7) the pattern does not appear extremely variable. The intra-Regional share of total trade fluctuated in a range of five percentage points between 33 per cent and 38 per cent; falling in 1950-3, rising 1953-8 and 1958-63. The shares of the other main areas fluctuated less, but more irregularly. West Europe's share fluctuated four percentage points between 23 per cent and 27 per cent; rising slightly in 1950-3, falling slightly in 1953-8 but rising considerably in 1958-63. The USA's moved only within three percentage points between 19 per cent and 22 per cent: falling from 21 per cent to 19 per cent in 1950-3, rising reciprocally from 19 per cent to 22 per cent in 1953-8, falling reciprocally from 22 per cent to 19 per cent again in 1958-63. The share of the rest of the world fluctuated four points: rising by the whole four points in 1950-3; to fall to about the same extent in each of the two next periods. The share of the sterling area – to be considered separately, as overlapping with the ECAFE and 'rest of world' categories – remained, however, remarkably stable, at 30 per cent throughout except for a slight rise to 32 per cent in 1953.

Overall (1950-63) the Region increased the share of its imports coming from West Europe and from the Region itself, reduced the share of its imports from the USA and the rest of the world; while that of the sterling area remained unchanged.

Table 4.7. Distribution of the Region's total trade
(imports plus exports)

Amount (US $ million)		ECAFE countries	West Europe	USA	Rest of world	Sterling area
				Distribution %		
1950	12,783	36%	24%	21%	19%	30%
1953	15,822	33%	25%	19%	23%	32%
1958	19,397	35%	23%	22%	20%	30%
1963	20,386	38%	27%	19%	16%	30%

Variability in import-sources

Analysis of the Region's *imports* (Table 4.8) shows, however, rather more extreme variations. The intra-Regional share of total imports dropped by six percentage points from 37 per cent to 31 per cent in 1950-3, but resumed the 1950 level in 1958 and remained at it in 1963. West Europe's maximum swing was by three percentage points (less than the swing in its total trade) but it was in the 'see-saw' pattern: 23-25-23-26 per cent. The USA's swing was four percentage points between 20-24 per cent, falling slightly in the first quinquennium, rising four points in the second, falling slightly in the third. The share of the rest of the world swung unevenly in an amplitude of five points: falling by the whole five points in 1950-3, recovering two points in

1953-8, only to fall reciprocally by two points in 1958-63.

Taking the sterling area, its share in the Region's imports fluctuated much more drastically than its share in the total trade: by nine percentage points, to which extent it rose in 1950-3, to fall three points in 1953-8 and two in 1958-63.

Table 4.8. Distribution of the Region's total imports

Amount (US $ million)		ECAFE countries	West Europe	USA	Distribution % Rest of world	Sterling area
1950	6,058	37%	23%	21%	19%	21%
1953	8,882	31%	25%	20%	14%	30%
1958	10,568	37%	23%	24%	16%	27%
1963	11,097	27%	26%	23%	14%	25%

Variability in export-destinations

Taking finally the various areas' shares in the Region's *exports* (Table 4.9), that of the Region itself varied in an extreme range of seven percentage points, remaining stable at 36 per cent in the first two quinquennial years, falling to 32 per cent in 1958 and rising to 39 per cent in 1963. West Europe's showed a range of five percentage points, similarly remaining stable in the first two specified years (at 25 per cent), falling to 23 per cent in 1958 and rising to 28 per cent in 1963. The shares of the United States and the sterling area declined: the US's by six percentage points, the sterling area's by eight. Both of these, however, divided their declines fairly evenly in the first and third periods and remained on a stable trend in the second. The share of the 'rest of the world', in contrast, fluctuated between four percentage points but actually rose in the first period and declined to its original level thereafter.

Table 4.9. Distribution of the Region's total exports

Amount (US $ million)		ECAFE countries	West Europe	USA	Distribution % Rest of world	Sterling area
1950	6,725	36%	25%	21%	18%	38%
1953	6,940	36%	25%	18%	21%	34%
1958	8,829	32%	23%	18%	17%	34%
1963	9,289	39%	28%	15%	18%	30%

All this illustrates how extremely unstable and irregular has been the layout of the Region's trade between the different areas. In sum the shares by areas in total trade, exports and

I = IMPORTS   E = EXPORTS   T = TOTAL TRADE

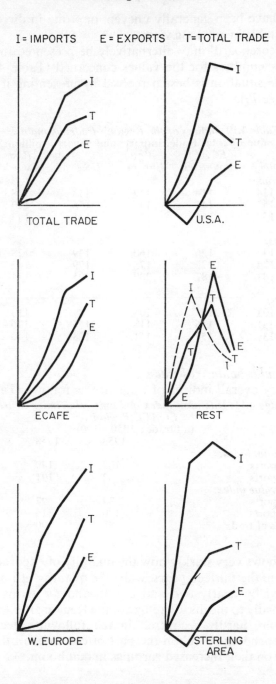

TOTAL TRADE

U.S.A.

ECAFE

REST

W. EUROPE

STERLING AREA

imports have been generally uneven, opposite in direction and unpredictable in any long view.

The 'scoreboard' may alternatively be presented in terms of the index numbers for the values concerned (Table 4.10); and the whole situation is best perceived by presenting it in graph form (page 79).

Table 4.10. *Indices of the Region's trade, by main areas*
(value of total trade, imports and exports, million $)

	Total	ECAFE countries	West Europe	USA	Rest of world	Sterling area
(a) Total trade:						
1953	124	114	129	113	148	132
1958	152	145	144	156	170	154
1963	159	166	177	145	137	159
(b) Imports:						
1953	147	126	160	139	178	216
1958	174	177	175	199	142	232
1963	183	187	209	195	133	222
(c) Exports:						
1953	103	103	104	89	119	91
1958	131	116	118	116	196	116
1963	138	151	151	128	140	128

The irregular balance of trade

The key overall indices of trade are as follows (Table 4.11).

Table 4.11. *Quantum index and unit value index of trade,*
ECAFE Region
(all trade: 1950=100)

	1953	1958	1963
Quantum index:			
Exports	108	149	191
Imports	132	191	246
Unit value index:			
Exports	98	97	99
Imports	110	115	115
Terms of trade	88	90	92

This shows very starkly how the quantity of exports less than doubled in the thirteen years, while the quantity of imports was multiplied by nearly two and a half; and the terms of trade, turning badly to the disadvantage of the Region after the Korean War boom, hardly recovered in the following decade. The 'import spending spree' on the part of countries in the Region followed on their increased earnings in that boom.

If the total trade balance is considered (Table 4.12) it is clear that a favourable balance of some US $670 million in 1950 changed into an adverse balance of nearly 2,000 million in 1953 and remained almost at the latter level for the following decade. The favourable balance in 1950 was distributed as follows: principally with Western Europe (46 per cent) and the ECAFE countries (32 per cent), secondly with the USA (15 per cent) and thirdly with the rest of the world (7 per cent). The sterling area – cutting across two of these categories, the ECAFE Region and the rest of the world – was really the big contributor, with a favourable balance of over $1,300 million. That is about double the total overall favourable balance in 1950; in other words, in the boom at that time the Region earned on the favourable balance of visible trade about fifteen times as much sterling as it earned dollars.

In 1953 the favourable balance was transformed into an adverse balance three times as large. The balance with all regions was unfavourable and was distributed more evenly than the favourable balance of five years earlier, as follows: USA 29 per cent, West Europe 24 per cent, ECAFE countries 15 per cent, rest of the world 32 per cent. The largest change – a swing with an amplitude of over $1,600 million – was in relation to the sterling area. The next largest change, a downward shift in the balance by over $700 million, was in relation to Western Europe. The shift in respect of the United States was almost as great ($650 million); the undermining of the dollar-earning position of the Region was, therefore, a particularly serious aspect. The drop in the balance with ECAFE countries themselves from above the credit line into 'the red', was also large ($500 million in round terms). The loss of the relatively small credit balance with the rest of the world (other than the West Europe, the USA and the Region itself) and its transformation into a deficit of $625 million was a change of greater amplitude than the change in the account with the United States.

1950-3 was thus the most adverse of the three periods, the big downswing from the balance of trade point of view. In the two subsequent five-year periods the Region continued to 'live with' overall deficits of approximately the same magnitude as the one in 1953 (1953: $1,900 million; 1958: 1,700 million; 1963: 1,800 million). The total deficit balance in 1958 was some 10 per cent less than that of 1953. The pattern was, however, very significantly different in this period 1953-8. Though the Region increased its own internal deficit with its own countries some three and a half times, increased its deficit with the United States by two-thirds and reduced its deficit with West Europe only very slightly, its account with the rest of the world improved by over $1,300 million; its balance with the sterling area also moved (more moderately, with a swing of $350 million) to the credit side.

In 1958-63 the overall deficit increased slightly (by 4 per cent); but the pattern again changed strikingly. The largest deficit in 1963 was with the United States: at over $1,100 million it was approximately the same as the deficits with the Region itself and with the US in 1958. The deficit within the Region itself was reduced by two-thirds, that with West Europe by 23 per cent. A smaller surplus was earned from the rest of the world ($150 million, about one-fifth of the 1958 figure); but a larger one from the sterling area (nearly five times the 1958 figure, though only 40 per cent of the surplus gained from the sterling area in 1950).

Table 4.12. *Balance of trade, ECAFE Region*
(million US $)

	ECAFE countries	West Europe	USA	Rest of world	Sterling area	Total
1950	+215	+306	+99	+47	+1,331	+667
1953	−292	−462	−562	−626	−343	−1,942
1958	−1,114	−426	−942	−743	+112	−1,739
1963	−471	−372	−1,163	−153	+543	+1,808

Variations in the size of the deficit

For the world as a whole, on the above basis, exports were some 9-10 per cent less than imports before the war, and again in 1948; but only 4-5 per cent less than imports in 1959 and 1964. For our East Asian group, there was in contrast an excess of exports over imports before the war by some 18 per cent. In 1948 and 1954, however, this was reversed to an import excess of some 17 per cent. The adverse balance fell further, to about 10 per cent, in 1959; but rose to some 30 per cent in 1964.

The actual shortfall of the value of imports below the value of exports, for the world as a whole, in 1948 was about double what it had been in 1937; in 1954 it was, however, only about one-third of what it was in 1948, and in 1952 two-thirds, though in 1964 it was some 17 per cent larger than in 1948. In East Asia, besides the transformation from a favourable balance in 1937 to an unfavourable one in 1948, the actual shortfall of the value of imports below that of exports increased much more formidably than for the world as a whole; it was about one-third larger in 1954 than in 1948, moderating in 1959 to only about 14 per cent larger than in 1948, but leaping in 1964 to a figure more than five times that of 1948.

It will be noted (Table 4.14) that the Region was in surplus in 1937 – its exports exceeding its imports by over 16 per cent. Post-war, however, a large part of the world's overall deficit is due to the Region – varying in the last ten years between 20 per cent and 50 per cent, if Japan is excluded. Taking 1948 and 1964, the world's deficit increased 17 per cent; that of the Region excluding Japan and Mainland China increased 629 per cent. Japan's deficit increased 300 per cent.

The absolute sums are, of course, enormously more meaningful if presented as percentages of the respective areas' total trade. In 1937 the Region's exports were some 18 per cent greater than its imports, whereas the world was importing 9 per cent more than it was exporting. In 1948 the region's imports exceeded exports by some 17 per cent, the world's by some 10 per cent. In 1954 imports continued to exceed imports by 16 per cent in the region, while the world's figure fell to only 2 per cent. In 1959 the corresponding figures were 10 per cent for the region and 4 per cent for the world; in 1964 no less than 30 per cent

Table 4.13. *Deficit on the balance of trade as a percentage of total trade:*
ECAFE countries
(+ indicates a surplus)

	1937	1948	1964
Burma	+36%	+17%	−4%
Ceylon	+16%	+1%	−2%
Hong Kong	−5%	−13%	−32%
India	..	−8%	−30%
Indochina	+25%	−34%	−46%
Indonesia	+32%	−8%	−3%
Japan	−9%	−45%	−9%
Korea: South	..	..	−54%
Malaysia	+15%	−1%	−1%
Pakistan	—	+1%	−33%
Philippines	+ 10%	−35%	−8%
Taiwan	..	..	−13%
Thailand	+20%	−22%	−5%
Total	+8%	−8%	−13%

for the region, against 5 per cent for the world.

The incidence of the deficit on the various countries, as a percentage of their total foreign trade (imports plus exports) is shown in Table 4.13.

Japan, alone in Asia, ranks as one of the great industrial nations of the world; its requirements of imports of materials and food are accordingly great, while on the other hand its international shipping and business services are very highly developed and represent enormous invisible exports; nevertheless, on balance Japan tends to have a deficit on the 'invisible' account. Hong Kong and Singapore are – on their relatively mini-scale – centres of similarly phenomenal industrial and commercial development. These countries can 'afford an overdraft' – indeed it is even normal in their contemporary business situations. For the other countries the condition of chronic and worsening deficit, reversing the credit position of pre-war days, is a very serious aspect. To emphasize the divergence of the Region's trend from that of the world as a whole, other UN figures are given as a recapitulation in Table 4.14.

Table 4.14. Balance of visible trade: E. Asian and world trends[14]

	1937	1948	1954	1959	1964
World:					
excess of imports					
over exports (m. $)	3,168	6,085	2,200	3,800	7,100
(%)	9%	10%	2%	4%	5%
index	52	100	36	62	117
E. Asia:					
excess of exports					
over imports (m. $)	530				
(%)	18%				
excess of imports					
over exports (m. $)		883	1,189	1,010	4,596
(%)		17%	16%	10%	30%
index		100	135	114	525

Depletion of exchange assets

The impact on the developing ECAFE countries (the region excluding Japan) should be especially stressed. It is interesting to set alongside the trade results the external-reserve position of this group of countries – as is done in Table 4.15. In the period 1956 to mid-1964 these countries consistently imported far more than they exported: to a total of over US $72,000 million worth of imports against nearly 61,000 of exports, imports thus exceeding exports by nearly 20 per cent. Their stocks of gold and foreign exchange assets were depleted. Between 1956 and 1959, for example, world gold and foreign exchange holdings (excluding international monetary institutions) increased 2.5 per cent while those of the underdeveloped East Asian countries fell 9 per cent. The latters' total holdings represented some 8 per cent of those of the world in 1956, barely 7 per cent in 1959. The deficit almost doubled in some years; only once was it reduced, otherwise it increased at least 30 per cent even in a 'good' year.

*Table 4.15. Trade deficits and exchange reserves:
developing ECAFE countries*[15]
(in US $000 million): (indices in brackets)

	Exports	Imports		Deficit	Gold and exchange reserves
1956	7.5 (100)	8.6 (100)	115%	1.1 (100)	4.4 (100)
1957	7.8 (104)	9.8 (114)	126%	2.0 (178)	3.7 (83)
1958	7.2 (97)	8.7 (101)	121%	1.5 (131)	3.6 (81)
1959	8.0 (107)	8.6 (104)	107%	0.9 (82)	4.0 (91)
1960	8.5 (114)	10.3 (120)	121%	1.8 (159)	4.1 (94)
1961	8.4 (112)	10.5 (122)	125%	2.1 (190)	4.0 (92)
1962	8.6 (115)	10.6 (124)	123%	2.0 (183)	3.9 (88)
1963, first half	4.6 (122)	5.3 (123)	115%	0.7 (138)	4.1 (94)

(E) THE TERMS OF TRADE

It is on all this background that the Region's gains from international trade must be evaluated.

Value shares

Indications were given above that Asia ranked low in many respects in comparison not only with the developed Regions, but also with other underdeveloped ones in various respects. Unfortunately the same applies to the development of its trade. ECAFE found that the world's underdeveloped areas as a whole increased their total trade between 1938 and the 1959-61 average by three and a half times, whereas the developed areas increased theirs by four and a half times.

The relative values of the staple commodities involved in trade are an important factor. For example, the figure just given for the underdeveloped countries is raised by the inclusion of some with large export earnings from petroleum; the developing countries of the ECAFE Region, which are not significantly petroleum-exporters, increased their total trade by less than 200 per cent in 1938-1959/61.

The dependence of the world economy on international trade in fuels is striking; and it must increase, given the pattern of modern development. The second largest 'resource' item in world imports in 1960 (after food and raw materials, which totalled $40,000 million) was fuels ($11,000 million). The trade in fuels grew much more than that in food and raw materials: in 1960 it was 70 per cent above 1938 and 80 per cent above 1950 (in quantity). Many countries are grossly dependent on fuel imports for their present activity and hopes of future development; not least the East Asian countries.

In 1950-60 the exports and imports of the world's developed countries each increased on the average 6.9 per cent per annum in volume. The corresponding figures for the developing countries were some 35 per cent to 50 per cent lower; and their imports grew more than 25 per cent faster than their exports. Their exports increased in volume by 3.6 per cent a year, their imports by 4.6 per cent a year. During that decade imports and exports everywhere rose in value; but the lion's share of the value-increases went to a startling extent to the developed countries, as the following figures emphasize.

The increase in the whole decade (1960 over 1950) in the unit value of exports of the developed countries was 17.5 per cent; the increase in the unit value of exports of the developing countries was only *one per cent*. In imports, however, the unit value for the developing countries rose almost as much as for the developed countries: viz. for the developing countries 10.2 per cent, for the developed countries 11.3 per cent. In this sense the trend of the terms of trade was severely unfavourable, especially to the East Asian and other underdeveloped areas which export largely food and agricultural raw materials.

If the shares in the world export value are considered, another scale of comparison emerges: in 1950 the developed countries took just under 60 per cent and the developing countries just 30 per cent, in 1960 the developed countries exactly two-thirds (66 per cent) and the developed countries 20.4 per cent. Since the East Asian group's trade grew less than the average for all underdeveloped areas, its share in the export-value fell from distinctly under 30 per cent to distinctly under 20 per cent. The remainder – 11.2 per cent in 1950 and 13.6 per cent in 1960 –

refers to the Communist world, the 'developed' and 'developing' countries in the above paragraphs being the non-Communist ones. Both the Communist countries and the question of the terms of trade are treated below.

Prices and terms of trade

The 'real' world-market prices of primary staple commodities fell greatly in 1948-60, and especially after the Korean war boom of 1950-1 (Table 4.16). This vitally affected the Region, where it is most vulnerable.

Table 4.16. *World index of export prices of food and raw materials; in terms of constant prices of exported manufactured goods*[16]
(UN index of export prices, food and materials, deflated by export prices for manufacturers. 1953 = 100)

1938:	68	1954:	101
1948:	100	1955:	100
1950:	115	1956:	96
1951:	116	1957:	96
1952:	101	1958:	89
1953:	100	1959:	86
		1960:	83

Breakdowns for specific commodities are generally difficult, because of many changes in standards or classifications, exchange rates and price-maintenance arrangements; but some of them can be accurately traced (Table 4.17).

This shows two things graphically: the acute shift in the terms of trade largely in favour of manufactures as against agricul-

Table 4.17. *World price-indices of some basic-resource commodities; in terms of constant prices of exports of manufactured goods*[17]
(1947 = 100)

	Copper	Cotton	Sugar	Wheat
1938	71	48	38	52
1948	95	86	79	112
1949	91	89	82	98
1950	88	115	94	76
1951	91	96	97	71
1952	119	86	73	77
1953	118	85	61	80
1954	116	86	58	68
1955	163	75	58	66
1956	148	63	58	60
1957	96	62	86	59
1958	85	60	58	58
1959	102	56	48	58
1960	105	60	51	58

tural products, and the extreme fluctuations in values from year to year (with an amplitude in the post-war period of 78 percentage points for copper, 59 for cotton, 49 for sugar and 40 for wheat).

Here is an aspect of the Asian paradox that has perhaps not been fully noticed. In a long-term view of the worldwide market, basic material products are generally in glut rather than scarcity. Yet in underdeveloped Asia, particularly, there is absolute *per capita* scarcity in these items and a reduced earning power associated with dependence on producing them.

(F) DEVELOPMENT GOODS AND CONSUMPTION GOODS

Finally it is necessary to analyse the composition of the trade as between the main types of commodities. In the backward-looking or negative view great importance has been attached to the composition of the trade as between raw materials on the one hand and manufactures on the other; dependence on the export of the former and the import of the latter is the 'colonial' economic situation. In the forward-looking view, striving for positive development in terms especially of industrialization, high significance attaches to the pattern of trade-flows as between producer goods and consumer goods.

For the latter part of our period UN figures give a breakdown of Regional imports into the main 'consumption' and 'capital' categories. Table 4.18 gives the results for the (non-Communists) developing countries of the Region.

This clearly illustrates the efforts of this group of countries

Table 4.18. *Imports, consumption goods and capital goods: developing countries of the Region*[18]
(value, million $)

	1958	1959	1960	1961	1962	1963
Food	1,628	1,415	1,565	1,495	1,488	1,821
Other consumption goods	1,391	1,313	1,548	1,581	1,532	1,565
Materials for consumption goods	1,612	1,817	2,125	2,186	2,429	2,409
Total for consumption	4,631	4,545	5,238	5,262	5,449	5,795
Materials for capital goods	838	854	891	854	831	888
Capital goods	2,025	2,106	2,756	2,827	3,074	3,361
Total, for capital	2,863	2,960	3,647	3,681	3,905	4,249
Grand total	7,494	7,505	8,885	8,943	9,354	10,044

towards industrialization; the grand total increased over the whole period by one third (34 per cent) but the group of imports for consumption purposes increased at half the rate at which imports on capital-goods account increased : 25 per cent and 48 per cent respectively. The category of imports of finished capital goods increased the most (by 66 per cent); as a proportion of the whole it rose quite strongly from just above a quarter to one-third (27 per cent in 1958, 28.1 per cent in 1959, 31 per cent in 1960, 31.6 per cent in 1961, 32.8 per cent in 1962, 35.5 per cent in 1963).

The category of 'materials chiefly for capital goods' meanwhile declined quite distinctly as a proportion of all imports (11,2 per cent in 1958 and 11.4 per cent in 1959, 10.1 per cent in 1960, 9.6 per cent in 1961, 8.9 per cent in 1962, 8.8 per cent in 1963).

To some extent this was healthily based on increased home-supply of these basic means of industrialization, to some extent it might be deemed to evince a less satisfactory increase in reliance on procurement of 'complete' equipment from the advanced countries. The former may be better or preferable in some circumstances and cases; the latter in others. Prejudices in this respect relaxed more and more in the Region during this period.

One thoughtful study termed the process of world-industrialization 'The Road to Huddersfield';[18a] it is too much to say that it became generally considered in this period that ' all the roads lead to Huddersfield' in the same sense that proverbially (in a different context) all roads lead to Rome, but at least it became increasingly understood that the routes to industrialization were varied and the choices not mutually exclusive. When there is an ecumenical congress of all the dogmatists of industrialization, the world may be ready for a great step forward.

The category of imports of 'materials chiefly for consumption goods' also involves these philosophical issues. It too showed an increasing trend as a proportion of the whole (21.5 per cent in 1958, 24.2 per cent in 1959, 23.9 per cent in 1960, 24.4 per cent in 1961, 26 per cent 1962 and 24 per cent in 1963); evidence that the development of consumption-goods industries is very important in the wishes and policies of these countries. The influence of these various categories in the total propensity to import will be examined below.

The category of imports of finished consumer goods (other than food) declined however : 18.6 per cent in 1958, 17.5 per cent in 1959, 17.4 per cent in 1960, 17.7 per cent in 1961, 16.4 per cent in 1962 and 15.6 per cent in 1963. The import of food declined in somewhat the same ratio : 21.7 per cent in 1958, 18.8 per cent in 1959, 17.6 per cent in 1960, 16.7 per cent in 1961, 15.9 per cent in 1962, rising again to 18.1 per cent in 1963. The percentages for these two categories are commonly considered to be too high for countries in this position at this stage of development; their progress would be deemed much more healthy if they produced more food and consumer goods themselves (without necessarily reducing their imports of the same). Comparisons will be stated below with an advanced country, to illustrate the perspectives in this respect.

The totals for the two broad categories of imports thus moved as follows.

	1958	1959	1960	1961	1962	1963
Consumption a/c:	63.8%	60.5%	59.9%	57.8%	58.3%	57.7%
Capital a/c:	36.2%	39.5%	41.1%	42.2%	41.7%	42.3%
	100%	100%	100%	100%	100%	100%

This shows a very creditable shift in the six years away from consumption-purposes towards capital-formation in the overall picture of the imports. Unfortunately a proper analysis of the

Table 4.19. *Changes in the percentage shares of consumption goods and capital goods in total imports: developing countries of the Region*[19]

(value, million $)	(minus sign = decrease, plus sign = increase)				
	1959	1960	1961	1962	1963
Total increase in imports	11	1,380	58	411	790
%	0%	18%	1%	5%	8%
Change in the percentage share of :					
Food	−13.4%	−6.4%	−5.1%	−4.8%	+13.2%
Other consumption goods	−5.9%	−0.6%	+1.7%	−7.3%	−4.9%
Materials for consumption goods	+12.5%	−1.2%	+2.1%	+6.5%	−4.9%
Total consumption group	−21%	−2.7%	−0.2%	−0.9%	−1.0%
Materials for capital goods	+1.8%	−11.4%	−5.0%	−7.3%	−1.1%
Capital goods	+4.1%	+10.3%	+1.9%	+3.8%	+2.1%
Total, capital group	+3.4%	+4.8%	+0.2%	+1.2%	+2.7%

propensity to import cannot be attempted here, as the interpretation of the national income figures would be lengthy and intricate, especially for international value comparisons. The following indications derive, however, from these import figures (Table 4.19).

Total imports increased every year: but in very fluctuating proportions. In 1959 and 1961 the increase was insignificant in percentage terms. In the intervening year 1960, however, the imports of this group of countries soared by 18 per cent in value. In 1962 they increased by 5 per cent and in 1963 by 8 per cent.

The share of food imports, as a percentage of these five categories of imports, fluctuated the most. It shrank impressively by over 13 per cent in 1959, then took a more moderately and evenly contracting course in 1960 to 1962; only to expand again by over 13 per cent in 1963. The dependence of these developing countries on food imports is a factor of high uncertainty which can drastically upset their pattern of progress. In a run of good years such as 1959-62 the proportion of food to other imports can fall – on a diminishing scale of reductions, showing presumably diminishing returns to favourable circumstances – but it can leap upwards again in a bad year like 1963 by as much as it fell in the good year 1959.

The food-consumption problems of the region have been widely – if still far from exhaustively – studied. The field of other consumption goods has been comparatively little surveyed.They are of vital importance in the process of development as incentives (to earn, produce and market) and as the nuclei through which there operates that greatest of all human chain-reactions, the 'demonstration effect'. The share of these has declined moderately and somewhat irregularly. It is influenced by many factors: the pressures of absolute and relative poverty, vagaries in the terms of trade, changes in policies or controls and in their effectiveness, changes in liquidity preference, credit conditions, etc. These pressures certainly apply in the other category, capital-goods; but in these development-planning countries the latter tends to be given guiding priority and financing from the resources 'mobilized' by the State, while consumption goods in particular are in the private sector and are the controlled residuum.

The share of 'other consumption goods' in imports fell in 1960 despite the notably lessened reliance on food imports, fell insignificantly in 1961, but contracted rather more drastically (much more than the percentage for food) in 1962; then fell considerably in 1963, though not in proportion to the percentage for food.

The share of materials for making consumption goods expanded in 1959 by almost as much as the share of food contracted. Possibly an improved food balance encouraged the hopeful expansion of domestic consumer-goods industries. However, it fell slightly in the next year, rose in 1961 and more substantially in 1962, only to fall in 1963 in the same proportion as food.

The total share of the three consumption categories in imports was reduced by no less than 21 per cent in the year of good food supplies 1959, slightly in the following years (including 1963, although that year saw the large increase in food imports).

Turning to the capital account, the share of imports for capital goods rose only slightly in 1959, fell disproportionately in 1960, rose in 1961 by half as much as it had fallen the previous year, fell again by a factor of one half in 1962 and fell slightly in 1963; while the import of capital goods rose throughout: by some 4 per cent in 1959, 10 per cent in 1960, 2 per cent in 1961, 4 per cent in 1962 and 2 per cent in 1963. The total for the capital goods category thus rose throughout, but by very modest percentages.

No very cogent correlations can thus be drawn directly from the study of the layout of the import-expenditures of this group of Asian developing countries; the possible inferences are very broad and loose. Certainly the period is too short – and probably too idiosyncratic – for the attempt to be justifiable. This aspect has, however, been pursued in some detail here to illustrate the very uncertain and highly variable circumstances of these developing countries. It would be dangerous to apply sweepingly to them many of the aggregative macro-econometric approaches of Keynesian and post-Keynesian economics. Presumably these techniques may usefully be applied for international or group comparisons among the industrialized countries, where the matrix is highly formed, both through a long and sequential evolution and through the consequent swift and effective interaction of the economic and social mechanism in all its parts.

Generalizations about these developing countries, in the same terms, may, however, obscure rather than clarify their real situation and trends. Suppose for example that it is attempted to analyse the 'propensity to import' in these countries.

This has not been attempted here, primarily because the national income figures are uncertain – especially from the point of view of international comparisons. The national income figures would, however, whatever their ranges of error, in any case show a much more stable trend (minutely rising, even in *per capita* terms) than the figures of imports. The marginal or total propensity to import – the proportion of income devoted to imports – fluctuates in these countries almost chaotically, in comparison with its degree of relative stability in more advanced countries, both in the aggregate and in each of the five economic categories here distinguished. The sectoral or factor interactions are far less coherent or regular in these countries, their policies far more variable in kind and in effectiveness. Their economic, social and political framework is quite different. They also differ among themselves much more than any group of advanced countries in the modern world.

Before proceeding to consider the East Asian developing countries individually, it may be useful to make a comparison with developed countries; in the first instance with the Region's own developed country, Japan. Table 4.20 gives the corresponding figures for Japan.

Table 4.20. *Japan's imports, consumption goods and capital goods*[20]
(value, million $)
(official figures in yen, converted at Y359 = $1)

	1958	1959	1960	1961	1962	1963
Food	523	485	530	641	704	1,051
Other consumption goods	59	64	86	120	139	201
Materials for consumption goods	1,524	1,821	2,192	2,607	2,563	3,147
Total for consumption	2,106	2,370	2,808	3,362	3,406	4,399
Materials for capital goods	527	816	1,210	1,767	1,398	1,454
Capital goods	401	418	478	686	840	887
Total, for capital	928	1,234	1,688	2,453	2,238	2,341
Grand total	3,034	3,604	4,496	5,815	5,644	6,740

The position of this industrialized country is in strong contrast to that of the underdeveloped group. Japan's total imports increased two and a half times in the period, theirs by one third; in the consumption sector Japan's imports more that doubled while the others' increased by one quarter, in the capital sector Japan's imports increased two and a half times while the others' increased 50 per cent.

Japan's imports of food nearly doubled, while the others' increased by only 12 per cent. Its intake of other consumer goods more than trebled, while that of the underdeveloped group increased only 12 per cent. Japan's international purchases of materials for consumption goods doubled, while the others' increased 50 per cent.

Of the total of this Asian market for the exports of the rest of the world Japan took nearly 30 per cent at the beginning of the period, rising to 40 per cent in 1963. In the consumption group it took 31 per cent of the total at the beginning of the period rising to 43 per cent at the end. In the capital group Japan's corresponding percentages were 24 per cent and 19 per cent; here its position is evidently different, as a major and rising industrial power. Japan's imports of materials for capital goods nearly trebled during the period, while those of the developing countries increased only 6 per cent. Its imports of capital goods increased by some 120 per cent (in current value terms, throughout) while those of the underdeveloped group increased by 66

Table 4.21. *Changes in the percentage shares of consumption goods and capital goods: Japan*[21]

(value, million $)   (minus sign = decrease, plus sign = increase)

	1959	1960	1961	1962	1963
Total increase in imports	570	895	1,319	−171	1,096
%	19%	25%	29%	−3%	20%
Change in the percentage share of:					
Food	−23%	−12%	−6.8%	+13.6%	+19.8%
Other consumption goods	−10%	+5.5%	+5.2%	+14.2%	+25%
Materials for consumption goods	+0.6%	+3.4%	−8.4%	+1.6%	+2.8%
Total for consumption	−5.2%	−5.1%	−7.6%	−4.3%	+8.3%
Materials for capital goods	+30%	+19%	+13%	−18.5%	−13%
Capital goods	−12.2%	−8.7%	+11.3%	+26.2%	−12.1%
Total for capital	+11.7%	+9.6%	+12.5%	−6%	−12.6%

per cent, or roughly half Japan's proportion. As a customer for materials for the manufacture of capital goods Japan became larger than all the developing countries of East Asia together in 1960; by 1963 it imported 64 per cent more than the developing group.

The point here is not merely to reiterate the economic pre-eminence of Japan in the Region. If the percentage rates of increase in the respective shares are scheduled in full (Table 4.21) as was done for the group of developing countries (Table 4.19) the much higher degree of stability and integration in the more developed economy is evident: compare Tables 4.19 and 4.21.

The year-to-year fluctuations in the case of Japan are thus marked, but may be described as much less frenetic than those in the underdeveloped group; much clearer trend-lines, reciprocal effects and correlations are discernible. The industrialized country shows fluctuations of much greater amplitude in all these percentages, but the pattern of its progress is much more strongly established and much more regular. The changes are not dislocatory in its case; it can 'take in its stride' variations which may cause an underdeveloped country to stumble or deviate. The comparison of the two types of import structure may be illustrated further by noting the actual percentages in these categories, as in Table 4.22.

Table 4.22. *Percentage distribution of imports, capital goods and consumption goods*[22] (value, million $) Per cent:

	Japan		Underdeveloped countries of the Region	
	1958	1963	1958	1963
Food	17.2%	15.6%	21.7%	18.1%
Other consumption goods	2.0%	3.0%	18.6%	15.6%
Materials for consumption goods	50.2%	46.7%	21.5%	24.0%
Total for consumption	69.4%	65.3%	61.8%	57.7%
Materials for capital goods	17.4%	21.6%	11.2%	8.8%
Capital goods	13.2%	13.1%	27.0%	33.5%
Total for capital	30.6%	34.7%	38.2%	42.3%
Grand total	100%	100%	100%	100%

The weight of primary products

Characteristically for an underdeveloped area, the exports of the Region consisted – in quantity terms especially, even more than in value – of primary products. Three groups should be distinguished: foodstuffs, agricultural materials and minerals (Table 4.23).

Table 4.23. *Quantity of exports of primary products from the Region*[23]
(million tons)

A. *Food*

	1950	1953	1958	1963
Fish, fresh or simply preserved	0.10	0.15	0.09	0.10
Rice and rice products	2.75	2.65	3.06	3.98
Sugar	1.03	1.75	1.91	2.28
Tea	0.36	0.44	0.47	0.47
Spices	0.05	0.06	0.09	0.12
Total	4.29	5.05	5.62	6.95
B. Agricultural materials				
Hides and skins, raw	0.05	0.02	0.03	0.03
Oilseeds	1.26	1.08	1.11	1.34
Rubber	1.75	1.61	1.74	1.89
Wood and lumber	2.04	2.28	3.32	6.62
Cotton, raw	0.25	0.35	0.21	0.29
Jute, raw	0.94	0.98	0.91	0.74
Hemp, raw	0.11	0.13	1.09	0.13
Total	6.40	6.45	8.41	11.04
C. Minerals				
Tin, ore and conc.	0.04	0.04	0.03	0.03
Iron ore	1.21	3.73	5.88	16.60
Manganese ore	0.82	1.59	1.98	0.92
Coal	1.05	2.20	1.80	1.22
Crude petroleum	3.77	6.96	36.80	66.00
Total	6.89	14.52	46.49	94.77
Grand total	17.58	26.02	60.52	112.76

Between 1953 and 1958 the quantum index of all exports from the Region rose nearly 28 per cent (see Table 4.11). That of the exports of primary products (Table 4.23) rose by more than 400 per cent; owing especially to the minerals (which rose nearly 700 per cent) and the agricultural materials (which nearly doubled) while food exports increased less than 14 per cent.

This is in terms of quantities. The classification of exports in value terms for accurate comparison with Table 4.22 is available for a few countries only; as follows.

Table 4.24. *Percentage distribution of exports, capital goods and consumption goods*[24]
(value, million $) Per cent:

	Japan		Malaya and Singapore		India	
	1958	1963	1958	1963	1958	1963
Consumption goods	46.5%	35.9%	22.3%	19.5%	67.6%	69.4%
Materials for consumption goods	12.6%	14.3%	60.1%	51.4%	22.4%	20.6%
Total for consumption	59.1%	50.2%	82.4%	70.9%	90.0%	90.0%
Materials for capital goods	6.0%	4.7%	14.4%	25.2%	9.3%	8.7%
Capital goods	34.9%	45.1%	3.2%	3.9%	0.7%	1.2%
Total for capital	40.9%	49.8%	17.6%	29.1%	10.0%	9.9%
Grand total	100%	100%	100%	100%	100%	100%

In the main underdeveloped country available for example here, India, the shift towards the industrial pattern of the predominance of manufactures and machinery is seen to be extremely slight. The progress of industrialization is more broadly the topic of another chapter.

D

Chapter 5

THE RAW MATERIAL BASE

For the present and prospective development of the Region certain basic materials are of great importance, either as necessary resources for its own industrialization on any foundation of major or partial 'self-supply', or as valuable earners when exported. In the latter aspect dependence on exporting raw materials is, however, the sign of the abhorred colonial status. Moreover, the instability of the basic materials situation – owing to the changing technical requirements for them on the one hand, the fluctuating production and markets on the other – is an anxiety for the developing countries almost as great as the crisis of food. In none of these respects is the material base of the Region satisfactory and it appears broadly to be worsening in comparison to the general progress of the world, especially in terms of *per capita* calculations against the growth of population.

MINERALS

The minerals should be considered first. Textbook economics in any case brands them broadly with the doom of diminishing returns. We are always aware that their extraction typifies the exhaustion, without replacement, of national stocks or assets. In the political history of development mining settlements and the like have been typical enclaves of foreign interests. Against all this can only be set the realization that the mineral resources of the Region and of the underdeveloped world in general are still very largely unexplored. Many of the areas are still not even mapped. The work of exploration and assessment is being pursued; its results sustain the hope that great resources are untapped.

(a) Fuels

The leading mineral item is currently *coal*.

World production of coal was about 1,300 million tons in 1948, 1,819 in 1958 and 1,929 in 1963. The Region outside Mainland China thus accounted for only 5 to 6 per cent of

Table 5.1. *Production of coal*[1]
—monthly averages, in 000 tons
(index: 1948=100)

	1948	1953	1958	1963
China: Taiwan	138	199 (144)	265 (192)	401 (291)
India	2,557	3,046 (119)	3,839 (150)	5,576 (218)
Indonesia	45	75 (167)	51 (113)	49 (109)
Japan	2,810	3,878 (138)	4,139 (147)	4,338 (156)
Korea: South	67	72 (107)	223 (333)	737 (1,100)
Pakistan	20	49 (245)	51 (255)	104 (520)
Total of above[a]	5,663	7,343 (130)	8,568 (151)	11,205 (198)
China: Mainland	..	5,548	22,517	35,000[b]
Philippines	..	13	19	13
Vietnam: South	..	..	1.7	8.7

Notes: [a] Includes Malaya and other minor producers.
[b] 1960.

world output, throughout these years; Mainland China for about 17 per cent in 1958, rising to over 20 per cent in 1963.

There have also been efforts pressed by ECAFE to discover and use local deposits of *lignite and brown coal*, but these remain quantitatively insignificant. Japan produced just over 2.5 million tons in 1948 (0.8 per cent of world output), declining to about 1.5 million in 1953 and 1958 (0.3 per cent of the world figure) and less than 1 million in 1963 (about 0.1 per cent). Malaya produced 381,000 tons in 1948 (about 0.1 per cent of the world total), some 25 per cent less in 1953, only 67,000 in 1958 and virtually none in 1963. A very small production began in Thailand in the later 1950s (127,000 in 1958, 137,000 in 1963). An interesting regional exception is North Korea, where production was nearly 2 million in 1948, fell drastically during the Korean War (to 400,000 in 1953) but rose again to 2.4 million in 1958 and 6 million claimed in 1963. In total the production in the non-Communist countries of the region fell from some 3 million in 1948 (1 per cent of the world's) to 1 million in 1963 (0.1 per cent).[2]

The region has taken some part in the worldwide expansion of the use of *natural gas* (Table 5.2).

The production of *petroleum* has greatly increased in the region, but still represents only about 2 per cent of the world output of crude (Table 5.3). Some two-thirds of the region's output is in Indonesia, which ranks with such producing countries as Rumania and Mexico, while a country so large as India

Table 5.2. Production of natural gas.[3]
(million cubic metres)

	1948	1953	1958	1963[a]
Burma	..	..	9	503
China: Taiwan	19	20	26	51
Indonesia	369	1,366	2,087	2,798
Japan	51	111	368	1,878
Pakistan	—	—[b]	547	1,401
cf. Netherlands	6	25	208	626
USA	146,000	238,000	312,000	418,000

Notes: [a] Estimated.
[b] began in 1955, with 39.

produces about as much as Yugoslavia, which has about 4 per cent of India's population. Supplies in the region have, however, been greatly improved recently (as elsewhere in the world) by the establishment of many refineries.

Table 5.3. Production of crude petroleum[4]
(000 m.t.)

	1948	1953	1958	1963[a]
World	468,600	659,900	909,700	1,303,800
Brunei	2,687	4,881	5,209	3,485
Burma	43	141	462	638
China: Mainland	121[b]	622	2,264	5,500[c]
China: Taiwan	3	3	2	3
India	251	272	425	1,653
Indonesia	4,326	10,225	16,110	22,275
Japan	159	296	267	785
Pakistan	65	237	302	470
Sarawak	47	50	58	52
cf. UK	156	161	146	125
Yugoslavia	36	172	462	1,611
Mexico	8,372	10,364	13,548	16,433
Rumania	4,149	9,058	11,336	12,233
USA	273,007	318,532	330,955	372,001

Notes: [a] Estimated.
[b] 1949.
[c] 1960.

The mineral fuel basis is thus on the whole poor – not providing broad, even or firm supplies of power for the proposed industrialization. World production of coal increased about 40 per cent between 1953 and 1963, of petrol about 100 per cent. The region's production of coal meanwhile increased about 50 per cent, of petrol about 75 per cent; while its population increased more rapidly than the world average, so that it has not greatly improved on its relatively poor position, despite great efforts. The same applies broadly to electric power, which is considered below in the chapter on Industrialization.

Next must be taken two large and complex groups of materials which are important as factors in industrialization, or for their value in trade.

(b) Metals

World production of *iron ore* increased about 150 per cent between 1948 and 1963. Meanwhile that of the Region (excluding Communist China) increased enormously more – over ten times – chiefly because of an increase in that proportion, very largely in the early 1960s, in India and in Malaya (Table 5.4) which raised the share of the Region (without China) in world output from less than 2 per cent in 1948 to some 8 per cent in 1963.

The latter figure is a better 'self-supply ratio' for industrialization, but still a modest one. However, India (already before its recent increase) and Malaya now rank with the United Kingdom as home-producers of iron ore; Japan roughly with such countries as South Africa and Yugoslavia. Japan like Britain relies heavily on imports; the trade implications are reviewed elsewhere in this book, the assessment here being of the endogenous physical resource-base.

Mainland China was a large and greatly increasing producer; the figures are not reliably available, but production was apparently 30 million tons in 1959.

Many other countries elsewhere are notably increasing their production.

Table 5.4. Production of iron ore[5]
(Fe content : 000 m.t.)

	1948	1953	1958	1963
World[a]	103,500	159,300	182,500	250,600
Hong Kong	—	62	60	64
Portuguese India	4	519	1,700 ⎱	12,464
India	1,483	2,458	3,739 ⎰	
Japan	297	915	1,144	1,363
Korea: South	—	9	131	250
Malaya	—	605	1,590	4,133
Pakistan	—	—	3	—
Philippines	10	682	615	789
Thailand	—	5	10	10
c.f. UK	3,990	4,500	4,008	4,091
Yugoslavia	377	382	1,006	812
South Africa	699	1,228	1,840	2,844

Note: [a] Excluding Mainland China.

A dozen countries in the world have most of the estimated reserves of iron ore which can be considered significant in terms of metal-content in good ores. At the beginning of the 1950s these were reckoned somewhat as follows (in million tons)[6]:

Brazil	7,800	Sweden	1,400
India	6,100	Cuba	1,200
S. Africa	3,700	UK	700
Canada	3,000	Australia	700
France	2,500	Venezuela	600
China	2,100		
USSR	2,000	Total	33,700
USA	1,900		

India and China thus have significant shares of the reserves in this 'major league'. Reserves elsewhere in S. Asia are relatively small.

World production of iron ore (in terms of metal content) was nearly 90 million tons in the immediate pre-war period. The 1949-51 average was some 20 per cent higher than pre-war, the 1958-60 average (at 228 million tons) some 150 per cent above pre-war. Productions in China varied between 1 and 3 per cent of the world total before the war, was around 1 per cent in 1949-51 but soared to about 10 per cent (claimed) in 1958-60. India's share remained at 2 or 3 per cent throughout. Great as the developments in iron-ore production have been in Asia, they are vastly overshadowed by the developments in N. America, Europe and the USSR. They are at least rivalled by the developments in South America; while developments in Australia and Africa compare not insignificantly with those in Asia.

In 1950 there was the world's largest giant centre of iron-ore production, defining the 'giant' scale at over 15 million tons per annum, around Lake Superior in the United States; and another adjoining it in Michigan. In the 'large' category (in the order of 5 million tons p.a.) there was one other centre in North America (Birmingham, Alabama). Well up in the 'large' category were two centres in Russia (Krivoi Rog and Magnitogorsk) and four in Europe (France: Lorraine, North Sweden, South Sweden and England). There were no other such large or giant centres anywhere else in the world.

There were about ten minor centres (100,000-2,500,000 tons) in North America, about twenty-four in Europe and ten in the USSR. In East Asia there were about fourteen centres, all low down in the 'minor' category (notably China: Anshan, Suanhwa, Tangshan, Tayeh and Lanchow; Japan: Tomakomai and Kamaishi; North Korea; Malaya: Dungun and Yong Peng; S. Borneo; two in the Philippines and one in N.E. India). There were two similarly 'small' centres in Mexico, seven in South America, seven in North Africa, one in West Africa, four in South Africa, one in Australia.

By 1960, N. America had added another giant (Labrador-N. Quebec) and developed nearly thirty other centres of the medium or minor size. In Europe at least one area (Lorraine) had joined the 'giant' category and medium or minor centres numbered about fifty. In the USSR at least six major areas and twelve minor ones were prominent. In Asia six medium to large centres had developed (China: Anshan, Luanping and Maanshan; N.E. India, S. India; Malaya) and some eighteen small or minor ones. South America had now six medium-sized and five minor centres, North Africa nine considerable centres, West Africa three and Oceania five.

The only specially notable exporter of iron ore in the region has been Malaya (supplying especially Japan) but its pre-war share of the world exports (4 per cent) was halved in 1950 and barely resumed in 1960. At the latter date India had, however, entered the export market with a very modest percentage, 2 per cent from India plus 3 per cent from the former Portuguese colony of Goa. Japan took some 7 per cent of world imports of iron ore in 1938, only 5 per cent in the restricted period 1949-51, rising to 8 per cent by 1960 - still only about her pre-war percentage.

World exports and imports of iron ore were around 45 million tons before the war, declined by some 10 per cent by 1949-51 but increased to nearly three times pre-war in 1958-60. Asia thus played little part in this international movement; in China and India especially, great national production movements occurred but they have not been vastly impressive in comparison to the scale of developments elsewhere.[6]

With iron should be considered particularly certain *alloys*. In *manganese ore* the Region (without China) contributed over 13 per cent of the world output in 1948, just over 10 per cent in 1963; very largely from India (Table 5.5). Half the world's production is in the Soviet Union; output in the United States is small and the capitalist industrial countries must draw their supplies from outside their own circle. The greatly increased production in India and elsewhere in the Region in the Korean war boom period was not subsequently maintained.

Table 5.5. *Production of manganese ore*[7]
(Mn. content: 000 m.t.)

	1948	1953	1958	1963[a]
World[b]	2,100	4,800	5,000	6,000
Burma	..	5n	0	0
India	253	897	594⎫	510
Portuguese India	3	75	31⎭	
Indonesia	—	12	23	..[c]
Japan[d]	19	69	108	100
Korea: South	..	1	1[e]	2
Philippines	12	9	9	4
China: Mainland	..	82[f]	255	300

Notes: [a] Estimated.
[b] Excluding Communist China.
[c] Severely declined: three in 1962.
[d] Metallurgical grade only.

In *chrome ore* there is a notable contributor in the Region – the Philippines (some 13 per cent of the non-Communist world's supplies in 1948, 16 per cent in 1963) – plus relatively small amounts from India, Japan and Pakistan (Table 5.6).

Table 5.6. *Production of chrome ore*[8]
(Cr_2O_3 content: 000 m.t.)

	1948	1953	1958	1963
World[a]	650	1,410	1,350	1,000
India	11	32	29	31
Japan	4	13	15	15
Pakistan	9	12	12	7
Philippines	89	206	187	161[b]

Notes: [a] Excluding East Europe and USSR.
[b] A peak of 249 was recorded for the Philippines in 1960 (over 18 per cent of world production).

There is no production of *vanadium* or *cobalt* in the Region.[9] Its output of *molybdenum* is trifling, except for that of Communist China; the United States largely monopolizes the production and Chile supplies about half of the remainder (Table 5.7).

In contrast there is *tin*: the only metal in which the Region really has a strong position. If Mainland China is included (in this case it is effectively in the market) the Region had some 57 per cent of the world production (excluding the USSR and other

Table 5.7. Production of molybdenum ore[10]
(Mo content: in metric tons)

	1948	1953	1958	1963[a]
World	12,840	28,630	21,430	34,000
Japan	2	181	314	332
Korea: South	19	9	37	70
Philippines	—	—	44[b]	107
China: Mainland	..	..	1,000	1,500
cf. USA	12,114	..	..	29,488

Notes: a Estimated
       b 1959.

Communist countries) in 1948, 62 per cent in 1953, 67 per cent in 1958 and 69 per cent in 1963 (Table 5.8). Taking 1948 as 100 the world production of tin concentrates rose to 117 in 1953 over the Korean War boom, fell to 89 in 1958 and went to 109 in 1963; the corresponding index for the Region (including China) was 1953: 127, 1958: 104 and 1963: 134. Thus the region did better than the world at large in this essential commodity; in which it occupies a vital position. Malaya is by far the world's largest producer; Mainland China, Thailand and Indonesia may be viewed as in the second rank alongside Nigeria and the Congo. The extreme fluctuations are, however, most notable.

Table 5.8. Production of tin concentrates[11]
(Sn. content: metric tons)

	1948	1953	1958	1963[a]
World[b]	153,900	179,800	136,600	168,500
Burma	1,165	1,383	910	1,016
China: Mainland[a]	4,900	6,400	18,300	24,400
Indonesia	31,104	34,365	23,573	13,155
Japan	120	745	1,123	874
Laos	32	268	306	406
Malaya	45,534	57,309	39,074	60,909
Thailand	4,308	10,288	7,850	15,835
Total	87,163	110,758	90,936	116,595
cf. Nigeria	9,384	8,347	6,330	8,869
Bolivia	37,935	35,384	18,016	22,603

Notes: a Estimated
       b Excluding Communist countries.

Such is the tin situation in outline. It has, however, many complexities. Some of these are worth pursuing in detail as a good illustration of the uncertainty and instability of the Regions' position. World production of tin increased swiftly in various preceding periods (early 1920s, early 1940s, late 1940s) but post-war export controls and political disturbances restrained production. Though there was much prospecting in the mid-1960s total production was not expected to rise in future much beyond the fairly stable level shown in the first line of Table 5.8.

World consumption of tin increased 50 per cent in the two post-war decades. That is much less than other non-ferrous metals; yet the rise in the price of tin was much larger (Table 5.9).

Table 5.9. Non-ferrous metals: world consumption and prices[13]

		World Consumption (million tons)			Prices (£ per ton)	
	1945	1964	Index	1945	1964	Index
Aluminium	0.9	4.7	(522)	£222	£239	(108)
Copper	1.9	4.1	(216)	£213	£271	(127)
Tin	0.1	0.15	(150)	£261	£1,200	(470)

Tin has always been expensive. When its price is especially high the competition of substitutes (mainly materials for containers – steel, aluminium, plastics, glass) becomes effective. Improvements in the substitutes – centred in the developed countries – continue. A new challenge in the mid-1960s was the marketing of a 'tin-free can' (sic) in the United States. The tin industry has also improved its techniques; thin-plating in particular has offset the advance of alternative materials.

All the main importing countries have reduced their consumption of tin except Japan. Incidentally this is another expression of the present and prospective importance of Japan in the Region (Table 5.10).

Table 5.10. Consumption of tin in various countries[14]

	Total (metal, 000 tons)				Per capita (lbs.)	
	1929	1939	1948	1963	1939	1963
USA	85	67	60	55	1.6	0.7
UK	24	27	25	21	1.2	0.9
West Germany	16[a]	11[a]	2[b]	11[b]	0.6[a]	0.4[b]
France	12	8	7	11	0.6	0.5
Japan	5	10	3	16	0.2	0.4

Notes: [a] All Germany.
[b] West Germany.

Another aspect of the question is the course of stockpiling operations and general regulation under international agreements. The first International Tin Agreement was for 1956-61, the second for 1961-6 and the third for 1966-71. To equilibrate supply and demand, stabilize prices, conserve resources and develop production economically, the Agreements set floor and ceiling prices and established buffer stocks – both of metal and of cash funds – for supply to or withdrawal from the market according to circumstances.

This did not work out well; in the early 1960s the buffer stock was exhausted (though it had operated well in the First Agreement), prices have not been stabilized, the ceiling price has been raised. The USA and USSR have not been members; the USA has collaborated generally with the countries in the agreement, the USSR less completely. On the administering International Tin Council 1,000 votes are allocated to the producing countries and 1,000 to the consuming countries, ranked in order of importance (producing countries: Malaysia 440 votes, Bolivia 170, Indonesia 140, Thailand 110, Nigeria 70, Congo 70 – consumer countries: UK 260, Japan 180, France 130, Italy 70, Canada 70, India 60, Australia 60, Netherlands 50, Belgium 40, Denmark 20, Mexico 20, Spain 20, Turkey 10, Austria 10, Korea 10).

Despite large releases from the US stockpile in 1961-4 the price soared (Table 5.11).

Table 5.11. *International Tin Council's Buffer Stock and market price*[15]

	Buffer Stock (000 tons) (at year end)	Sales from US Stockpile (000 tons)	London (average per ton, £)
1957	15.3	—	£755
1958	23.3	—	£735
1959	10.0	—	£785
1960	10.0	—	£797
1961	nil	—	£889
1962	3.3	1.4	£897
1963	nil	9.3	£910
1964	nil	29.0	£1,239

At the mid-1960s all these uncertain prospects were further shadowed by the expectation of continued falls in the reserves of tin-in-concentrates (i.e. tin at the mine) in the various countries. Even at the favourable 1964 prices, the expectations were as follows (Table 5.12).

Table 5.12. *Reserves of tin,* 1960 (*actual*) *and* 1970 (*projected*)[16]
(000 tons: tin-in-concentrates)

Region:	1960	1970	*percentage change*
Malaysia	1,000	600	− 40%
Thailand	1,000	1,400	+ 40%
Indonesia	560	560	0
	2,560	2,560	0
Others:			
Bolivia	700	500	− 28%
Nigeria	100	80	− 20%
Congo	100	60	− 40%
Others	100	80	− 20%
	1,000	720	− 28%

In this respect the Region's position is less unfavourable than others', though the swing from Malaya to Thailand is striking.

The East-West 'Cold War' confrontation is another factor. In the early 1960s exports of this metal from the Western 'bloc' to the Eastern increased, reversing the predominance of the latter (Table 5.13). These exports comprise some 9 per cent of current world output.

Table 5.13. *East-West trade in tin*[16]
(tin metal, 000 tons)

		Exports		
	From Western Countries	*from Eastern*	*Balance in favour of*	
	to Eastern[a]	*to Western*[b]	*East*	*West*
1960	0.2	13.0	12.8	—
1961	2.5	8.3	5.8	—
1962	5.0	5.7	0.7	—
1963	6.2	7.5	1.3	—
1964	6.7	6.1	—	0.6

Notes: [a] From Belgium, Malaysia, Netherlands, Nigeria, Indonesia, UK and W. Germany, to USSR and East Europe.

[b] From USSR and China to Japan, Netherlands, UK, W. Germany and others.

World production of *nickel* is heavily concentrated in Canada (approximately 78 per cent in 1948, 70 per cent in 1963) and the Soviet Union (over 11 per cent in 1948, rising to near 30 per cent in 1963). Production in the Region is virtually negligible (Table 5.14).

The list must be continued, but it is timely to stress the extreme variability of the results from year to year, This is per-

Table 5.14. *Production of nickel ore*[17]
(Ni content: metric tons)

	1948	1953	1958	1963[a]
World	153,000	218,000	252,000	280,000
Burma	—	82	454	102
Japan	168[b]	99[c]	45[d]	—
Korea: South	..	33	2	26

Notes: [a] Estimated.
[b] 1945.
[c] 1955.
[d] 1956.

haps especially marked in the case of the Asian countries; it certainly has a great impact on their livelihood and outlook. Such fluctuations are evident in the foregoing figures and will claim further attention in those which follow.

Tungsten notably exhibits the kinds of variations and uncertainties which are here in question. The Region is a main contributor in the widely fluctuating supply of this mineral (if China is excluded, nearly 20 per cent of the non-Communist world's output in 1948, nearly 30 per cent in 1953, about 25 per cent in 1958 and nearly 40 per cent in 1963). Communist China in this case has a monopolistic position, with a large and increasing production (which by 1963 exceeded that of the rest of the world). Burma's share reached 19 per cent of world production before the war, but was only in the order of 2-3 per cent after the war. Thailand's was 3-4 per cent after the war. Details are in Table 5.15.

Table 5.15. *Production of tungsten ore*[18]
(WO_3 content: metric tons)

	1948	1953	1958	1963[a]
World[b]	11,800	27,600	14,300	12,830
Burma	947	1,170	762	449
Hong Kong	—	92	25	5
India	—	9	1[c]	2
Japan	5	437	480	466
Korea: South	871	4,985	1,958	3,655
Thailand	297	1,054	396	124
China: Mainland	7,300	12,200	9,000	13,500

Notes: [a] Estimated.
[b] Excluding Mainland China, USSR and North Korea.
[c] 1957.

The production of *copper* ore in the non-Communist world increased only 7 per cent between 1948 and 1953, while production in non-Communist East Asia approximately doubled. In the next five-year period also, production in the region expanded notably faster than the world total, the comparable figures being: world 20 per cent increase, region 77 per cent. In the third quinquennium they kept pace, each increasing by 37 per cent (Table 5.16). However, the region's output was only in the order of 1 per cent of the world's in 1948, rising to 3 per cent in 1953 and about 4.7 per cent in both 1958 and 1963.

The percentages in the last paragraph exclude Communist countries, but these are also small producers by world standards. Communist China raised its production above that of the Philippines and near to Japan's while North Korea approached India's level (which is roughly that of Spain, for example). Japan's production is roughly comparable to that of Australia, though the latter has risen much more strikingly and should be vastly more expansible in future.

Table 5.16. Production of copper ore[19]
(Cu content: 000 m.t.)

	1948	1953	1958	1963a
Worldb	2,120	2,470	2,960	4,050
Burma	—	0.1	0.1	0.2
China: Taiwan	..	0.4	1.5	1.6
India	8.1	6.0	8.9	10.6
Japan	25.7	58.9	81.5	107.2
Korea: South	0.1	0.7	0.5	0.5
Philippines	2.0	12.7	47.0	63.7
Total	35.9	78.8	139.5	183.8
Korea: North	2.0	0.4	4.0c	8.0
China: Mainlanda	0.5	10.0d	30.0	90.0
cf.Spain	4.2	7.6e	8.6	6.7
Australia	12.6	38.1	76.9	114.6
USA	757	840	888	1,101

Notes: a Preliminary figures or estimates.
b Excluding USSR, Mainland China, Albania, Czechoslovakia and Hungary.
c 1957.
d 1955.
e 1952.

The production of *zinc* ore in the non-Communist world increased from 1.8 million metric tons in 1948 to 2.5 in 1953 (40 per cent) with further rises of 8 per cent in 1953-8 and 15 per cent in 1958-63. Production in non-Communist East Asia is almost entirely in Japan, which nearly trebled its production in 1948-53, increased it a further 50 per cent by 1958 and again 38 per cent by 1963. Four other countries in the region are very minor suppliers, though they have increased by large percentages on their small bases. Communist China's production has risen to about half that of Japan, and North Korea has produced more than China; these countries are on the level of Germany or Italy in this respect (Table 5.17).

Table 5.17. Production of zinc ore[20]
(Zn content: 000 m.t.)

	1948	1953	1958	1963[a]
World[b]	1,790	2,500	2,710	3,130
Burma	1.7	3.6	11.2	8.1
India	—	2.2	3.9	6.2
Japan	33	97	143	198
Korea: South	0.2	0.3[c]	0.3	1.1
Philippines	—	0.7	0.3[d]	3.9
Korea: North	13	58[e]	85	110
China: Mainland	..	28[e]	45	100

Notes: [a] Estimated.
[b] Excluding USSR and Mainland China.
[c] 1952.
[d] 1957.
[e] 1955.

In the production of *lead* ore the region shows a similar pattern of large increases on a very small share of the world's total. Excluding the Communist states, world production increased 32 per cent in 1948-53 while the region's multiplied more than four times. In 1953-8 the region's output doubled again, while the world's increased only 9 per cent. In 1958-63 the region's rate of progress in this item slowed down to 27 per cent; but much less than the world's, which sank to 3 per cent. However, the region's production figure represented about 0.5 per cent of the world's in 1948, 1.8 per cent in 1953, 3.2 per cent in 1958 and 4 per cent in 1963 (Table 5.18).

Mainland China produced about as much as the rest of the Region in the mid-1950s, and slightly more by the early 1960s. The volume of Japan's production is comparable with that of such countries as Poland; Australia's is eight times as large. The only other significant regional producer, Burma, ranks (for example) with Tunisia. In the same kind of analogy, gigantic and industrially ambitious India ranked only with Congo-

Brazzaville, prior to the latter's troubles (reflected in its 1962 figure). Production in the Philippines declined to a mere 100 tons from 1960 onwards.

Table 5.18. *Production of lead ore*[21]
(Pb content: 000 m.t.)

World[b]	1948	1953	1958	1963[a]
	1,370	1,810	1,980	2,040
Burma	—	5.6	19.8	20.1
India	0.4	2.0	3.9	4.5
Japan	6.7	18.7	36.7	52.7
Korea: South	0.3	0.1	1.2	1.9
Philippines	0.1	2.4	1.3	0.1
Thailand	—	3.4	1.0	2.1
Total	7.5	32.2	63.9	81.4
China: Mainland[a]	..	30	50	100
Congo: Brazzaville	2.7	4.8	3.8	0.3[c]
Tunisia	13.2	24.0	22.5	13.8
Poland	14.5	37.9	33.1	38.7
Australia	220	274	334	417
USA	359	311	243	230

Notes: [a] Estimated.
[b] Excluding USSR, Mainland China and North Korea.
[c] 1962.

In the case of *antimony*, out of a world production (excluding the USSR) of some 45,000 m.t. in 1948 (Sb. content) Communist China recorded 3,250. In 1953 world production fell about one-third, to 33,400, of which Mainland China accounted for nearly one-third. The world total rose again to 40,600 in 1958 (of which China claimed well over one-third) and declined again to 35,000 in 1963 (of which China recorded 15,000, or over 40 per cent). The other countries of the Region recorded small amounts (Japan, 1948: 135, 1953; 321, 1958: 270, and 1963: 192. Thailand, 1948: 118, 1953: 46, 1957: 2 only, 1962: 66. And Pakistan a trace).[22]

The region is a small producer of *mercury*; the non-Communist world's production (from ore) fluctuated between 3,000 and 6,000 metric tons. Italy's share in this was around one-third, that of Japan one-half or one-third of Italy's, the United States' around 10 per cent of the total; the Philippines' small contribution being the only other entry for East Asia. Communist China's quantity is undetermined. Such countries as the Soviet

Union, Yugoslavia and Turkey have outputs in the order of 5 per cent of the total.[23]

In the metallic domain there is further *bauxite*; in which the Region's production, though increasing, remains relatively small (Table 5.19).

Table 5.19. Production of bauxite[24]

	1948	1953	1958	1963
Worlda	8,430	13,000	19,360	26,720
India	23	72	169	505
Indonesia	438	150	344	493
Malaysia	—	226	406	609
Pakistan	—	—	2	—
China: Mainland	—	—	150	400

The processing of bauxite into aluminium requires much ore and consumes much electricity.

In the non-Communist world's production of *magnesite* a modest contribution was made by India (some 5 per cent throughout, of a total of nearly 1 million tons in 1948, 2 million tons in 1953, 2.3 million tons in 1958 and 3 million tons in 1953).[25]

Asbestos is another material in which the Region's home resources are extremely slight. Production in the non-Communist world roughly trebled from 1948 (870,000 m.t.) to 1963 (2.4 million). Regional producers made large increases in their outputs: Japan 5,000 in 1958 to 17,000 in 1963, India 100 in 1948 to 2,700 in 1963. Taiwan and the Philippines produced small amounts.[26]

(c) Chemicals and others

A group of chemical items should be next considered. Japan is a fairly notable supplier of *sulphur* (about 10 per cent of the world's production of 17,000 tons in 1948, 12 per cent of 24,000 in 1953, 16 per cent of 30,000 in 1958 and over 20 per cent of 32,000 in 1963); Taiwan and the Philippines produce comparatively minute quantities. The United States furnished one-third of world output in 1948 and one-sixth in 1963.[27]

The Region is not a producer of *potash*. Its output of *phosphate rock* is almost imperceptible in the world total.[28] It is a considerable producer of *salt*; comparable world totals unfortunately cannot be given, but this important commodity merits another table (5.20). The variations are again striking, though broadly the region kept up with the world trend of approximately doubling production since the war, it has done so with rather more unevenness than other Regions. In this common commodity as in others its position is not especially strong.

Table 5.20. Production of salt[29]
(000 m.t.)

	1948	1953	1958	1963[a]
Burma	43	62	111	161
Cambodia	..	41	30	..
Ceylon	79	58	17	22
China: Mainland	..	3,569	10,400	10,500
China: Taiwan	376	171	444	626
India	2,300	3,216	4,232 }	4,539
Portuguese India	20	16	5 }	
Indonesia	..	268	315	304
Japan	293	455	1,170	747
Korea: South	90	193	460	236
Philippines	118	48	140	70
Thailand	..	354[a]	427	258[b]
Vietnam: South	6[c]	84	62	128
Total	..	8,535	17,813	17,591
Index		100	209	206
cf. USA	14,867	18,859	19,873	27,800
USSR	5,700	..	6,200	9,560

Notes: [a] Estimated.
[b] 1962.
[c] Including North Vietnam.

(d) Diamonds, gold and silver

Finally, certain precious materials have to be specially noticed. World production of *diamonds* doubled between 1948 and 1953 and increased further by one-third by 1958, though 1963 showed a slight decrease. The Region contributes – through India only – a minute percentage of gem diamonds, but no industrial diamonds (which were of increasing importance, being 43 per cent of the total output in terms of carats in 1948 and 75 per cent in 1963).[30]

The significance of *gold* needs no emphasis. The seven gold-producing countries in the region – if the Communist countries are omitted, for lack of data on them – doubled their production by the 1960s, while the world output rose comparatively less (72 per cent). But again their progress was uneven and they represent a very small proportion of world output (some 2.5 per cent in 1948, 4.3 per cent in 1953, 3.5 per cent in 1958, 2.9 per cent in 1963). The region's largest producers, the Philippines and Japan, rank roughly with such countries as Colombia in this respect, India with (for example) Sweden or Nicaragua, Malaya (at its peak production) or Taiwan with Finland. The Region's indigenous resource-base for industrialization cannot therefore be described as gilt-edged (Table 5.21).

Table 5.21. Production of gold[31]
(kilogrammes)

	1948	1953	1958	1963[a]
World[b]	698,000	753,000	934,000	1,203,000
China: Taiwan	555	846	664	986
India	5,625	6,934	5,291	4,304
Indonesia	1,000	..	..	..
Japan	3,105	8,030	9,594	13,454
Korea. South	108	494	2,242	2,802
Malaysia	337	536	656	341
Philippines	6,507	14,948	13,152	11,696
Total[c]	17,237	32,788	32,599	34,583
cf. Finland	352	606	786	635
Sweden	2,236	2,745	3,968	3,660
Nicaragua	6,850	8,058	6,492	6,870[d]
Colombia	10,428	13,601	11,562	10,094
S. Africa	360,329	371,395	549,177	853,655

Notes: [a] Estimated.
[b] Excluding USSR, Mainland China and Rumania.
[c] Assuming Indonesian production maintained at 1948 level.
[d] 1962.

Nor is there any deep lining of *silver*. Production in the region more than doubled in 1948-53 and again in 1953-63; its share in the output of the non-Communist world rose from about 2.5 per cent in 1948 to nearly 8 per cent in 1963. Burma is a producer of approximately the size of Chile (73 tons in 1963), Japan compares with West Germany (478 in 1962); the whole Region produces about half as much as each of the three main producers (Mexico, USA and Canada, which divide approximately one half of the total between them with some 1,000 tons each).[32]

Chapter 6

INDUSTRIALIZATION

Industrialization has been the most urgent preoccupation in East Asia in the post-war period. The perspectives of its success must now be considered.

THE SCALE OF WORLD PROGRESS

The course of East Asian industrial development must be compared with that of the world's other Regions. Taking the indices for all industrial production (mining, manufacturing, electricity and gas) the first notable feature lies in the differing effects of the war. The overall industrial output doubled between 1938 and 1948 in North America (Table 6.1). In Latin America it increased by more than one-third. In German-occupied Europe it fell (by 25 per cent in the present EEC area) but this was offset in non-occupied Europe, the index for all Europe remaining the same in 1948 as in 1938. In East and South East Asia as a whole the war reduced industrial production in a slightly larger proportion than in Axis Europe – by 27 per cent. This again was due mainly to the destruction and attrition in its Axis heartland, Japan. If Japan is excluded the rest of the region *increased* its industrial production by over 13 per cent.

In the post-war reconstruction period of 1948-53 the corresponding overall indices show rises by: North America 35 per cent, Latin America 25 per cent, EEC 72 per cent, all Europe 44 per cent and all E. and S.E. Asia 66 per cent; but the Asian recovery centred heavily in Japan, the rise for the rest of the region excluding Japan being only 18 per cent.

We take next the whole decade 1953-63. The overall index again rose 36 per cent in North America, 80 per cent this time in Latin America, exactly 100 per cent in the European Community area, 77 per cent in Europe as a whole; but no less than 340 per cent in South and East Asia. The region's industrialization thus distinctly gathered speed in the last decade, though this was again due largely to the inclusion of Japan, the figure without Japan being 164 per cent. The weight and impetus of Japan may be described as quantitatively more than double the whole of the rest of its region; qualitatively, Japan's industrial progress is even more outstanding.

Unfortunately the comparisons cannot be extended to the Communist countries.

Table 6.1. *General index of industrial production*[1]
(mining, manufacturing, electricity and gas)
$(1958 = 100)$

	North America	Latin America	E. & S.E. Asia	E.S.E. Asia excluding Japan	Europe	ECC
1938	35	34	48	44	53	51
1948	72	57	35	50	52	40
1953	97	71	58	59	75[b]	69
1963	132	128	197	156	133	138

From this blunderbuss overall indicator we must pass to sectoral and specific-industry perspectives. A closer sighting is given by the index for all manufacturing industry (Table 6.2). Somewhat similarly this index shows in the first place the effects of the war and the post-war periods. In 1938-48 it rose 118 per cent for N. America, 66 per cent for Latin America and 14 per cent for the Asian region without Japan, but fell 30 per cent if Japan is included, while remaining unchanged for Europe as a whole.

In 1948-53 the results were increases in: North America 34 per cent, Latin America 22 per cent, all E.S.E. Asia 77 per cent, the region excluding Japan 22 per cent, Europe 45 per cent, EEC 80 per cent.

In 1953-63 the increases were: North America 34 per cent, Latin America 82 per cent, E.S.E. Asia 260 per cent, but excluding Japan 156 per cent, Europe 81 per cent, EEC 106 per cent. The region's progress is marked but when the field of manufacturing is spotlighted it appears that the overall index of Asian progress is more weighted with the extractive and power industries, relative to manufactures, than that of other Regions.

It is useful to distinguish heavy manufacturing industries from light (Table 6.3). This further emphasizes the effects of the war period. Heavy industries increased massively more than light industries between 1938 and 1948 in North America, by 188 per cent for heavy industry against 63 per cent for light; and even in Latin America by 84 per cent against 55 per cent.

Table 6.2. *Index of production: all manufactures*[2]
(1958 = 100)

	North America	Latin America	E.&S.E. Asia	E.S.E. Asia excluding Japan	Europe	ECC
1938	34	35	46	43	52	50
1948	74	58	32	49	51	38
1953	99	71	57	60	74	68
1963	133	129	205	155	134	140

In Europe as a whole light industries' production was reduced through the war by 8 per cent, while heavy industries' rose 5 per cent. In the EEC area both were heavily reduced, the light industries slightly more than the heavy ones (25 per cent against 21 per cent). In E.S.E. Asia as a whole both were, however, even more reduced – heavy industries' output by 35 per cent, light industries' by 27 per cent – owing to the damage in Japan, as the rest of the region increased in heavy industries by 19 per cent and in light by 11 per cent. The comparative weakness of the wartime impetus to heavy industry in British India is also shown by these figures: heavy industrial output in the region minus Japan rose 19 per cent, i.e. only about one and a half times the rise in light industrial output (and the same is true of Latin America), whereas in North America heavy industrial production rose three times as much as light industrial production.

Table 6.3. *Production indices: heavy industry and light industry*[3]
(1958 = 100)

	North America	Latin America	E.&S.E. Asia	E.S.E. Asia excluding Japan	Europe	ECC
(a) Heavy industries:						
1938	24	25	27	36	44	43
1948	69	46	24	43	46	34
1953	104	62	49	50	70	63
1963	139	144	254	183	139	146
(b) Light industries:						
1938	49	44	56	47	65	61
1948	80	68	41	52	60	46
1953	92	79	67	66	81	77
1963	125	117	153	141	126	127

In the first post-war period, 1948-53, the indices proceeded to increase. In North America the increase in heavy-industries' output was treble the increase in that of light industries, in Latin America double, in all Europe 50 per cent greater, in the EEC area 27 per cent greater. In the E. Asian region as a whole it was 65 per cent greater, in the region excluding Japan 69 per cent greater. In the post-war reconstruction phase the stress on heavy relative to light development therefore appears far less than in the USA and Canada; and less than in the Southern Americas, but somewhat greater than in Europe (especially in what is now the European Community area, where it was then surprisingly low).

Moreover the ratios do not in this period diverge so much between Japan and the rest of the region: it was the region outside Japan which was then beginning to emphasize heavy-industrial development more than did Japan, whose economy was still badly reduced, in that sector particularly. All this is in relative terms; what is attempted here is to measure the comparative speed of industrial development in respect of these sectors in these countries, which are extremely various in their industrial structures and levels. The absolute dimensions will be considered later.

In 1953-63 there was in contrast a very notable relative increase in industrial production altogether in the Asian Region, which included a stress on heavy industry comparatively much greater than in any other Region. This is again to be imputed largely to Japan, where a prodigious expansion and evolution of industry occurred. In the East Asian Region as a whole heavy industrial output increased by over four times; more than three and a half times as much as light-industrial production. In the Region excluding Japan, however, industry increased by 266 per cent, light industry by 114 per cent.

In Europe total production roughly doubled, with heavy industries' production increasing twice as much as that of light industries. In the EEC area both the total increase and the preponderance in it of heavy industry were somewhat more marked than in the rest of Europe. From the viewpoint of those who measure progress in terms of industrialization East Asia did moderately better than Europe in this period. The percentage increases in the United States – on its gigantically greater base – were comparatively small, at about one-third, and there the growth in the light-industrial production slightly exceeded the heavy-industrial one.

Table 6.4. *Changes in industrial production in various periods*[4]
(percentage change in the index of production)
1958 = 100 (—) indicates a decrease

	North America	Latin America	E.&S.E. Asia	E.S.E. Asia excluding Japan	Europe	ECC
All mining:						
1938-48	59	67	−10	8	−14	−22
1948-53	16	27	18	−2	28	42
1953-63	21	77	115	185	13	18
Coal:						
1938-48	57	36	−23	−2	−16	−22
1948-53	−27	21	35	28	18	28
1953-63	−6	30	40	135	−6	−7
Metal minerals:						
1938-48	20	3	−40	−35	−23	−38
1948-53	18	26	74	65	59	93
1953-63	25	51	33	18	23	10
Crude petroleum and natural gas:						
1938-48	67	112	47	52	133	83
1948-53	29	31	−38	−40	271	264
1953-63	23	93	410	420	277	398
Non-metallic minerals:						
1938-48	128	118	−30	8	−7	−19
1948-53	25	48	131	96	40	63
1953-63	38	73	212	198	81	103
Chemicals, petroleum and rubber products:						
1938-48	160	96	43	19	11	−11
1948-53	48	35	65	−24	91	91
1953-63	91	136	290	221	146	189
Paper products:						
1938-48	78	78	−63	23	−7	−32
1948-53	27	31	262	156	42	82
1953-63	45	114	238	339	94	101
Food, drink and tobacco:						
1938-48	63	53	−14	16	−7	−25
1948-53	13	28	54	25	40	73
1953-63	33	50	77	73	56	59
Textiles:						
1938-49	100	73	−47	−5	−10	−21
1948-53	6	4	74	24	33	55
1953-63	24	37	118	91	27	41

	North America	Latin America	E. & S.E. Asia	E.S.E. Asia excluding Japan	Europe	ECC
Basic metals:						
1938-48	758	58	−48	−17	−11	−34
1948-53	19	27	139	36	46	76
1953-63	3	115	249	209	73	91
Metal products:						
1938-48	230	109	−25	56	5	−20
1948-53	67	28	117	46	53	91
1953-63	28	175	679	366	96	138
Electricity:						
1938-48	147	95	24	55	47	28
1948-53	62	44	51	59	49	50
1953-63	112	131	200	243	109	114

RATES OF PRODUCTION-INCREASE

A more itemized study of the movements in production by particular industries leads to a more detailed impression of the changes that have occurred.

For the same regional groupings as in the preceding tables, Table 6.4 sets out the indices of production for twelve industrial groups in terms of increases or decreases for each industry and region in each of the periods taken above (1938-48, 1948-53 and 1953-63). Used as a 'scoreboard' these tables conveniently chart the trends in the world's industrial production – so far as the *pace* of increase in each area is concerned.

(a) 1938-48

In minerals and metals, textiles and paper the war-period hit Japan particularly hard: in most items, distinctly more than Germany and German-occupied Europe. In petroleum Japan in that decade (1938-48) achieved some increase. But it was of the order of half the percentage increase the Germans achieved; and less than in other regions also, for the whole group of petro-chemical and rubber products. In the foodstuffs group the attrition in Japan was perhaps half that in German-held Europe; but double that in the rest of Europe (in terms, throughout, of percentage reduction).

In the rest of the East Asian region, excluding Japan – i.e. in this context mainly in the then British India and to a lesser extent in Japanese-occupied Manchuria – manufacturing industry fared somewhat better over the wartime decade, with the following significant variations. Mining other than petroleum was severely reduced. The foodstuffs and paper industries' production increased considerably, in contrast to Japan. The production of basic metals declined considerably, but that of metal manufactures rose by more than 50 per cent. In that aspect unoccupied Asia's wartime processing boom was proportionately much greater than that of unoccupied Europe, but only half that of Latin America, and a quarter of North America's.

In Latin America – an underdeveloped Region not directly involved in the warfare – all these indices rose distinctly, though variously. In the uninvaded developed Region, North America, they rose prodigiously – on their already gigantic base – the output of basic metals being multiplied by more than eight, metal products by more than three, the generation of electricity by nearly two and a half, chemicals, petroleum and rubber products by a similar proportion, while textiles doubled and the rest notably increased.

(b) 1948-53

The Asian Region thus entered on the stage of post-war rehabilitation in a very poor situation, due especially to the crippling of the economy of Japan and some of the other industrial centres under Japanese occupation. The five years 1948-53 were largely affected, not only by the intrinsic difficulties of post-war rehabilitation and reconstruction and by the political ferments and disturbances in Asia at the time but also by the rise and fall of the 'Korean War Boom'.

The hostilities in Korea (1950) caused first an upsurge of demand for various raw materials, in particular the 'strategic' items, owing to rearmament and stockpiling in the industrial countries. In the second place, the boom greatly stimulated the resumption of industrial activity in Japan, which served largely as the rear-base for the United Nations military operations in Korea. Japanese entrepreneurship seized this opportunity swiftly and effectively, so that this boom may well be said to mark Japan's 'take off' into its subsequent flight of prodigious economic and technical progress.

In the third place, the boom greatly benefited the underdeveloped regions, particularly East Asia, through raised demand for their primary products, better terms of trade and improved balances of payments. Unfortunately the boom did not last long; recession followed and the underdeveloped East Asian countries (which are accused broadly of not having conserved their gains during the boom, or used them wisely for their own development) did not enjoy any such take-off into sustained development as ensued in Japan.

The output of petroleum, rubber and manufactures from these materials fell notably in the Asian region outside Japan in this period, owing especially to the political disturbances in the centres of production of these materials. In this group Europe doubled its production, East Asia including Japan increased by two-thirds (but fell by one quarter if Japan is excluded) Latin America by one-third, North America by half. Mining in general increased in the region in somewhat less proportion than in Europe (where the Marshall Plan gave a special impetus) and Latin America. The percentage increase in the much larger mining activities in North America was meanwhile distinctly slighter : it will be noted that the relative decline of coal had already become a marked feature in North America, though not yet in Europe and the other regions.

In the other industries which had sunk lowest through the war – basic metals, paper, foodstuffs, textiles, metal products, nonmetallic minerals – the East Asian region, principally Japan, achieved great percentage increases in the rehabilitation period. Japan in particular may be said to have progressed rather similarly to Europe in these respects. The increases in the region were distinctly creditable in this period, in comparison especially with Latin America, while industrial progress in affluent North America continued at much less than its wartime frenzy.

Overall, South East Asia roughly equalled the rate of industrial progress of the EEC area in this period, which was much higher than that of the rest of Europe and that of North America. This was, however, due mainly to Japan. The East Asian index including Japan rose 77 per cent, excluding Japan only 22 per cent (equal to the figure for Latin America, and half that of Europe).

Noteworthy features are the concentration in this period by the Asian region on minerals and on the simpler lower-value manufactures – and the failure of the sources of power (electricity, coal, petroleum) to develop proportionately to metallurgical and other outputs. They are especially marked if the

region excluding Japan is considered. Such features are concomitants of the relatively low level of industrial progress in that
period, despite the index-number rises which it displayed; it is
often stressed that these are also concomitants of its *de facto*
(even if no longer *de jure*) 'colonial' situation.

(c) 1953-63

In the third period – in strong contrast – most of the figures
for East Asia soared. The *rate* of industrialization in the region
in that decade may be described as phenomenal – if it may be
emphasized once more that it is (so to speak) merely the speedo-
meter or revolution-counter readings that are being compared
here, on vehicles which differ greatly in their kinds and capaci-
ties. Moreover, in this later period the figures for the region
excluding Japan for the most part no longer appear to be quite
so markedly inferior to those for the region including Japan,
though the industrial preponderance of Japan in the region
remains very marked.

The features noted in the last paragraph – the relative concentration on primary minerals especially coal and the simpler
manufactures, the relative lag in the application of power –
continue to be considered as negative aspects, even as denoting
some degree or kind of 'semi-colonial' or 'neo-colonial' situation, despite such striking credit-entries as an almost eightfold
increase in the last five years in metal products (if Japan is
included – three-and-a-half fold if Japan is excluded).

Nevertheless the industrial advance of the Region in 1953-63
was somewhat impressive. At the end of the period Japan came
definitely into the 'advanced' or industrialized category of
nations; the rest of the region was making large increases under
several headings, in fact greatly exceeding Europe and America
in current growth-rates in almost all of the industry-groups.

These figures have given some impression of the course of
world industrialization, in terms at least of the tempos of development in various regions. The aspect of 'pacemaking' is
important in the Asian outlook. Nevertheless it must be admit-
ted that it is mainly a question in East Asia of large percentage
increases on small bases. Outside Japan especially, and if the
other major industrial units India and China are further sub-
tracted, indeed there is little left. It was noted in the preceding
chapter in respect of the basic raw material commodities how

small a percentage (in comparison especially with the area, populousness and poverty of Asia) each of them represented of the total world output or market. The same assessment must now be attempted in respect of industrial products: what is the weighting of Asia's industry, for all its recent increase, in the total of the world's industrial activity?

MEASURING THE PROGRESS OF INDUSTRIALIZATION

On what scale is the degree of industrialization to be judged and recorded? Many 'yardsticks' are applied. The *consumption of steel* per head of population is one common measure of progress in industrialization. In the United States saturation may be said to have been reached in this respect about 1950; during the 1950s the *per capita* consumption of steel in the US fell some 10 per cent, though it was still about 500 kg. per inhabitant per year. In Canada it was still rising slightly (to about 360 kg.). In the United Kingdom it rose some 14 per cent (to about 330 kg.). In Japan production was very restricted in 1950; it more than trebled in the following decade, reaching half the UK figure by 1960 and rising sharply thereafter.

The figures for the other countries of the region are exceedingly low. They were approximately as follows for 1960, expressed as percentages of the United States: Hong Kong 18 per cent, Malaya with Singapore 6 per cent, Mainland China 4 per cent, Taiwan 4 per cent, Philippines 3 per cent, India 2 per cent, Thailand 2 per cent, Indonesia, Indochina and Pakistan 0.5 per cent. Great percentage increases were achieved in most of these countries in this period over the crippled conditions of 1949; e.g. Mainland China increased about tenfold, Taiwan and Hong Kong more than doubled, India nearly doubled, the Philippines doubled. Indonesia increased by about one-third, Malaya by about one quarter, Ceylon by about 10 per cent. Yet steel consumption *per capita* actually fell in this period in Cambodia, North and South Vietnam and Pakistan (by some 30 per cent).

Moreover, the movements in these countries were considerably more irregular than in the western lands; with much larger percentage changes either way from year to year than in the developed countries. Communist propaganda made much of the instability of capitalism. This was especially marked in the underdeveloped Asian capitalist or semi-capitalist countries, but the instability was in fact more marked in Communist China where a series of 'great leaps' on the scale of doubling at times alternated with recessions and dislocation on the scale of 30-40 per cent reduction at other times. In contrast colonial Hong Kong's *per capita* consumption progressed quite steadily, as did Japan's. India's grew fairly steadily. The percentage swings in the advanced capitalist countries such as the US and UK were relatively small, being in the order of 10 per cent.[5]

Quite a different general measure of the extent of industrialization is the *occupational distribution of the population* between rural and other pursuits. In the diminishing dependence on agrarianism also, East Asia has made marked but uneven progress.

Table 6.5. Distribution of the working population between agriculture, manufacturing and other occupations[6]
Percentages of the economically active population in:

		Agriculture, forestry and fishing	Manufactures	Others
Ceylon	1946	53	10	37
	1953	53	10	37
	1963	53	7	40
China: Taiwan	1930	69	9	22
	1940	64	10	26
	1956	56	12	32
Hong Kong	1961	7	40	53
India	1951	67	10	23
	1951	72	9	19
	1961	74	10	17
Japan	1930	50	19	31
	1947	53	17	30
	1960	33	22	45
Korea: South	1955	78	..	..
Malaya: Fed.	1947	65	8	27
	1957	59	6	35
Singapore	1947	8	19	73
	1957	9	14	77
Pakistan	1951	77	6	17
	1961	75	8	17
Philippines	1939	73	10	17
	1948	71	7	22
	1960	61	12	27
Thailand	1937	89	2	10
	1947	85	2	13
	1960	82	3	14
cf. Australia	1933	21	20	60
	1947	15	25	59
	1961	11	27	62
New Zealand	1936	27	24	49
	1945	19	20	61
	1961	16	26	58

The declining share of agriculture is evident. This shift was most rapid in Japan. Corresponding gains are divided differently in various countries between the manufacturing and 'other' (tertiary and service) occupations, according to the countries' circumstances. Taking broadly the decade of the 1950s, in India only was there a shift towards agriculture; albeit only a marginal one (2 per cent rise in the share of agriculture). In Singapore and Ceylon there was virtually no change; in Pakistan and Thailand a marginal relative decline in agriculture's share (2 per cent). The movement away from agriculture can, however, be said to be strong in Taiwan (8 per cent), the Malayan Federation (10 per cent) and the Philippines (12 per cent) – similar to that in New Zealand (10 per cent) – and very strong in Japan (nearly 30 per cent – cf. Australia 21 per cent).

Alternatively the econometrics of development may deal largely in terms of *production-increases* in key items. Under this heading *iron and steel may* naturally be emphasized.

In terms of crude steel, over 80 per cent of world production was in the USA and West Europe before the War. In 1949-51 this percentage had fallen to 70 per cent, by 1958-60 to 58 per cent. The western Communist countries have taken up most of this change: here again the progress in East Asia certainly does not rival developments elsewhere in the world, especially in *per capita* terms.

World production of crude steel was about 110 million tons before the war. Trade in pig iron, ingots and castings increased by about one-third by 1959-51 and was nearly three times pre-war by 1960, having increased by one-third between 1950 and 1960. Over a quarter of this was from the United States, throughout. Between pre-war and 1960 the UK's share fell from 10 per cent to 7 per cent, West Germany's from 15 per cent to 7 per cent, France's from 6 per cent to 5 per cent. The USSR increased its share from 15 per cent to 20 per cent, Poland and Czechoslovakia moved from 3 per cent to 5 per cent each. China greatly increased its efforts in this field, rising from a negligible percentage pre-war to some 5 per cent in 1960. Japan, despite much progress, remained at the same figure of 6 per cent.[7]

Capacity must be considered as well as immediate output. The methods of the economic geographer are particularly useful in the analysis of changes in the number and location of plants. The mapping of industrial locations illustrates other essential perspectives. This may be applied for example to the case of steel.

Taking 'giant' centres of the steel industry as those with an output in the order of 10 million tons p.a., there were, around 1950, three such in the United States, two in the United Kingdom, two in West Europe and two or three in the USSR. Medium or minor centres (100,000 to 5 million tons) numbered about fifteen in North America, twenty in West Europe, eleven in the USSR, two in Mexico, six in South America, one in South Africa and two in Australia. In East Asia there were only about nine (Japan: Yawata, Kobe, Kawasaki, Fukushima, Kamaishi and Muroran; China: Anshan only; India: Asansol and Jamshedpur).

By 1960 these markings on the map of Asia had certainly greatly increased. Especially in China, where Anshan had grown into the largest category and two others had appeared (Wuhan and Paotow) while some seventeen minor centres had also been established. Japan's centres had become larger. Six medium or minor centres could now be distinguished in India (Durgapur, Burnpur, Jamshedpur, Rourkela, Bhilai, and Bhadravati), expansions in North Korea, Taiwan (Kaohsiung) and minor new developments also in the Philippines (Iligan) and Burma (Yama).

There were, however, by then five centres in the largest category in North America and about twenty-five others, four or five in the largest category and about forty others in West Europe, at least five in the 'giant' class and thirty others in the USSR. While the number of minor centres in South America had increased to about twenty and those in Africa to six. In addition important new development areas in various regions had been prospected and planned or were under construction: five in China (Tunghwa-Anshan, Chungking, Chengtu, Tsungi and Kwangsi), one in India (Bokaro) two in Pakistan (Karachi and Chittagong). There are, however, four such additional new developments in East Europe, about seven in the USSR and one in South America (Orinoco).

There were in all in 1950 about seventy-five centres of the steel industry in the world, of which only nine were in the Asian Region. By 1960 the number in East Asia had risen to forty-three out of a world total of a hundred and ninety.[8]

If there were free trade, not overridden by national-development considerations, the basic prices of iron and steel might still largely favour their procurement by the developing Asian countries from the developed countries (including Japan). The terms of trade for international purchases of these materials have been and remain more favourable than those in other commodity groups. The relative plenty of steel and steel-products is evident in this fact. For example the basic (f.o.b. USA) price of iron just over doubled between the 1934-8 average and that of 1947-51 and trebled by 1960 (from $24 to $73 per ton). The corresponding basic price of steel billets rather more than doubled ($35 pre-war to $88 in 1960). This is much less than the price-increase in most groups of commodities.[9]

Iron and steel development also depends especially on the supply of alloys. Their use is constantly being extended; the demand for them is likely to expand increasingly and their technical importance to grow. The production of manganese ore was about 2.3 million tons a year before the war, increasing to 3 million in 1949-51 and 5.8 million in 1958-60. India's production was about 20 per cent of the world's pre-war, falling to about 10 per cent in 1960. There is some production in Japan (about 2 per cent of the world's output, both before and since the war), South China, the Philippines, Malaya and Indonesia. Balaghat in the middle of India is one of a dozen major centres of production in the world. A few other centres have developed in Asia, but much less numerously or significantly than in other regions of the world. India contributed 37 per cent of world exports of manganese ore in 1938, 27 per cent in 1949-51, 22 per cent in 1958-60. The Philippines contributed about 2 per cent pre-war and again at the end of the 1950s. These aspects are examined more fully in other pages; they are mentioned here only to remind that many interrelated processes are involved, so that industrialization cannot be measured only by counting steelworks.[10]

Some other industries may be similarly considered. *Chemicals* serve almost all aspects of industrial advance and are most complicatedly involved in the whole process of industrialization and technical change. The intricacies in this field make it difficult to postulate overall comparisons such as are attempted for iron and steel, shipbuilding, etc. It is possible to take one key product as an indicator, for this sulphuric acid may be the most suitable. 14.6 million tons of this material were produced annually in the world before the war. This was increased to over

E

23 million on the 1949-51 average and doubled again to 46 million a year in 1958-60.

Production of sulphuric acid has certainly become diffused over the world, though the predominance of the United States is still marked. The USA had 28 per cent of world production pre-war and 34 per cent in 1958-60. The USSR raised its share from 7 per cent to 11 per cent. Canada increased from 1 per cent to 3 per cent and Spain from 1 per cent to 2 per cent. All other main producers suffered a reduction in their percentage share of the world's total production – though all substantially increased their output, as the total had more than trebled. Japan had 14 per cent of the world production pre-war, 9 per cent in 1958-60. West Germany similarly declined from 13 per cent to 7 per cent; the figures for others are UK 7 per cent to 5 per cent, Italy 6 per cent to 5 per cent, France 8 per cent to 4 per cent, Belgium and Luxembourg from 5 per cent to 3 per cent, Australia from 3 per cent to 2 per cent. Production in all the rest of the world increased from 7 per cent pre-war to 13 per cent at the end of the 1950s.

Sulphuric acid is not, however, an extremely satisfactory indicator – and less so as time goes on, with the increasing diversification of the patterns of activity involved. In particular it overweights Japan in the above ranking of countries, owing to the nature of fertilizer production in that country.

Mapping may be attempted, with greater looseness than for the other industries previously considered. Taking the whole range of chemical industries from the heavy to the lightest (from fertilizers and dyestuffs through plastics, synthetics, detergents, etc.) and observing the major and minor locations as before, the following is the general picture. In 1950 there were about thirteen major centres in the eastern half of North America and two in California, plus nearly thirty minor ones in the whole continent; or about fifty altogether. The map of Europe was closely packed with similar centrings: about twenty major nodes and about forty minor. The USSR might in this war-damaged phase count no such major units as North America and West Europe, but had at least thirty in the lesser category in operation. Japan had two centres of 'major' calibre (Osaka and Shimonoseki) and nine minor (Sunagawa, Toyama, Tokyo, Nagoya, Yokkaichi, Niihama, Fushiki, Omuta and Yawata). The whole of the rest of the region had only minor locations:

Mainland China had Shanghai and six others, Taiwan three, the Philippines one, Indonesia three, India seventeen (Sindri, West Bengal and two others in the east, four in the south, Bombay, Kathiawar and three others in the west, four in the north), while Pakistan had Karachi and four in the north: a grand total for the whole region of about forty-seven, mostly of third-rank size.

Australia had six minor centres. South Africa had one major (Johannesburg) one medium sized (Durban) and five small centres. South America had one first-rank (Sao Paulo) one medium (Buenos Aires) and sixteen small centres. Mexico had one second-rank centre (Mexico City) and four minor ones.

The Asian region thus had perhaps fifty centres of chemical industries, about a quarter of them in Japan, out of over 200 in the whole world; but the average size and technical standard were far higher in N. America and Europe.

The map for 1960 is much more complex, with the very great extension and evolution of these industries. The number of major centres in N. America had risen to about twenty, of minor to about forty. Europe had some twenty-six major and about fifty minor. The USSR counted at least seven major and about forty minor, or some fifty altogether on a conservative estimate.

The Asian Region had certainly expanded very greatly also. The number of centres in Japan had not changed, but many new ones had emerged elsewhere. Mainland China now counted one major centre (Peking) and twenty others (Harbin, Kirin, Mukden and four others in Manchuria; Shanghai, Wuhan, Nanking and five others in the Yangtse Basin; Taiyuan, Tientsin and three others in North China; two in the Canton area). The rest of the region continued to have minor centres only. Taiwan still had three, the Philippines now two, Malaya, North Vietnam and South Vietnam entered the list with two each, North Korea, South Korea and Thailand with one each. Indonesia increased its number to seven. India had now twenty-three (Sindri, Durgapur, W. Bengal and three others in the east; Madras and five others in the south; Bombay, Kathiawar and four others in the west; Ajmer and four others in the north). Pakistan had important new construction at Karachi and five centres in the north. The grand total for the region about 1960 was thus approximately ninety.

Great increases had, however, occurred in the other parts of the world. South America counted no less than forty-seven centres of the chemical industry by 1960, plus two new constructions under way in Peru. There were now sixteen in Mexico and about seven elsewhere in Central America and the Caribbean. There were forty-six altogether in Africa (fourteen in the north; sixteen in the west; ten in South Africa, where a second major centre, Modderfontein, was added besides Johannesburg; and six elsewhere in Africa). There were fourteen in Australia, five in New Zealand and thirteen in W. Asia. Summarizing grossly, the East Asia region had about ninety chemical centres out of about 415 in the whole world in 1960 compared with about fifty out of 200 in 1950. Despite large developments, in this respect as in practically all others the Region has not really increased its weight in the world economy. On a *per capita* reckoning it has progressed much less than all other Regions.[11]

One of the most important and striking worldwide increases has been in the production and use of *cement*. The pre-war production of the USSR and China is not known; without these countries it was about 68 million tons a year. By 1958-60 this had risen to 292 million tons a year. Before the war the United States produced about 25 per cent of the total, on the average of 1958-60 about 20 per cent. The USSR had 13 per cent of the world production at the latter date, China about 4 per cent. All Germany produced 16 per cent pre-war, West Germany 8 per cent in 1958-60. The corresponding figures for Japan are 8 per cent and 6 per cent, Italy 6 per cent and 6 per cent, France 7 per cent and 5 per cent, the UK 10 per cent and 4 per cent, India and Poland 2 per cent each in both periods. This leaves a large entry for all the others – some 25 per cent pre-war and 30 per cent post-war. Note that owing to the lack of pre-war figures for Russia and China the pre-war percentages exclude these countries and overstate the pre-war share of the others compared to the figures given for them in the post-war period.

The location-mapping technique used in preceding pages cannot be applied for pre-war and post-war comparisons in the case of cement owing to the inadequacy of the data. It may be attempted summarily for the 1958-60 period as follows. There were five or six 'giant' producing centres in N. America (manufacturing over 400,000 tons each per year) and about thirty-five others. Europe counted just about a hundred smaller ones. In East Europe there were at least fifteen more under construction or under effective expansion. In the USSR there were about forty, also to be classified as in construction and expansion rather than currently big producers. There were six minor centres in Australia and four in New Zealand. There were twenty-seven in the Middle East.

The East Asian Region had about eighty-five, some fourteen centres in the southern half of Japan and four in the northern (notably Fukuoka, Yamaguchi and Saitama), one or two in N. Korea, plus three under construction, two in S. Korea; six in Taiwan, Mainland China had thirty-one (eight in Manchuria and two under construction, Peking, Sian, Yungteng, three others and two in formation in the north, Shanghai, Wuhan, Chungking and three others along the Yangtse, eight in S. China). Hong Kong, Ceylon, Burma and N. Vietnam counted one each. The Philippines had four, Malaya and Indonesia two each. India had nine (notably Bihar, Rajasthan, Punjab, Gujerat and Madras). Pakistan had Karachi and three others. Some of the concentrations in Japan were the only ones in the Region which could be classed in the highest category of size.

Mexico had seven, the rest of Central America and the Caribbean eleven, South America fifty and Africa about forty (including two under construction). None in the underdeveloped regions was of major size. Thus in 1960 the East Asian region had eighty-five cement producing centres, out of a world total of

Table 6.6. *Share of industry in gross national product*[13]
(index, 1952-5 = 100)

	Manufacturing			Other non-agricultural		
	1952-4	1961-2	(index)	1952-4	1961-2	(index)
Burma	10	15	(140)	44	45	(104)
Ceylon	5	5	(111)	42	48	(114)
China: Taiwan	11	16	(119)	48	51	(105)
India	16	16	(101)	35	40	(114)
Indonesia	9	7	(81)	34	33	(90)
Japan	24	31	(129)	53	55	(103)
Korea: South	7	13	(193)	48	47	(97)
Malaysia	5	6	(117)	49	50	(102)
Pakistan	10	14	(150)	32	34	(106)
Philippines	11	16	(144)	46	52	(113)
Thailand	12	11	(97)	46	52	(113)
Vietnam: South	10	11	(117)	61	56	(91)
Average	11	13	(125)	45	47	(104)
Average, excluding Japan	10	12	(123)	41	46	(113)

some 415; a proportion strikingly similar to its rating for the chemical industry.[12]

Another method of gauging the progress of industrialization is the measurement of the proportions of the *national income* generated in various occupational sectors (Table 6.6).

This shows the relatively high industrialization in Japan and its continued increase (77 per cent of GNP from non-agricultural pursuits in 1952-4, rising to 86 per cent in 1961-2). By this criterion Indonesia, Thailand and Vietnam fell back in this period, all the others made some advance, for the most part small and on a small base. In all except the last-mentioned countries and India the manufacturing did, however, increase more than the other non-agricultural product.

One basic measure of industrialization is the *production and consumption of power*. The United Nations calculations give the following overall picture.

Table 6.7. Increase in the total production of energy[14]
(in million metric tons of coal equivalent: coal, lignite, crude petroleum, natural gas, electricity)

	1951		1963		*Increase %*
World	2,808		4,793		71%
N. America	1,279	(46%)	1,626	(34%)	29%
Latin America	167	(6%)	339	(7%)	103%
W. Europe	532	(19%)	575	(12%)	8%
Middle East	132	(5%)	487	(10%)	269%
Far East	107	(3.8%)	192	(4%)	79%
Oceania	23	(0.8%)	35	(0.7%)	52%
Africa	31	(1.1%)	87	(1.8%)	181%
Others	538	(19%)	1,451	(30%)	170%
		(100%)		(100%)	

The figure for the Far East thus increased much less than that of other underdeveloped regions; and its pitifully small share in the world total remained static at 4 per cent. 'Others' means largely the Communist states. It is further interesting to note the composition of this production (Table 6.8).

West Europe is most dependent on coal; 95 per cent of its energy-production in 1951 was from coal and lignite, falling to 86 per cent in 1963. The Far East's power-basis is not so dependent on coal, which shows a similar decline there, the figures for the Far East being 78 per cent and 70 per cent, compared with 42 per cent falling to 27 per cent only for North America, and world averages of 59 per cent and 45 per cent. The Far East is, however, much more concentrated on the use of crude petroleum than is Europe (17 per cent in 1951 rising to 20 per cent in 1963, compared to Europe's 1 per cent and 4 per cent) though much less so than North America (34 per cent in both 1951 and 1963) or the world as a whole (29 per cent and 36 per cent). In respect of natural gas and hydroelectricity the Far East's percentages are similar to those of West Europe. Natural gas provided less than 1 per cent of the total energy production of West Europe in 1951, but 4 per cent in 1963; in East Asia the figures were similarly 1 per cent and 4 per cent (cf. 11 per cent and 17 per cent for the world as a whole, but 22 per cent rising to 37 per cent for North America). Hydroelectric power represented only 2 per cent of the total in both 1951 and 1963, both for the world and for North America; but 3 per cent rising to 6 per cent and 4 per cent rising to 6 per cent for Western Europe and the Far East, respectively.

The Far East's basis and trend are thus somewhat analogous to those of West Europe. The consequence for the Far East is, however, a more extreme dependence on imports, which grew suddenly from 1960 to 1965. North America imported 24 million tons (coal equivalent) in 1951, equal to less than 2 per cent of its energy production, in 1963, 120 million tons or over 7 per cent. West Europe imported 129 in 1951, or over 24 per cent;

Table 6.8. *Total and* per capita *consumption of energy, East Asia*[15]

| | 1955 | | 1963 | |
	Total (mn. m.t.)	Per cap. (kg.)	Total (mn. m.t.)	Per cap. (kg.)
All Far East	139	178	281	295
Burma	0.66	33	1.30	55
Cambodia	0.08	20	0.28	48
Ceylon	0.76	87	1.22	114
China: Taiwan	3.42	383	6.71	573
Hong Kong	0.95	407	2.04	567
India	43.87	114	78.36	170
Indonesia	9.46	116	11.08	111
Japan	65.87	740	146.87	1,532
Korea: South	2.98	138	10.51	391
Malaya: Fed.	1.30	220	2.17	285
Malaya: Singapore	1.00	650	1.46	821
Pakistan	3.50	42	8.16	83
Philippines	2.76	126	5.79	191
Thailand	1.03	50	2.41	84
Vietnam: South	0.46	37	0.95	62

rising to 414, or 72 per cent in 1963. The Far East imported 6, or nearly 6 per cent in 1951, but 107, or 56 per cent in 1963. There is further the question of bunker requirements. World bunker-intakes remained steady at 2.9 per cent of world energy production, 1951-63, and North America's at 1 per cent. West Europe required 22 million tons of bunkers (in coal equivalent) in 1951, 4.1 per cent of its energy production, rising to 42 or 7.3 per cent in 1963. The Far East took only 5 in 1951 or 4 per cent of its energy output, but 20, or 20 per cent in 1963.

Per capita consumption of mechanical energy certainly increased in the Region at a reasonable rate, especially since the mid-1950s (Table 6.8). It remains, however, at low rates for the most part: for example the highest, Japan, is about at the level of Italy (1570 kg. in 1963) and Taiwan or Hong Kong at about that of Greece (341 in 1955, 562 in 1963).

ELECTRICITY

Electric power increased very greatly in the world in the post-war period. The installed capacity in all countries of the globe multi-

Table 6.9. Electricity: installed capacity in the region[16]
(000 kw)

	1948	1963	Index, 1963 (1948 = 100)
Burma	..ª	252	—
Cambodia	5	23ᵇ	460
Ceylon	17	172	894
China: Taiwan	..ᶜ	1,118	..
Hong Kong	94	499	531
India	1,809	6,902ᵈ	382
Indonesia	..ᵉ	404ᶠ	..
Japan	10,379	34,295	330
Korea: South	..	622	..
Malaya Fed.	..	284ᶠ	..
Malaya: Singapore	32	224	700
Pakistan	76	839	1,039
Philippines	191	958	501
Thailand	29	293ᵍ	1,034
Vietnam: South	..	116	..
Total	12,632	46,900	371
cf. USA	69,615	228,589	328
UK	13,766	44,139	321
USSR	15,157	93,050	614

Notes: ª 10 in public plants. ᵇ 23 in 1961. ᶜ 275 in public plants; nearly one half hydroelectric, throughout. ᵈ 1962. ᵉ 1949. ᶠ 1961. ᵍ 1962.

plied by a factor in the order of three and a half, from somewhat less than two million kW. in 1948 to over six and a half in 1963. Particulars for East Asia are shown in Table 6.9.

The region thus conformed to the world trend, its capacity roughly trebling. The smaller countries showed particularly large percentage increases. The weight of the figures is, however, very clearly with Japan, which has nearly three-quarters of the region's capacity (excluding its Communist countries); which capacity totals little more than that of the United Kingdom. On a *per capita* basis the Asian figures are obviously very low; especially for the rural masses. Kilowatts *per capita* of the whole population work out roughly as follows for 1963: Burma .01, Cambodia .004, Ceylon .01, Taiwan .10, Hong Kong .14, India .01, Indonesia .004, Japan .36, South Korea .02, Malayan Federation .04, Singapore .13, Pakistan .008, Philippines .03, Thailand .01, South Vietnam .008: cf. USA 1.2, UK .75, USSR .41.

In this field as in all others it is the *per capita* comparisons which are ultimately significant. These are next taken (Table 6.10) from the *consumption* side of the matter.

Table 6.10. Per capita *total consumption of energy: by Regions*[17] (solid and liquid fuels, natural and imported gas, hydro-, nuclear and imported electricity: kg. of coal-equivalent)

	1951		1963		
	kg.	% of world	kg.	index (1951=100)	% of world
World	1,070	100%	1,201	112	100%
N. America	7,486	6,996%	7,562	101	6,296%
Caribbean	507	47%	672	132	56%
Other America	372	35%	444	119	37%
W. Europe	2,092	196%	2,332	111	194%
Middle East	200	19%	318	159	26%
Far East	151	14%	295	195	25%
Oceania	2,546	238%	2,552	100	212%
Africa	203	19%	277	136	23%
Others	600	56%	834	139	69%

The power-consumption per person in the world increased 12 per cent – less than 1 per cent a year. This was the rate in West Europe also. In affluent North America and Australasia it remained stable, at their high levels. The developing countries made notable advances; the oil-rich ones particularly, the Middle East and Caribbean. Africa's overall effort and the Communist countries' are quite remarkable. The Far East achieved the greatest percentage increase of all, nearly doubling its *per capita* consumption. But the gains in the non-Communist developing countries were swallowed up by the increase in population. The consumption per head in the Far East rose only from one seventh of the world average to one quarter. The Far East was the lowest in this table in 1965, below even Africa; and only just surpassed the latter in 1963.

The countries under 'Far East' in Tables 6.9 and 6.10 are those taken in this book plus Afghanistan, West Irian, Laos and the Ryukyus. (For the countries included in the other regions see the sources given in footnotes 16 and 17.)

Table 6.11. Per capita *consumption of energy, East Asia*[18]
(kg. of coal equivalent)

	1955 kg.	1963 kg.
Burma	33	55
Cambodia	20	48
Ceylon	87	114
China: Taiwan	383	573
Hong Kong	407	567
India	114	170
Indonesia	116	111
Japan	740	1,532
Korea: South	138	391
Malaysia: Brunei	214	139
Malaysia: Federation	220	285
Malaysia: Sabah	36	211
Malaysia: Sarawak	1,266	681
Malaysia: Singapore	650	821
Pakistan	42	83
Philippines	126	191
Thailand	50	84
Vietnam: South	37	62

The output of *coal gas* in Japan was just over 800 million cu. metres in 1948, rising sevenfold to 5,754 in 1963. Production declined 40 per cent in that period in the United States. In the United Kingdom it increased only about 5 per cent. Japan's output was about 2 per cent of the United States' in 1948, 25 per cent in 1963; about 4 per cent of the United Kingdom's in 1948, 26 per cent in 1963. Figures for India are unfortunately not available. The other East Asian countries are small producers but do have gas and have mostly expanded it greatly: Ceylon declined (8.5 in 1948 to 6.1 in 1963) but Taiwan increased from 1 to 54, Hong Kong from 8 to 25, Indonesia from 13.5 to 72 (in 1962), Malaya from 7 to 27 and the Philippines from 7.2 (in 1955) to 17. The smallness of such figures may, however, be emphasized by comparing for example: (in 1963) Finland 77, Luxembourg 24, Tunisia 16.

TEXTILES

Textile industries are the first, the easiest and the most immediately necessary to develop in any industrial revolution; naturally they have played this part in East Asia also. *Cotton spinning* may first be considered. Between the beginning of 1950 and the end of 1963 the number of spindles in operation in the whole world increased 26 per cent. The number in operation in East Asia increased 131 per cent (Table 6.12).

Table 6.12. Cotton spinning: number of ring spindles installed[19]
(thousands)

	Beginning of 1950	End of 1963	Increase %
Ceylon	..	53	—
China: Taiwan	—	465	—
Hong Kong	82	633	(672%)
India	10,220	14,559	(42%)
Indonesia	..	305	—
Japan	3,739	13,353	(252%)
Korea: South	305	591	(94%)
Pakistan	164	2,416	(1,372%)
Philippines	..	620	—
Thailand	18	111	(517%)
Vietnam: South	..	515	—
Total	14,528	33,621	(131%)

The number in Mainland China is estimated to have slightly more than doubled, from just over 5 million in January 1950 to about 10.5 million in December 1963.

The countries in Table 6.12 thus roughly doubled their share in the world's total spindleage from 14 per cent in 1950 to 27 per cent in 1963. India was the largest of them in 1950, with 1 per cent of the world total and some 70 per cent of the East Asian total, followed by Japan with about one-third of these percentages (while Mainland China had about half India's figure). By 1964 Pakistan had increased prodigiously, Hong Kong and Thailand greatly, on their much smaller bases, but the region's spindleage was divided thus: India 43 per cent, Japan 40 per cent, Pakistan 7 per cent, the rest 1-2 per cent each. Mainland China had increased to about one-third of these eleven countries' total.

The production of cotton yarn was as follows (Table 6.13).

Table 6.13. Production of cotton yarn[20]
(000 m.t.)

	1948	1962	*Increase %*
Burma	..	5.0	—
Ceylon	0.7	1.5	(214%)
China: Taiwan	0.7	48.1	(589%)
Hong Kong	10.8	109.1	(910%)
India	657.0	893.0	(21%)
Indonesia	1.4	7.6	(543%)
Japan	124.0	470.0	(379%)
Korea: South	5.9	62.6	(961%)
Pakistan	13.5	213.9	(1,633%)
Philippines	1.2	8.9	(732%)
Thailand	..	0.7	—
Vietnam: South	..	6.8	—
	845.2	1,827.2	(116%)
World total	5,839.2	9,348.7	(60%)

Communist China's 1963 figure is unknown; it had 327,000 in 1948 and 1.6 million in 1960.

Meanwhile this industry was apparently declining in the developed countries. For example the number of spindles in the United Kingdom fell from 10.3 million to 5.3 million (just over 50 per cent), in the United States from 23.3 million to 19.3 (17 per cent), in Canada from 1.1 to 0.8 (30 per cent). The output of cotton yarn in the UK fell from 413,000 metric tons to 237,000 (43 per cent), the USA's remained unchanged at 1.7 million, Canada's fell from 82,000 to 73,000 (11 per cent). At the same time these figures point to technical improvements in this group of countries; in 1963 the USA was producing the same amount of yarn with 17 per cent fewer spindles, the UK's spindleage had fallen rather more than its output, Canada's much more. In Asia also the increase in production per unit of machine-capacity was above the world average – though well below the Western levels. The world as a whole increased the output of cotton yarn by 60 per cent, but had increased its spindleage by almost double that proportion; the Region increased its yarn output 116 per cent on only a slightly larger increase in spindle-age (131 per cent).

Problems of productivity are considered elsewhere in this book. Here we are considering principally the increase in plant. However, the kind of plant must also be considered. Turning to the *cotton-weaving* industry, it may be noted that the United Nations statistics distinguish usefully (though broadly) between 'ordinary' and 'automatic' cotton looms (Table 6.14). Automatic here includes semi-automatic looms or those with power-attachments. Ordinary includes all other power looms in establishments primarily engaged in cotton manufacturing; i.e. domestic handloom weaving is excluded.

Table 6.14. Cotton looms installed in factories[21]
(numbers)

| | Mid-1952 | | | End 1963 | | |
	Ordinary	Auto-matic	Total	Ordinary	Auto-matic	Total
China: Taiwan	..	..	..	8,097	7,132	15,229
Hong Kong	440	10,060	10,500	4,000	15,938	19,938
India	189,160	9,313	198,473	187,357	20,766	208,123
Indonesia	..	..	..	2,000	3,500	5,500
Japan	238,350	51,843	290,193	324,816	51,973	376,789
Korea: S.	2,379	1,234	3,613	12,285	4,472	12,757
Pakistan	8,249	1,335	9,584	12,500	21,470	33,970
Philippines	..	..	..	500	16,000	16,500
Thailand	672	—	672	3,000	5,214	8,214
Vietnam: S.	..	..	..	6,000	2,654	8,654
Total	439,250	73,785	513,035	560,555	103,119	663,674
World total	1,774,155	918,970	2,693,125	1,379,498	1,314,258	2,693,756
cf. USA	—	398,501	398,501	—	294,772	294,772
UK	309,501	40,301	349,802	89,700	47,000	136,700

In Japan, it should be noted, a large part of the older equipment was 'sealed' (disused).

The total of looms in the whole world thus showed no significant increase in these twelve years. The number in the USA declined by about a quarter, the total in the UK by nearly two-thirds. For the Region full figures are unfortunately not given for 1952, but evidently there was a substantial increase, in the order of 20 per cent. It must be recalled, however, that this was somewhat less than the increase in population in the Region in that period.

Some of the large percentage increases are recorded among

the smallest producers, which are also those with the smallest populations: such as Thailand, which increased over twelve times, and South Korea whose increase approached the fourfold. Pakistan's increase, it must also be noted, was about three and a half times. Others were Hong Kong 90 per cent, India only 5 per cent, Japan 30 per cent. It should be added that there was probably a fivefold increase in Communist China, the estimated figures being:

	1952	1963
Ordinary	56,000	200,000
Automatic	8,000	100,000
Total	64,000	300,000

The distinction here between 'ordinary' and 'automatic' is merely a rough guide to the technical status in this industry. 86 per cent of the looms in the Region were in the 'ordinary' category in 1952; about the same proportion (84 per cent) in 1963.

In the world as a whole two-thirds were non-automatic in 1952, but this proportion had been reduced to just over a half in 1963. In the United States there were no non-automatic looms. In the United Kingdom their proportion of the total was reduced from over 88 per cent in 1952 (even higher than the proportion in the Region) to 66 per cent in 1963. It is interesting to note that Communist China strongly surpassed the UK in this field and changed from ordinary to automatic in the same proportions.

There are, however, great differences among the Asian countries. In Taiwan almost half the looms are automatic. In Hong Kong the number of ordinary looms increased about ninefold, automatics 50 per cent; the proportion of the latter fell from about 98 per cent to 80 per cent but was still very high. In India the automatic installations more than doubled, but increased their share in the total only from about 5 per cent to 10 per cent. In Japan the increase was almost entirely in the ordinary looms, the automatics increasing only slightly and representing only 18 per cent and 14 per cent in the two years: in this industry Japan is not so highly automated as is widely imagined. In South Korea and Vietnam the development has been mainly with ordinary looms; in Pakistan, the Philippines, Thailand and Indonesia, as in Hong Kong, automatics predominate in the recent development.

Changes in the percentages of automatic looms in the national totals (1952-63) were thus: Hong Kong 96-80 per cent, India 5-10 per cent, Japan 18-14 per cent, South Korea 34-35 per cent, Pakistan 14-63 per cent, Thailand 0-63 per cent, Region 14-15 per cent.

The output of *cotton cloth* developed as follows (Table 6.15) according to the limited data available.

Table 6.15. Production of woven cotton fabrics[22]
(including mixed fabrics)

	Unit	1948	1952	1963	Increase % (1963/52)
Ceylon	m. sq. metres	6	8	..	.. [a]
China: Taiwan	m. metres	13	88	221	150%
India	m. metres	3,950	4,205	4,423	5%
Japan	m. sq. metres	773	1,871	2,938	57%
Korea: South	m. sq. metres	29	50	169	238%
Pakistan	m. metres	81	159	668	320%
Philippines	m. metres	7	6	124	1,967%

Note: [a] Ceylon's increase was slight; production in 1959 was still 8.

Mainland China increased from 1,890 million metres in 1948 to 3,830 in 1952 and 7,500 in 1963, i.e. by about 100 per cent in 1952-63. These increases are quite striking. Except in the case of India (and apparently Ceylon) they are well ahead of the increase in the population. *Per capita* calculations would emphasize, however, the very low amounts available for the average individual (from home production) in these countries. And in some cases it will be apparent that production of cotton cloth has not increased in proportion to the increase in the number of looms (compare Tables 6.13 and 6.14). These two aspects will be examined in the chapter on productivity and standards; it is, however, immediately evident here that South Korea quadrupled its number of looms but much less than quadrupled its output of cloth, in Pakistan the increase in looms was also rather larger than the increase in output, while the two figures were even in India at the very low rate of 5 per cent increase. In Japan, however, the increase in the output was almost double the increase in the number of looms.

Compare the Western countries. In the United States output was 8,815 million metres in 1948, 8,701 in 1952 and 8,770 in 1963; thus output rose slightly in 1952-63 even though the number of machines fell by one quarter. In the United Kingdom output was 1,768 in 1948, 1,546 in 1952 and 1,223 in 1963, so output declined about 20 per cent even though the number of looms was reduced about 63 per cent.

On the *per capita* count it is evident that annual home production of cotton cloth per person is in the following orders of magnitude: in Japan about 30 square yards, in Mainland China about 6 yards, in other East Asian countries about 10, in the United States and the United Kingdom about 45.

The *woollen* industry is much less developed in the Region, where it is important only in Japan. Japan had only 547 spindles for wool at the end of 1948; but increased more than threefold to 1,798 by the end of 1963; i.e. nearly half the number in the United Kingdom in 1963 (where the number had declined over 20 per cent since 1948) and slightly more than Italy, but some 40 per cent more than the United States (where the number had declined much more sharply, by some 60 per cent). The only other country in the Region significantly equipped in this respect was India, which had 117 wool spindles in 1950 and 207 in 1962 – i.e. only slightly more than such countries as Austria, Portugal and New Zealand. The number in the world increased about 15 per cent in this period – despite the falls in the three largest countries, the UK, USA and France, which had respectively about 40 per cent, 27 per cent and 22 per cent of the world total in 1948, falling to 27 per cent, 9 per cent and 8 per cent in 1963. Japan had less than 5 per cent of the total in 1948, but 12 per cent in 1963; India had slightly less than 1 per cent in 1948 and slightly over 1 per cent in 1963.[23]

In the production of woollen yarn (pure and mixed) Japan rose from being a minor producer in 1948 (11,000 metric tons, similar to such countries as Denmark, or one-thirtieth of British or United States output) to fourteen times that amount in 1963, or about 60 per cent of the UK output (which had increased about 15 per cent in the period) and about 75 per cent of the US output (which had decreased about 45 per cent in the period). India trebled its 1948 production of 7,700 m.t. by 1963, but remained a minor producer, ranking with such countries as Rumania and Yugoslavia. There was also a small production in Taiwan (900 m.t. in 1955 – rising to 2,600 in 1963), Hong Kong (1,000 in 1955 – 5,100 in 1963), South Korea (100 – 3,600) and Pakistan (2,700 in 1957, 3,100 in 1958, but declining to 2,400 in 1963).

The Japanese wool-spinning industry has concentrated increasingly on pure wool yarns, the proportion of worsteds diminishing. In 1948 for example the division in Japan was 20 per cent pure to 80 per cent mixed, in 1958 to 1963 this was reversed to 80 per cent pure and 20 per cent mixed; in the United States the ratio was 73 per cent pure to 27 per cent mixed in 1959 and 78 per cent to 22 per cent in 1963.

Japan produced about 20 m.t. of yarn per spindle in 1948, over 70 in 1963. The UK produced about 40 per spindle in 1951 and 50 in 1963. The United States produced over 100 in 1948, but over 200 in 1963. This illustrates the rise of Japan from wartime destruction to the West European levels of industrial performance – but also how much higher are the American levels in such instances. On this basis, however, this industry was still more efficient in India, where output was about 70 tons per spindle in 1948 and about 100 in 1963. Unfortunately it is not possible to extend this analysis to the other countries in the Region.[24]

The comparisons are entirely crude in omitting considerations of quality of the products, intensity of working of the machinery and other factors. Nevertheless the basic textile industries have made marked progress in the developing regions; while they are (in some senses at least) declining in the developed countries. The demand that the latters' markets should not be closed to the new production of the former, the implication also that a further shift in the international division of labour (with the advanced countries concentrating still more on technically advanced industries and products and letting the developing countries supply more of the older basic manufactures) would now be rational and equitable, is a case that is urged with increasing strength.

Another textile group is of some interest in this connection; namely *artificial fibres*. In the 1950s some countries of the Region entered significantly into this field. World production in the category of continuous filaments of rayon and acetate increased 47 per cent between 1948 and 1955, and a further 18 per cent between 1955 and 1963 (0.7 million m.t. in 1948, 1.0 in 1955 and 1.2 in 1963). Production in the United States declined about 20 per cent in the whole period; in the UK output increased about 30 per cent. Japan produced over 16,000 m.t. in 1948, 89,000 in 1955 and 133,000 in 1963. Taiwan began production in 1957 with 800 m.t., rising to 1,900 in 1963. Mainland China began in 1958 with 200, rising to 11,800 in 1963. Hong Kong's figures were 3,200 in 1956, declining, however, immediately thereafter to 100-200, India began in the early 1950s, with 6,900 in 1955 rising to 33,200 in 1963 (i.e. about 10 per cent of the UK's output).[25]

In the category of discontinuous filaments of rayon and acetate world production even more strikingly increased – nearly trebling – in 1948-55 and increased a further 50 per cent in 1955-63. In the UK output approximately trebled in the whole period, in the United States it more than doubled. In Japan it increased from 16,000 m.t. in 1948 (about 2 per cent of the world total) to 329,000 in 1963 (18 per cent of the world total, nearly two and a half times the UK's output and 14 per cent larger than that of the USA). Mainland China began production in 1957 with 200 m.t., increasing to 15,000 in 1963. India's figures were 5,700 in 1955 and 32,100 in 1963, Taiwan's 600 in the first year of production (1958) and 2,900 in 1963.

The production of fabrics woven from rayon and acetate increased only about 8 per cent in the UK between 1948 and 1963; in the USA it declined about 20 per cent. In Japan it was very small in 1948, but from 1955 onwards it was at the United States level. In India it almost doubled between 1955 and 1963 and at the latter date was nearly 50 per cent greater than the UK's. There was also a small production throughout these years in the Philippines and South Korea; the percentage increases in these countries are larger than the average or median in most other countries in the world.[26]

The Asian development in these cellulosic fibres (though principally in Japan) thus deserves at least a passing credit. One other category is, however, of interest in juxtaposition. It is almost a *per contra* entry, for in this field only Japan in the Region has greatly advanced and this is an instance of the importance of changes at the higher level of research and techniques, with the evolution of new or substitute products in which developing countries can hardly compete. The category (in the UN statistical definition) is that of

'non-cellulosic man-made fibres, excluding textile glass fibre. These fibres are either of non-cellulosic natural polymers which are based on materials such as casein or groundnuts or are made of synthetic polymers, which are based mostly on coal or petroleum . . . among the best known are nylon, terylene, orlon and saran.'

Total world production in this category soared from 34,000 m.t. in 1948 to 1.3 million in 1963. Some 75 per cent was from the United States in 1948; production there multiplied almost twenty times by 1963, but the US share in the world total was reduced to just under 40 per cent. There were thirteen producing countries in 1948 – none of which was in the Region. Japan began in the early 1950s with a production of 7,220 m.t. (about 2 per cent of the world total) rising to 341,000 in 1963 (about 25 per cent of the world total, and 60 per cent of the USA's). Mainland China began a very small production (230 tons) in 1960, doubling this by 1963. Taiwan began with a token 100 tons in 1959, increasing sixfold by 1963. India began in 1962 with 230 tons and produced 730 in 1963. South Korea's figures were 90 tons in 1959 and 400 in 1963. These last represent levels very low down in the world scale – broadly above the smallest South American producers but below the smallest European ones. Only Japan is in the first-league, in most aspects where technical progress and innovation are concerned.[27]

To emphasize this point it is appropriate to mention immediately here one of the latest developments, which might be portentous.

INCEPTION OF A SYNTHETIC RUBBER INDUSTRY IN JAPAN

Synthetic rubber competes strongly with the natural rubber which is one of Southern Asia's main commodities; and Japan has been a good customer for the latter. It was therefore ominous that Japan began to produce synthetic rubber in 1959. The scale of this start was very small – 1,200 tons. This was a negligible amount compared to the USA's 4 million and others'. It was smaller than the amount with which France inaugurated this industry in the same year (6,000 tons). But it was 50 per cent larger than the start the UK had made two years earlier (800 in 1957) which grew into 11,500 in 1958 and 58,000 in 1959.

Unfortunately later figures cannot be given here. If, however, this industry grows in Japan as it has in other industrial countries the effects in South Asia might be considerable. The US production in 1959 showed an increase of 182 per cent on the nearly 500,000 tons made there in 1948; East Germany's output trebled from 29,000 in 1948 to 86,000 in 1959, Canada's increased two and a half times from 41,000 in 1948. West Germany produced 900 in 1948 and more than five times as much in 1959; and Italy started with an estimated 20,000 in 1958, rising at once to 48,000 in 1959. The other countries of the Region, apart from Japan, are not in this field at all. Here is a cloud, no larger as yet than a man's hand, but it might portend a radical change in the present climate of Asian development.[28]

IRON AND STEEL

Meanwhile the focus of attention in industrialization still remains iron and steel, as the heavy basis of the 'black' industrial revolution which is still the accepted goal.

World production of *pig-iron and ferro-alloys* increased nearly 150 per cent from 113 million m.t. in 1948 to 281 in 1963. The increase in the United States was 19 per cent, from over 56 million in 1948 to nearly 67 in 1963; in the United Kingdom 57 per cent, from nearly 9.5 million to nearly 15. Production in Japan was 836,000 m.t. in 1948 – less than 1 per cent of world production – but increased more than twenty times, to 20,434 or 7.3 per cent of world production in 1963. India's output rose about four and a half times, from (000 m.t.) 1,487 to 6,740 (1.3 per cent of the world total to 2.4 per cent). Taiwan produced 14 in 1948 and 54 in 1963, South Korea 1 in 1948 and 5 in 1963, North Korea 106 in 1948 rising to eleven times as much in 1963. Mainland China produced nearly 3.9 million tons in 1955 – about twice as much as India – with a claimed increase to more than four times that figure (i.e. nearly three times India's output, and more than the UK's) in 1963. The percentages and *per capita* amounts remain, however, small in terms of world-wide comparisons.[29]

In *crude steel* similarly world output more than doubled (156 million tons in 1948, 387 in 1963), India's increased nearly five times (in 000 m.t. 1,277-5,971) from 0.8 per cent of the world total to 1.5 per cent, Japan's increased nearly sixteen times (1,715-31,501) from 1.1 per cent to 8.1 per cent of the world total. Taiwan and South Korea increased production greatly on their small bases (4-215 and 8-160 respectively). North Korea's figures were 115 and 1,220. The China Mainland is credited with 2.8 million tons in 1955 and 12 in 1963 (about 60 per cent of the United Kingdom at the latter date). The UK had increased production about 50 per cent, the USA about 25 per cent. The USSR increased production about fourfold (18.6 million to 80.2 – reaching about 80 per cent of United States' production). The basis of heavy industry in the Region is thus in fact still comparatively slender, especially if Japan is considered separately.[30]

The *pace* of this advance is further studied in Table 6.15, which shows that the major advance in the two important non-Communist countries of East Asia mainly gathered speed only from about 1959. Previous to that year the progress of India in particular was less than the world average. India's progress was throughout surpassed by that of Japan.

The most total efforts were evidently made in this field by Mainland China, resulting in huge percentage increases (which were, however, broadly matched, as percentage increases, by Taiwan). Mainland China's progress faltered heavily in the early 1960s, though the level was evidently well above that of the 1950s – just when the progress of the other East Asian countries accelerated. This was due to the extraordinary adventure of the 'Great Leap Forward' launched at the end of the 1950s, when the whole population in Communist China was mobilized to concentrate on the production of iron and steel everywhere by

Table 6.16. *Iron and steel production, East Asia and the world*[31]
(production in 000 m.t.)   (index: 1957=100)

(a) *Pig iron and ferro-alloys*

	World	Japan	India	Mainland China	Taiwan
(1951 production	150,000	3,227	1,853	1,448	8)
1951 index	100	100	100	100	100
1952	102	111	102	133	125
1953	112	144	97	166	100
1954	107	147	108	215	213
1955	129	168	104	267	200
1956	134	194	108	333	225
1957	142	221	104	410	250
1958	131	238	116	658	213
1959	150	305	172	1,416	413
1960	171	382	230	1,899	300
1961	171	508	275	1,036	662
1962	177	571	315	1,036	788
1963	187	633	364	1,174	675
(1963 production	281,000	20,434	6,740	17,000	54)

simple direct local 'backyard' methods. A vast quantity of mostly poor or industrially useless material was thus produced. It seriously clogged the transport system. The effort was abandoned in 1960. United Nations Headquarters noted against the 1958 figure for pig iron in Mainland China of 9.53 million tons 'excluding production by simple local methods which was estimated by the US Bureau of Mines to be 4 million metric tons which was probably reworked and included in the figure for 1959', but there is no clear evidence about this reworking.

In addition South Korea produced 3,000 tons in 1958 and the following amounts in the next five years (in 000 m.t.): 8, 14, 9, 2, 5. And North Korea produced in 1955 to 1963: 118, 194, 278, 392, 694, 872, 890, 1,213 and 1,159.

(b) *Crude steel*

(000 m.t.)   (index: 1951 = 100)

	World	Japan	India	Mainland China	Taiwan
(1951 production	210,800	6,502	1,524	900	16)
1951 index	100	100	100	100	100
1952	100	107	105	150	113
1953	111	118	100	197	125
1954	106	119	112	247	156
1955	128	145	114	317	250
1956	134	171	116	496	494
1957	139	193	114	594	556
1958	130	186	121	1,311	669
1959	145	256	162	1,483	994
1960	164	340	216	2,050	1,250
1961	166	435	268	1,056	1,156
1962	171	424	338	1,111	1,138
1963	183	484	392	1,333	1,344
(1963 production	386,600	31,501	5,971	12,000	215)

In addition South Korea produced (in 000 m.t.) 1 a year in 1951 to 1954 and the following from 1955 onwards: 11, 12, 17, 20, 38, 50, 66, 148 and 160, and Pakistan the following from 1951: 3, 8, 11, 10, 11, 11, 12, 10 11, 12, 12, 11, 12.

The production of *metallurgical coke* increased accordingly (Table 6.17) but the comparison shows that the methods in Japan and Taiwan are relatively economical on the side of fuel costs (per unit of increased output). Japan obtained well over six times the iron and five times the steel on three times the coke, Taiwan seven times the iron and thirteen times the steel on double the amount of coke; while India produced three and a half times the iron and nearly four times the steel on about three and a half times the coke, but Mainland China increased the output of coke *pari passu* with the increase in iron and steel production, about twelve times in each case. The relevance of this as an indication of technical levels or trends may be seen if it is noted that in the United Kingdom in the same period pig iron production increased 50 per cent and steel 44 per cent while the output of metallurgical coke declined 4 per cent; in the United States pig iron output increased 5 per cent and steel 4 per cent while that of metallurgical coke fell more than 32 per cent.

Table 6.17. Production of metallurgical coke, East Asia[32]
(000 m.t.)

	Japan	India	Mainland China	Taiwan
(1951 production	3,859	2,161	1,300	114)
1951 index	100	100	100	100
1952	99	98	220	114
1953	118	92	269	132
1954	109	106	308	120
1955	117	122	346	116
1956	137	118	423	103
1957	155	121	514	129
1958	155	142	1,385	161
1959	175	199	1,538	151
1960	212	221	1,923	170
1961	269	288	1,154	164
1962	283	326	1,154	202
1963	294	342	1,154	204
(1963 production	11,347	7,350	15,000	233)

MISCELLANEOUS INDUSTRIES

A wide variety of activities is important to the process of industrialization. A selection of these may immediately be noted before a summation in terms of general indices is attempted.

The *lumber* industry of the world increased considerably in the period – by 54 per cent, from a total of 219 million cu. metres of wood sawn (all timber, both home-produced and imported, but excluding sleepers) in 1948 to 337 in 1963. In the United States it decreased about 7 per cent (to 82 cu. metres), in Canada it increased about one third (to 23), while in the USSR it multiplied three times (to 106). In the East Asian region it increased about two and a half times, from about 15 million in 1948 to just over 30 million in 1962-3, i.e. in the order of 5 per cent to 10 per cent of world output. A major uncertainty in this calculation is India, for which figures are not available after 1948 (which was 610,000). Burma's output fell by some 30 per cent from 426,000 in 1948, but Japan's trebled from 9 million in 1948, Malaya's quadrupled from 400,000 in 1948, Ceylon's apparently trebled from the small figure of 8, Indonesia's doubled from 1,000, Cambodia's doubled from 70, Thailand's increased 40 per cent from 700, while the Philippines' and Vietnam's were maintained at around 1.1 million and 200,000 respectively.

Japan is the region's significant producer of *wood pulp*, with an output of 407,000 metric tons in 1948 (about 1 per cent of the world total) rising sevenfold to nearly 3 million in 1959 (over 5 per cent of the world total). World output almost doubled in this period – from 28.5 to 54.4 million m.t. Canada's output increased about 40 per cent (7-10 million m.t.), the United States' increased similarly (11.7-22 million); the United Kingdom's increased more than fourfold at its very much lower level (53,000-230,000). The USSR's trebled, from 1 to 3 million. Japan's production was about 6 per cent of that of Scandinavia in 1948 but rose to nearly one-third in 1959. The other countries of the region are minor producers of low quality. Paper shortage has been marked in Communist China.

Technical differences have been interesting. One third of the total world output was produced by mechanical means and two-thirds by chemical processes, in both 1948 and 1959. In Canada mechanical production predominated (59 per cent of output in 1948, 54 per cent in 1959) in the UK even more strongly, on its much smaller scale (91 per cent and 93 per cent). In the United States chemical production greatly predominated (83 per cent and 79 per cent in the same years) also in the Soviet Union (70 per cent - 73 per cent) and in Scandinavia. In Japan mechanical production predominated in 1948 (56 per cent) but this was shortly afterwards reversed (falling to 29 per cent in 1959).[33]

In newsprint similarly Japan is the region's significant producer, with 0.1 million tons in 1948 and 0.7 in 1959; i.e. about 1 per cent and 4 per cent respectively of world output, which rose 70 per cent from 7.5 million to 12.8 between those years. Japan's production had been one-third of the UK or Finland in 1948 but surpassed these countries' in 1959.[34]

In paper other than newsprint Japan again leads the region,

with an output of 260,000 m.t. (less than 1 per cent of the world total) increasing sevenfold to 1.8 million in 1959 (still less than 2 per cent of world production, which had nearly doubled meanwhile). India produced one-third as much as Japan in 1948, approximately trebling – to reach Japan's 1948 level – by 1959. South Korea produced 2,000 tons in 1948 and between five and ten times that amount in the following years. Pakistan produced 14,000 in 1948 and 25,000 in 1959, Taiwan at least 9,000 in 1948 (the figure 9,000 is based on very incomplete data) and 88,000 in 1959. The whole region outside Japan and Mainland China produced about the same quantity of non-newsprint paper as such countries as Poland, Austria or Switzerland.[35]

The UN Yearbooks record also the following miscellaneous items.

Table 6.18. Miscellaneous items of industrial production[36]

	Caustic soda (000 m.t.)		Soda ash (000 m.t.)	
	1948	1963	1948	1963
Burma				
China: Mainland	48(1951)	270(1958)	185(1951)	640(1958)
China: Taiwan	8(1951)	45	0	13
India	15	152	48	267
Indonesia				
Japan	325	1,082	221	1,500
Korea South				
Malaysia				
Pakistan				
Philippines	1(1953)	3(1961)		
World				
UK				
USA	2,156	5,275	4,151	4,247

	Super- phosphates (000 m.t.)		Nitrogen fertilizers (000 m.t.)	
	1948	1963	1948	1963
Burma				
China: Mainland				
China: Taiwan	28	172	10	93
India	22	580	24	221
Indonesia				
Japan	993	1,687	407	1,279
Korea: South				38
Malaysia				
Pakistan				24(1961)
Philippines				8
World			4,200	14,000
UK	1,121	597	277	563
USA	9,511	11,790	1,080	4,004

Table 6.18. *Miscellaneous items of industrial production*[36]—continued

	Petroleum products (000 m.t.)		Aluminium (000 m.t.)	
	1948	1963	1948	1963
Burma	38	598		
China: Mainland				100
China: Taiwan	211	1,413	3	12
India	..	7,163	3	53
Indonesia	4,588	10,056		
Japan	142	46,925	10	214
Korea South				
Malaysia	1,679	2,066		
Pakistan	45	1,998		
Philippines		2,737		
World	376,700	985,200	1,130	4,360
UK				
USA				

	Radio and TV receivers (000s)		Motor vehicles (000s)	
	1948	1963	1948	1963
Burma				
China: Mainland				
China: Taiwan				
India	25	419		52
Indonesia				
Japan	807	22,881	20	1,400
Korea: South				
Malaysia				
Pakistan				
Philippines		168		
World			6,670	20,500
UK	1,721	4,445		
USA	17,683	26,309		

	Cargo ships (000 g.r.t.)		Tankers (000 g.r.t.)	
	1948	1963	1948	1963
Burma				
China: Mainland				
China: Taiwan				15
India	11(1952)	23		
Indonesia				
Japan	434(1951)	2,367	71(1951)	1,301
Korea: South				
Malaysia				
Pakistan				
Philippines				
World	1,710	4,822	600	3,716
UK				
USA				

THE INDUSTRIAL STRUCTURE OF EAST ASIA

This chapter opened with some overall index number comparisons; it then proceeded to annotate some industries and products particularly. The structure and trends of East Asia's industries may next be considered synoptically by means of other available data.

The UN has analysed the total value-added in all industrial activities in the world (Table 6.19). The result shows (a) the pitifully small part played by Asia, especially if (b) Japan is considered separately. In mining as a whole Japan represented 44 per cent of the Region's total value added in 1953: in coal 79 per cent, in metal mining 20 per cent. In all manufacturing, Japan represented 48 per cent in 1953; in light manufacturing 34 per cent; in heavy manufacturing 67 per cent. Taking the various headings of manufactures, further comparisons follow. (The Communist countries are excluded for lack of data.)

Table 6.19. Percentage distribution of value added in mining and manufactures: at current prices[37]
(Communist countries excluded in 1958)

(a) *World total*

	1953	1958
Asia, East and South-east	4.5%	4.3%
Asia, excluding Japan	..	1.7%
Latin America	4.0%	3.0%
Africa and Middle East	2.2%	2.0%
North America	55.1%	35.8%
Europe	32.6%	26.5%
Oceania	1.6%	1.2%

(b) *Distribution of Asia's share:*

	1953	1958
Japan	47.7%	59.7%
Burma	0.9%	0.8%
Ceylon	0.4%	0.8%
China: Taiwan	1.1.%	1.0%
India	32.7%	18.1%
Indonesia	..[a]	3.1%
Korea: South	1.3%	2.7%
Malaysia	2.8%	1.5%
Pakistan	3.3%	3.2%
Philippines	2.5%	2.1%
Thailand	1.6%	1.1%
Rest	5.7%	5.9%

Note: [a] Included in Rest.

Table 6.20a. Index numbers of industrial production, world and East Asia[38]

	World			East and S.E. Asia		
	1950	1953	1963	1950	1953	1963
All mining, manufacturing, electricity and gas	62	78	144	43	58	197
Food, beverages, tobacco ..	69	80	125	57	74	131
Textiles, clothing, leather ..	72	82	126	46	68	153
Wood products and furniture ..	69	78	140	..	..	..
Paper and paper products ..	68	77	135	29	58	196
Coal and crude petroleum, chemical, coal petroleum and rubber products	59	73	147	56	55	174
Non - metallic mineral and products	57	71	143	43	62	181
Metal mining and basic metals	68	85	141	54	74	211
Metal products	55	79	158	21	39	304
Electricity and gas	40	65	154	49	62	186

Table 6.20b. Index numbers of industrial production: non-Communist World and East Asia[39]

(1958 = 100)

	World excluding USSR and E. Europe			East and S.E. Asia			E. and S.E. Asia excluding Japan		
	1948	1953	1963	1948	1953	1963	1948	1953	1963
All mining, manufacturing, electricity and gas	61	85	137	35	58	197	50	59	156
All mining	69	86	127	56	66	142	55	54	154
Coal	99	101	100	66	89	125	58	74	174
Metal	66	85	122	57	99	132	68	112	138
Crude petroleum and natural gas ..	58	81	146	50	31	158	50	30	156
All manufacturing ..	62	86	138	32	57	205	49	60	155
Light manufacturing	69	85	127	41	67	153	52	66	141
Heavy manufacturing	56	86	145	24	49	254	43	50	183
Food, beverages, tobacco	68	84	121	48	74	131	59	74	128
Textiles	75	91	124	39	68	148	54	67	128
Clothing, footwear ..	75	88	127	..	..	..	..	..	..
Wood products, furniture	74	88	129	..	..	..	..	..	..
Paper and paper products	58	78	134	16	58	196	16	41	180
Chemicals, petroleum and coal products	46	71	156	31	51	199	68	52	167
Non-metallic mineral products	60	82	134	26	60	187	27	53	158
Basic metals	76	99	135	28	67	234	55	75	232
Metal products ..	55	89	145	18	39	304	28	41	191
Electricity and gas ..	44	68	147	41	62	186	34	54	185

On the UN indices of overall industrial production, East and South East Asia was much below world averages before 1958, but thereafter showed increases much above the world averages (Table 6.20) in which East and South East Asia includes Brunei, Burma, Ceylon, China : Taiwan, Hong Kong, India, Indonesia, Iran, Japan, Korea : South, Malaysia (except Sabah), Pakistan, Philippines, Thailand and Vietnam : South.

Another UN series gives different particulars (Table 6.20b: East Asia defined as in the preceding Table) to the same effect, though it is notable here that Japan progressed more than the rest of the Region, especially in metallic and other manufactures and in heavy industry.

It is evident that the weight of the Region's industrial advance – apart from very substantial progress in Mainland China, which is however unfortunately not fully verifiable statistically – is in Japan. The UN figures underline this very heavily (Table 6.21).

Table 6.21. Shares of Japan and India in the total value added in industry in East Asia[40]

Japan's share in Regional total of value added:

	1953	1958	India's share 1953	1958
Food, beverages, tobacco	32%	41%	36%	30%
Textiles, clothing	52%	44%	48%	34%
Wood products and furniture	31%	57%	43%	23%
Paper and paper products	86%	86%	9%	7%
Chemicals, petroleum and rubber products	60%	49%	20%	10%
Non-metallic mineral products	51%	62%	36%	20%
Metal mining and basic metals	76%	69%	20%	16%
Metal products	69%	80%	21%	11%

Only scanty indications are available concerning the workforce in industry (Table 6.22). In the cases of Ceylon and Singapore, these indicate an actual decline in the numbers engaged in manufacturing industry since 1955, though there have been great increases in the other countries listed.

Table 6.22. Indices of non-agricultural employment[41]
(1958 = 100)

	1948	1963
Japan	82	127
Malaysia : Singapore	103	93
Philippines	79(1949)	114

Employment in manufacturing

	1948	1955	1963
Ceylon	..	101(1957)	92(1961)
China: Taiwan	43	99	153
Hong Kong	..	72	146(1961)
Indonesia	85	96(1957)	109(1960)
Japan	..	777	131
Malaya	..	89(1956)	137
Singapore	..	113	90
Philippines	..	94	114

In sum, prodigious efforts have been made in the direction of industrialization in East Asia. For the most part they have, however, been heavily offset by the size of the populations involved and by the rate of growth of those populations; so that betterment of the poor material situation of the Asian masses has not significantly resulted, particularly in the cases of the most populous countries. Success – especially in technical and quantitative terms – has been largely concentrated in Japan, and at most points in the industrial spectrum deep and rapid technological change makes it uncertain whether past and present investment-decisions and commitments, based on technical, market and cost conditions of past rather than present and oncoming decades, are economically optimal and operationally secure. For Asia as for Europe, the ultimate requirement may now be a complete re-thinking of the requirements for economic development – against the conditions and assumptions of the late, not the early or middle, twentieth century.

Chapter 7

TRANSPORT AND COMMUNICATIONS

The overland communications of the Region are slight. The Siberian railway and the traffic through West Asia are minor factors. Ocean traffic remains the main determinant of development, despite increasing activities within the national boundaries. For the developing countries of the Region this is one of the main aspects of dependence on foreigners – on the Western countries and Japan.

SHIPPING

The world's merchant shipping (counting vessels of over 1,000 tons) totalled nearly 80.3 million g.r.t. in 1948. This represented an increase of 20 per cent over 1938, despite the wartime sinkings. Japan is outstandingly the great shipping nation in East Asia; reduced by huge wartime losses, the Japanese fleet only recently recovered a leading position. Before the war Japan had some 7 per cent of the world's merchant tonnage, or nearly five million g.r.t. In 1948 this was reduced to little over one million (just over 1 per cent of the world total). Even so this was nearly twice as much as the tonnage of the whole of the rest of the Region. In the following ten years to 1958 the world tonnage increased by 56 per cent; Japan's by 43 per cent which, however, brought Japan to only 4.4 per cent of the world total. In the next five years to 1963 the world total increased by only about 17 per cent; Japan's by 86 per cent which, however, brought Japan to no more than her pre-war share of the world total (about 6.8 per cent).

Meanwhile, the rest of the Region had greatly increased its tonnage. It had less than two million tons in 1948 – about 2 per cent of the world total. It increased by 282 per cent by 1958; but this represented only 1.2 per cent of the world total. It increased by 214 per cent between 1958 and 1963; but still had hardly 2.2 per cent of the world tonnage. Japan thus had about two-thirds of the merchant shipping tonnage owned by the whole Region in 1948, nearly 80 per cent in 1958 and three-quarters in 1963.

Despite great increases in the rest of the Region, it takes a very small place in world ship-owning. The figures (Table 7.1) show the different countries' progress. Between 1948 and 1958 the following were the percentage increases: Hong Kong 382 per cent, India 114 per cent and the Philippines 28 per cent. Between 1958 and 1963 the increases were: Hong Kong 189 per cent, India 80 per cent, Indonesia 255 per cent, Pakistan 134 per cent and Philippines 230 per cent. Hong Kong had about 22 per cent of the tonnage of the Region excluding Japan in 1948, 29 per cent in 1958 and 26 per cent in 1963. The corresponding percentages for the others show India with a heavily declining share (60-40-38 per cent), Indonesia with a share rising in 1958-65 from 8 per cent to 13 per cent, Pakistan with about 9 per cent in both 1958 and 1963, the Philippines' share falling from 18 per cent in 1948 to 8 per cent in 1958 but recovering to 13 per cent in 1963.

The above excludes China. In 1948 there was quite a large tonnage under the Chinese flag; the United Nations figure is over 800,000 tons (80 per cent of Japan's and 60 per cent more than the whole of the rest of the Region). This must include 'Liberty Ships' and other wartime arrangements which were withdrawn in the following year. Mainland China had little ocean shipping till the mid-1950s when significant construction began. Taiwan's merchant fleet notably increased meanwhile, from a very low starting-point. The island had 520,000 g.r.t. in 1963; about 40 per cent of India's figure and about 20 per cent more than either Indonesia or the Philippines, and about 20,000 g.r.t. (4 per cent) more than Communist China's figure, which, however, relates to inland and coastal ships only, whereas Taiwan's merchant fleet plies worldwide.

In this period the world's shipping-pattern has greatly changed. The United States merchant marine declined in absolute tonnage (by 12 per cent in 1949-59 and 10 per cent in 1958-63) and as a percentage of the world total (from 36 per cent in 1948 to 20 per cent in 1958 and 16 per cent in 1963). The United Kingdom's increased only moderately in tonnage (by 13 per cent in 1948-58 and 6 per cent in 1958-63) and therefore decreased markedly as a percentage of the world total (from 22 per cent in 1948 to 16 per cent in 1958 and 15 per cent in 1963). The question is complicated especially by the great increase in the use of 'flags of convenience' – the registration of many ships in Liberia,

Panama and Greece – but clearly Asia has not increased in this respect so much as the Asian Region (including Japan) in 1948; it increased by 41 per cent in 1948-53 and 83 per cent in 1958-63, representing 2.6 per cent of the world total in 1948, 2.4 per cent in 1958 and 3.7 per cent in 1963.

A post-war feature was the increase in tankers. Of the total world merchant tonnage in 1948 over 15 million or 19 per cent consisted of tankers. By 1958 the world's tonnage of tankers had more than doubled and represented 27 per cent of all merchant shipping tonnage. In 1958-63 it increased by 50 per cent and came to represent 35 per cent of the aggregate tonnage. Japan is the only country in the Region with a significant tanker-fleet. Starting with a mere 10,000 tons in 1948, Japan multiplied this more than tenfold by 1958 and almost trebled her tanker tonnage in the following five years. The Japanese took the lead in the first half of the 1960s in building very large vessels of this kind; nevertheless Japan had only 3 per cent of the world's tanker tonnage in 1958 and 5.6 per cent in 1963. The figures for the UK, USA and USSR show trends similar to the general shipping situations of those countries: a very large increase in the USSR, a considerable increase in the UK and some decline in the USA.

Though the growth-rate is impressive, the traffic in the Region

Table 7.1. Merchant fleets of the world and the Region[1]
(000 g.r.t.)

	1948	1958	1963
All merchant ships:			
World	80,292	124,935	145,863
(of which tankers	15,337	33,590	50,563)
Hong Kong	114	435	821
India	315	674	1,211
Indonesia	..	119	422
Pakistan	..	128	299
Philippines	96	123	406
Total	525	1,481	3,159
Japan	1,024	5,465	9,977
(of which tankers	10	1,039	2,834)
cf. USA	29,165	25,590	23,133
(of which tankers	5,472	4,109	4,647)
UK	18,025	20,286	21,490
(of which tankers	3,528	5,929	7,792)
USSR	2,097	2,966	5,434
(of which tankers	..	230	1,716)

F

is really low in proportion to its size and population. The vessels entering East Asian ports in 1948 and in 1963 represented only 6-7 per cent of the world total.

Table 7.2. Shipping in East Asia: vessels entered (000 *n.r.t.*)[2]
(*index* 1948 = 100)

	1948	1953	1958	1963
Burma	1,420	1,253(88)	1,801(127)	1,706(120)
Ceylon	5,695	8,795(154)	7,005(123)	5,051[c](89)
China: Taiwan	2,588[a]	3,349(129[b])	5,676(219[b])	9,207(356[b])
Hong Kong	10,754	12,070(112)	16,855(157)	27,154(253)
India	8,100	8,999(111)	12,450(154)	15,796(195)
Japan	5,123	22,347(436)	32,461(634)	76,279(1489)
Korea: South	299	1,353(452)	5,550(1856)	7,546(2523)
Malaya: Federation	11,598	13,706(118)	12,804(110)	18,049(155)
Malaya: Singapore	..	..	5,770	7,979
Pakistan	2,895	5,288(183)	5,971(206)	8,863(306)
Philippines	6,402[a]	7,560(118[b])	7,911(124[b])	12,218(191[b])
Thailand	801	1,863(232)	2,814(351)	4,492(561)
Vietnam: South	1,802	3,363(187)	2,780(154)	4,444(247)
Total	57,477	89,946(156)	119,848(209)	198,784(346)

Notes: a 1952, b 1952 = 100, c 1962.

Japan had less than 10 per cent of the Region's ship-entries in 1948 but 38 per cent in 1963. Malaya and Hong Kong dominated the shipping traffic in 1948 (about 20 per cent each). Hong Kong remained second in 1963 with 14 per cent and Malaya third with 9 per cent.

The above measures the traffic in terms of the tonnage of ships entering ports; it is necessary to analyse further the figures of their cargoes, inward and outward. If the returns for all Asia are considered it is immediately noticeable (Table 7.3) that freight with the whole Asian continent increased between 1948 and 1963 very much more than freight to and from other parts of the world. Freight in the world as a whole increased 189 per cent, freight into and out of Asian countries multiplied five times. The corresponding particulars for the other Regions were as follows. In the same period loadings in Africa quadrupled unloadings increased 120 per cent. In South America loadings just over doubled, unloadings increased only 25 per cent. In both Europe and Oceania, loadings and unloadings increased evenly; each approximately trebled. In North America loadings increased 75 per cent and unloadings just over doubled. Whereas in Asia both quadrupled.

Table 7.3. *Goods loaded and unloaded by international shipping*[3]
million m.t. (index 1948 = 100)

	World		Of which, Asia:			
	Loaded and unloaded	(index)	Loaded	(index)	Unloaded	(index)
1938	470	(96)	84	(100)	68	(136)
1948	490	(100)	84	(100)	50	(100)
1953	680	(139)	170	(202)	93	(186)
1958	940	(200)	276	(329)	147	(294)
1963	1,360	(289)	426	(507)	251	(502)

The second direct observation from these figures is the marked excess in tonnage of loadings over unloadings in Asia – which is true also of the other underdeveloped regions, in contrast to the developed continents, where unloadings greatly exceed loadings. This obviously reflects the condition of under-development; the underdeveloped countries largely produce and ship out bulky or weighty raw materials, receiving (in the colonial relationship) compact manufactured goods in return.

It is further striking that in general this disparity greatly in-creased in the post-war as compared to the pre-war period. In Asia as a whole loadings exceeded unloadings by 24 per cent in 1938, 68 per cent in 1953, 88 per cent in 1958 and 70 per cent in 1963. Particulars for the three developed and the three under-developed Regions are given in Table 7.4. Note especially that the position of North America was reversed after 1948; in 1938 loadings in North America exceeded unloadings by 27 million tons (21 per cent), and in 1948 also outward freight loadings still exceeded inward freight unloadings there by 9 million tons (6 per cent), but from 1953 onwards the inward movements greatly exceeded the outward.

Table 7.4. *Cargo balance, Asia and the world*[4]
(million m.t. loaded/unloaded in the year)

	Excess of unloadings over loadings			Excess of loadings over unloadings		
	North America	Europe	Oceania	Africa	South America	Asia
1938	−27(−21%)	81(44%)	1(18%)	5(22%)	33(168%)	16(24%)
1948	−9(−6%)	118(109%)	2(27%)	4(15%)	69(239%)	34(68%)
1953	44(26%)	132(76%)	3(24%)	7(21%)	92(317%)	77(83%)
1958	50(24%)	232(113%)	9(6%)	8(18%)	143(376%)	129(88%)
1963	47(17%)	371(109%)	2(8%)	61(100%)	189(525%)	175(70%)

The imbalance for Asia is thus large, but not so extreme as for South America – and less than for Africa in the most recent period when it suddenly rose sharply for that Region.

Two very substantial qualifications must, however, be stressed. This 'colonial' imbalance in the volume of the interregional sea traffic is a strong feature (and the increase in the figures is especially noticeable) but these statistics seriously confuse the impression in the following respects, particularly in relation to the group of countries considered in this book. The tonnages represent all types of cargo, in which the contents of tankers bulked increasingly. Crude petroleum and petroleum oils represented 12 per cent of world total freight in 1937, 43 per cent in 1953 and 47 per cent in 1958; these went very largely to the developed continents, particularly from South America (which here also includes Central America and the Caribbean) and comparatively little from East Asia (though very much from West Asia, which is here included under 'Asia').

Concentrating strictly on the Region studied in this book, therefore – the fifteen countries of East Asia – the perspective must be modified as follows. (a) As far as the developing countries of the Region are concerned the factor of petroleum, just mentioned, applies only very marginally (slightly to Indonesia and very slightly to Burma), but the 'colonial imbalance' applies *a fortiori* to their position of supplying other primary products. (b) This Region does, however, include Japan, a major indus-

Table 7.5. *Goods loaded and unloaded, East Asia*[5]
(000 m.t.) (index 1953 = 100)

(a) Loadings

	1948	1953	1963
Burma	1,928 (148)	1,307	2,282 (118)
Ceylon	713 ((76)	942	997[d](106)
China: Taiwan	152 (11)	1,446	3,108 (215)
Hong Kong	1,242 (82)	1,511	2,250 (149)
India	6,458 (84)	7,722	7,199[d](93)
Indonesia	5,185 (42)	12,412	17,584 (142)
Japan	1,980 (40)	4,957	18,345 (370)
Korea: South	33[b](23)	143	864 (604)
Malaya: Federation	..	7,472	8,026 (107)
Malaya: Singapore	..	6,623[a]	7,979 (120)
Pakistan	1,149[a] (88)	1,307	2,561 (196)
Philippines	4,414[a] (98)	4,504	5,106 (113)
Thailand	1,779[a] (103)	1,723	3,277 (190)
Vietnam: South	265[c] (128)	207	741 (358)
Total	25,298 (50)	50,765	80,319 (158
Total excluding Japan	23,318 (50)	45,808	61,974 (135

Notes: [a] 1962. [b] excluding civilian aid. [c] 1949. [d] 1962. [e] 1956.

(b) *Unloadings*

	1948	1953	1963
Burma	1,425 (166)	858	960 (112)
Ceylon	1,694 (78)	2,185	4,039 (185)
China: Taiwan	259 (20)	1,304	3,596 (276)
Hong Kong	2,833 (85)	3,344	8,246 (247)
India	9,960 (108)	9,203	18,514[d](201)
Indonesia	1,924 (46)	4,203	3,322 (79)
Japan	6,756 (22)	31,289	138,959 (444)
Korea: South	37[b](3)	1,135	4,332 (382)
Malaya: Federation	..	11,062	4,882 (44)
Malaya: Singapore	..	11,052[e]	13,961 (126)
Pakistan	5,018[a](143)	3,519	7,391 (210)
Philippines	2,580[a](76)	3,391	5,143 (152)
Thailand	1,126[a](88)	1,280	2,969 (232)
Vietnam: South	590[c](46)	1,269	2,530 (199)
Total	33,202 (39)	85,094	218,844 (272)
Total, excluding Japan	26,646 (50)	53,805	79,885 (148)

(c) *Balance* (+ indicates excess of unloadings over loadings, i.e. inward balance)

	1948	1953	1963
Burma	503 (112)	449	1,322 (294)
Ceylon	+981 (79)	+1,243	+3,042 (245)
China: Taiwan	+107	142	+488
Hong Kong	+1,591 (87)	+1,833	+5,996 (327)
India	+3,502 (236)	+1,481	+11,315 (764)
Indonesia	3,261 (40)	8,209	14,262 (174)
Japan	+4,776 (18)	+26,332	+120,614 (458)
Korea: South	+4	+992	+3,468 (350)
Malaya: Federation	..	+3,590	3,144
Malaya: Singapore	..	+4,429	+6,082
Pakistan	+3,869 (175)	+2,212	+4,830 (128)
Philippines	1,834	1,113	+37
Thailand	653 (147)	443	308 (70)
Vietnam: South	+325 (31)	+1,062	+1,789 (168)
Total	+7,904 (23)	+34,329	+138,525 (403)
Total, excluding Japan	+3,128 (39)	+7,997	+17,911 (224)

trial country, and other industrial centres taking in not only oil-fuel imports but vast amounts of raw materials and food. If the East Asian countries are listed instead of all Asia, they thus show an inward, not an outward cargo balance (Table 7.4). Moreover (c) this situation has been accentuated in the post-war period by the import of food into most of the East Asian countries. Hence, even if Japan is excluded this Region shows a substantial net inward cargo-balance. Only Burma, Indonesia and Thailand are completely free of the plus-sign, indicating a net inward balance of freight, at the end of Table 7.5.

Loadings thus increased about 60 per cent in tonnage between 1953 and 1963, if Japan is included, or 35 per cent without Japan; but unloadings increased 172 per cent for the whole group, or 48 per cent if Japan is excluded. The inward balance quadrupled overall, and more than doubled if Japan is excepted. The Region's outward cargoes in 1953 were quantitatively more than double pre-war, by 1963 more than three times; but its inward cargoes had increased in five or six times that proportion.

RAILWAYS

The metabolism of economic and social development in the East Asian countries still depends greatly on the railways. In the developed countries recently road traffic has significantly displaced railway transport. In East Asia the roads (and contingent facilities) are few and bad, compared to those in the developed countries; with the partial exception of some present or former British colonial areas. Even in Japan, highway development is far below the extent and standard appropriate to that country's general level of development.

Table 7.6. Railway freight: East Asia and the world[6]
(000 million ton-km. carried) (index 1948 = 100)

	1938	(index)	1948	1953	(index)	1963	(index)
World	1,129	(63)	1,806	2,247	(124)	3,587	(199)
Africa	18	(58)	31	42	(135)	65	(210)
N. America	471	(46)	1,032	995	(96)	1,038	(101)
S. America	19	(73)	26	27	(104)	30	(115)
Asia	74	(94)	79	164	(234)	418	(529)
E. Europe ⎫			462	862	(179)	1,782	(386)
⎬	539	(92)					
W. Europe ⎭			165	181	(110)	236	(143)
Oceania	8	(73)	11	13	(118)	17	(155)

Table 7.6 above shows that railway freight in the world doubled between 1948 and 1963. In Asia it multiplied more than five times. In Asia – and in Communist countries – railways have been a main instrument of economic development in this period. Asia's share in the world total remains, however, very low, in comparison especially with its share of world popu-

lation. In the developed countries at the same time railways were, in contrast, significantly displaced by road transport.

Particulars for the East Asian countries are given in Table 7.7 below.

Table 7.7. *Railway traffic: East Asia[7]*

	Goods (m. net ton-kms.)			Passengers (m. passenger-kms.)		
	1948	1963	(index)	1948	1963	(index)
Burma	626	734	(117)	484	1,541	(318)
Cambodia	48[a]	68	(142)	44[a]	81	(184)
Ceylon	(255)[b]	303	(119)[c]	1,391[d]	1,634	(117)[f]
China: Taiwan	691	2,206	(319)	2,121	3,558	(168)
Hong Kong	3	159	(500)	116	146	(126)
India	37,200	92,000	(247)	62,470	88,000	(141)
Indonesia	434[a]	951	(219)	1,532[a]	6,262	(409)
Korea: South	1,041	4,067	(391)	2,829	6,575	(232)
Malay	316	618	(196)	(526)[b]	536	(102)
Pakistan	3,825	9,643	(252)	9,943	13,266	(133)
Philippines	139	192	(138)	416	1,068	(257)
Thailand	301	1,340	(445)	1,307	2,714	(208)
Vietnam: South	77	182	(236)	23	230	(1000)
Total	76,156	112,319	(147)	83,202	125,611	(151)
Japan	24,294	58,100	(239)	121,515	221,411	(182)
cf. UK	35,421	27,041	(76)	33,832	31,503	(93)
USA	935,996	912,733	(98)	66,344	29,803	(45)

The following figures are given for Mainland China:

	Goods		Passengers		
1949	1959		1949	1959	
18,400	265,260	(1441)	13,000	45,670	(351)

Notes: a 1949. b 1953. c index 1953=100. d 1954. f index 1954=100. g 1951.

Thus the totals of goods and passengers carried by rail in the developing East Asian countries each increased by some 50 per cent. Japan carried nearly one third as much goods traffic as all the thirteen South East Asian countries listed in 1948; over half as much in 1963. In passenger traffic, however, Japan's activity was 46 per cent greater than the thirteen countries' together in 1948, and 76 per cent greater in 1963. Communist China's enormous increase was concentrated heavily on the development of goods traffic. In the advanced Western countries, in contrast, there were significant declines in both categories. In Burma, Cambodia, Indonesia, the Philippines and Vietnam passenger-use of the railways increased more rapidly than goods-use; in the other Asian countries the opposite was the case.

MOTOR VEHICLES

Inland water transport plays a large part in the economic life
of several of the East Asian countries, but the statistical basis
is not available to provide an analysis. Road transport must,
however, be immediately considered, in direct relation to the
increase in rail transport. Particulars of the numbers of commercial and passenger vehicles are available (Table 7.8).

Table 7.8. *Motor vehicles in use: East Asia*[8]
(000s) (index 1948 = 100)

	Commercial vehicles			Passenger vehicles		
	1948	1963	(index)	1948	1963	(index)
Burma	22.0	19.1	(87)	10.9	24.8	(228)
Cambodia	1.2	8.2[a]	(683)	0.9	14.2[a]	(1578)
Ceylon	12.6	34.4	(273)	27.6	79.5	(288)
China: Taiwan	3.4	13.2	(388)	1.6	11.0	(688)
Hong Kong	2.9	15.1	(521)	6.4	47.2	(738)
India	86.1	302.0	(351)	119.9	353.0	(294)
Indonesia	18.7	98.5[d]	(527)	17.6	140.8[a]	(800)
Korea: South	7.9	20.0	(253)	2.9	11.1	(383)
Malaya	15.1	39.0	(258)	19.8	129.7	(655)
Pakistan	14.0	34.2[a]	(244)	21.9	69.4[a]	(317)
Philippines	51.4	99.3	(193)	34.6	102.3	(296)
Thailand	5.7	72.4	(1270)	6.3	60.3	(957)
Total	241.0	755.4	(313)	270.4	1,043.3	(386)
Japan	187.5	2,845.1	(1517)	35.3	1,233.6	(3495)
cf. UK	831.5	1,618.4	(195)	2,019.7	7,391.7	(366)
USA	7,734.5	12,874.1	(166)	33,350.9	68,683.0	(206)

Note: [a] 1962.

The number of vehicles in Japan has increased phenomenally
(and this increase was greatly gathering speed in the mid-1960s).
By 1963 the number of goods vehicles in Japan was nearly four
times the total of the other East Asia countries. The number of
commercial vehicles actually declined in Burma. In all the countries except Thailand passenger vehicles increased in a higher
ratio than goods vehicles – in most cases a much higher ratio.

Turning from transport to communications, the increased use
of modern methods of rapid and direct communication may be
considered first.

TELEPHONES

By the end of 1963 there were over 154 million telephones in
use in the world. Nearly 7 per cent of these were in the Asian

region, which had improved its relative position, as it had had only a little over 2 per cent in 1948 and had increased its total by some 500 per cent (Table 7.9).

Table 7.9. Number of telephones in use, Asia and the world[9]
(millions)

	1948		1960		Increase, 1960/48
World	66	(100%)	143	(100)%)	117%
Africa	0.7	(1%)	2	(1%)	173%
N. America	40.7	(62%)	79.8	(56%)	96%
Central America	0.5	(1%)	1.0	(1%)	118%
S. America	1.6	(2%)	3.3	(2%)	112%
Asia	2.1	(3%)	10.4	(7%)	387%
Europe[a]	19.0	(29%)	43.2	(30%)	116%
Oceania	1.4	(2%)	3.2	(2%)	125%

Note: a Including USSR.

The Asian scale is, however, heavily tipped by Japan, which had 78 per cent of the regional total in 1948 and even more – 82 per cent – in 1963. The other countries, despite three- to tenfold increases (fourfold for the region as a whole excluding Japan) hardly increased their percentage shares. The *per capita* comparisons must also be stressed. The United Kingdom had approximately one telephone for every six persons in 1963; the

Table 7.10. Telephones in use: Asian region[10]
(000s)

	1948	1963
Burma	5	21
Cambodia	2e	4
Ceylon	13	41
Taiwan	40e	132
Hong Kong	40e	178
India	117	681
Indonesia	29	148
Japan	1,310	8,430
Korea: South	50e	171
Malaya: Federation	20	98
Malaya: Singapore	13	74
Pakistan	17	107
Philippines	11	147
Thailand	6	55
Vietnam: South	10	21
Total	1,683	10,308
Total, excluding Japan	373	1,978

Note: e Estimated.

United States one for only just over two persons. Japan had one for every twelve inhabitants; the rest of the region excluding Japan had only one per 460 of population, the figures ranging from Hong Kong twenty, Singapore twenty-four, Federation of Malaya seventy-eight, Taiwan ninety, Philippines 205, South Korea 220, Ceylon 260, to leap upwards through Thailand 520, India 650, South Vietnam 765, Indonesia 800, to Pakistan 980 and Burma and Cambodia about 1,000 each.

The use of telegraphic services must next be considered.

INLAND TELEGRAMS

The figures for the use of telegraphic services within each of the Esat Asian countries are summarized in Table 7.11. They show great increases for some countries – but actual declines in others. In total, excluding Japan, the increase was by two-thirds; contrasting especially with the great decline of this means of communication in developed countries.

Table 7.11. *Number of domestic telegrams sent and received*[11]
(000s)

	1948	1953	1963	*increase or decrease* (–) 1963/53
Burma	..	746	889	19%
Cambodia	..	52	42[d]	– 19%
Ceylon	2,550	3,141	4,400[e]	40%
India	20,613	24,679	32,766[d]	33%
Indonesia	1,440	2,046	6,724[f]	229%
Malaysia	837	606[a]	1,214	100%
Pakistan	2,034	2,973	4,938	66%
Philippines	2,146[b]	..	5,521[e]	(100%)[g]
Thailand	..	1,301[c]	2,194	69%
Vietnam, South	..	574	547	– 5%
Total	29,620	36,118	59,235	64%
Japan	75,169	93,793	94,605	1%
cf. UK	43,396	34,195	10,523	– 69%
USA	189,964	153,889	92,231	– 40%

Notes: [a] 1954. [b] 1949. [c] 1955. [d] 1962. [e] 1959. [f] 1961. [g] Over 1949.

It will be noted that Japan's figure was two and a half times the total of the other ten Asian countries in 1948 and 60 per cent higher than their total in 1963, but had become comparatively stable in the last decade. Various factors are, however,

Table 7.12. Foreign telegrams sent (s) and received (r)[12]
(000s)
(r = incoming telegrams, s = outgoing telegrams)

		1953	1963	*increased or decreased (−)*
Burma	r	156	77	
	s	157	82	
		313	159	−41%
Cambodia	r	108	100[b]	
	s	75	116[b]	
		183	216[b]	18%
Ceylon	r	392	441[c]	
	s	1,076	565[c]	
		1,468	1,006[c]	−31%
India	r	2,302	1,388[b]	
	s	1,657	1,431[b]	
		3,959	2,819[b]	−29%
Indonesia	r	560	443[d]	
	s	660	513[d]	
		1,220	956	−22%
Malaysia	r	1,128	1,481	
	s	901	1,628	
		2,029	3,109	53%
Pakistan	r	771	808	
	s	622	938	
		1,393	1,746	25%
Philippines	r	400[a]	1,487	
	s	450[a]	797	
		850[a]	2,284	169%
Thailand	r	250[a]	349	
	s	250[a]	336	
		500[a]	685	37%
Vietnam, S.	r	117	131	
	s	193	166	
		310	297	−4%
Total	r	6,184	6,705	
	s	6,041	6,572	
		12,225	13,277	9%

		1953	1963	*increased or decreased (−)*
Japan	r	1,646	2,225	
	s	1,880	2,425	
		3,526	4,650	32%
cf. UK	r	9,986	9,342	
	s	10,271	8,849	
		20,257	18,191	− 10%
USA	r	..	..	
	s	..	..	
		19,661	18,896	− 4%

Notes: a estimated. b 1962. c 1959. d 1961.

involved. It must be noted that telegrams are of social as well as business use; in Japan's case the cheap internal *kana* telegrams have been much used for greetings, personal messages, etc. Civil disturbances affected the figures for some S.E. Asian countries in some of the years. It is also a question of such considerations as the relative cost and availability of telephone and mail services, in relation further to the time taken by surface mails (relatively long in large countries).

The use of telegrams has declined in developed countries. The *per capita* figures are, however, interesting. In the UK about one domestic telegram per head of the population was sent in 1948, only about one per four inhabitants in 1963. For Japan the figure has remained around one per head per annum. In the United States it was also at about this figure in 1948, but approximately halved by 1963. Whereas in Ceylon for example it has remained roughly one per two persons; in the large countries India and Pakistan approximately one per twenty persons.

FOREIGN TELEGRAMS

The figures for international telegrams are also highly indicative for our analysis (Table 7.12).

The complexities previously mentioned apply in this sphere also. In addition, the balance of international telegraphic exchanges is interesting – the marked but varying excess of incoming over outgoing cables, or *vice versa*. Note that the figures are of numbers of telegrams, not of wordage; this may presumably mean that they are not unduly inflated by press-cables, and in general may be assumed to relate almost entirely to business activity. The figures for the developed countries are fairly stable. Analysis of those for the developing countries would be an involved task. The decline in some of these countries is serious. It must mean some decline in their overseas business activity, in this most rapid sector of communication, though improved air mail connections offset this, to an extent that cannot be precisely determined. Table 7.12 may, however, be useful in giving an impression of this aspect of the metabolism of development, though it certainly does not lead readily to any specific diagnosis. We turn therefore to a consideration of letter-mail, which is clearly the broader medium of communication from the viewpoint of economic development.

INLAND LETTER MAIL

The use of inland postal services has greatly increased in the Region; as shown in Table 7.13. The increases are, however, very uneven between the countries, and (except in Japan) are very low in *per capita* terms.

Table 7.13. Domestic letter mail[13]

	1948	1953	1963	Increase, 1963/53
Ceylon	170,989	244,206	344,526	41%
China: Taiwan	..	61,000[a]	366,000	500%
Hong Kong	5,557	20,253	43,249	114%
Indonesia	43,020	134,447	200,111	49%
Korea, S.	..	146,000[b]	207,000[c]	42%
Malaya: Fed.	53,638	87,723	114,056	30%
Pakistan	272,625	357,378	684,885	92%
Vietnam S.	..	24,557[d]	44,213	80%
Total	545,829	1,075,564	2,004,040	86%
Japan	2,285,829	3,901,000	8,490,000	118%
cf. UK	7,700,000	8,658,000	9,709,000	12%
USA	40,280,000	50,948,000	67,853,000	33%

Notes: [a] 1952. [b] 1956. [c] 1962. [d] 1954.

The only figures for Burma are 11,512 in 1960, 12,582 in 1963. Cambodia's figure for 1953 is given as 1,442. In the case of India earlier figures are given only for *all* letter mail (including both domestic and foreign) as: 2,246,000 in 1948 and 2,667,000 in 1953. The corresponding figure for 1963 is 4,877,000 – an increase of 83 per cent over 1953. As this is almost entirely domestic (see below) these figures may be added for India.

FOREIGN LETTER MAIL

The use of international postal services also increased greatly in the Region (Table 7.14).

Table 7.14. Foreign letter mail[14]
(000s) s = sent (outgoing), r = received (incoming)
Balance: S = excess of s over r, R = excess of r over s

		1948		1953		1963	Increase, 1963/53
Ceylon	s	9,496		11,412		7,203	− 37 %
	r	13,110		16,628		11,445	− 31 %
	R	3,614	R	5,216	R	4,242	
China:	s	..		3,000a		8,000	167 %
Taiwan	r	..		5,000a		12,000	140 %
		..	R	2,000a	R	4,000	
Hong Kong	s	41,390		35,236		69,877	98 %
	r	60,649		25,925		62,916	143 %
	R	19,259	S	9,311	S	6,961	
Indonesia	s	36,366		5,394		7,355	36 %
	r	43,149		11,221		10,451	− 7 %
	R	6,783	R	5,827	R	3,096	
Malaysia	s	18,894		19,872		29,281	47 %
	r	26,477		27,034		30,404	12 %
	R	7,583	R	7,162	R	1,123	
Pakistan	s	22,348		35,112		52,849	50 %
	r	33,518		108,475		127,203	17 %
	R	11,170	R	73,363	R	75,354	
Vietnam, S.	s	..		11,941		13,202	10 %
	r	..		14,701		17,006	16 %
			R	2,760	R	3,804	

		1948	1953	1963	*Increase* 1963/53
Total	s	108,494	121,967	187,767	54%
	r	176,543	208,984	271,425	30%
	R	68,049	R 87,017	R 83,658	
Japan	s	4,648	21,505	60,065	179%
	r	4,211	26,348	73,178	178%
	S	437	S 4,843	R 13,113	
c.f. UK	s	358,000	444,000	528,000	19%
	r	..	294,000	414,000	41%
		..	S 150,000	S 114,000	
USA	s	409,236	471,014	528,973	12%
	r	..	661,691	1,733,000	162%
		..	R 190,677	R 1,204,027	

Note: ª 1954

The following figures are also available. Cambodia in 1953 sent 969 and received 1,505 (in thousands, as above). South Korea in 1956 sent 2,000 and received 4,000, in 1959 sent 3,000 and received 4,000. Burma in 1960 sent 1,852 and received no less than 65,433. The figures rose even further in 1962 – sent 2,224, but received 77,173. Only to fall drastically in the next two years : sent 2,685 in 1961 and 1,790 in 1962, received 6,718 in 1961 and 4,479 in 1962.

Figures for India are available only from 1959 : sent 68,000 in 1959 and 88,000 in 1963 (33 per cent increase), received 87,000 in 1959 and 92,000 in 1963 (6 per cent increase).

Thus foreign correspondence of these Asian countries increased greatly; in the total (inward plus outward) by some 60 per cent from 1948 to 1963 and nearly 40 per cent from 1953 to 1963. However, the drastic falls shown above for Ceylon, Burma and Indonesia were not paralleled anywhere else in the world, sadly reflecting declines in these countries' communications with the rest of the world.

The balance figures (S and R in Table 7.14) are intriguing, especially perhaps the tendency in the region to a marked (though diminishing) excess of inward over outward foreign mail. Serious analysis of this feature is difficult. Possibly it reflects the underdeveloped condition of passivity in outward dealings : cf. the excess of sendings by countries in a certain phase of trade expansion efforts (Hong Kong, Japan, UK). This curious feature appears worthy of passing emphasis – even at the risk of some apparent levity, in commenting for example that about 1,000 million foreign letters to the region (or about 40 per cent of the total) appear to have gone unanswered in those fifteen years. Note, however, that the United States 1963 figure is equally remarkable, to the same effect.

Per capita comparisons are interesting in this connection also. The UK sends about ten letters abroad per head of its population per year, and receives about eight. The United States' figures are about three outward and eight inward. The corresponding figures for others are (sent and received *per capita*) approximately:

	s	r
Ceylon	1.0	1.0
Taiwan	1.0	1.0
Hong Kong	20.0	20.0
Indonesia	0.07	0.1
India	0.1	0.1
Pakistan	0.5	1.3
Japan	0.6	0.7

Table 7.15. Ratio of domestic to foreign letter mail[15]
000s. d = domestic (see Table 7.13), f = total (incoming plus outgoing) foreign. Ratio = d : f

		1948	1953	1963	Increase, 1963/53
Ceylon	f	22,606	28,040	18,648	− 33%
	ratio	7.6 : 1	8.7 : 1	18.5 : 1	
China:	f	..	8,000	20,000	150%
Taiwan	ratio	..	7.6 : 1	18.3 : 1	
Hong Kong	f	102,039	61,161	132,793	117%
	ratio	0.05 : 1	0.3 : 1	0.35 : 1	
Indonesia	f	79,515	16,615	17,806	3%
	ratio	0.5 : 1	8.1 : 1	11.2 : 1	
Malaysia	f	45,371	46,906	59,685	27%
	ratio	1.2 : 1	1.9 : 1	1.9 : 1	
Pakistan	f	55,866	143,587	180,052	25%
	ratio	4.9 : 1	2.5 : 1	3.8 : 1	
Vietnam, S.	f	..	26,642	30,208	13%
	ratio	..	0.9 : 1	1.5 : 1	
Total	f	285,487	330,951	459,192	39%
	ratio	1.9 : 1	3.2 : 1	4.4 : 1	
Japan	f	8,859	47,853	133,243	178%
	ratio	258 : 1	82 : 1	64 : 1	
cf. UK	f	..	738,000	942,000	28%
	ratio	..	12 : 1	10 : 1	
USA	f	..	1,132,705	2,261,973	100%
	ratio	..	45 : 1	30 : 1	

PROPORTION OF DOMESTIC TO FOREIGN MAIL

Table 7.15 considers the totals of foreign mail for the respective countries and draws attention to the proportion of foreign mail in each country's total mail, which is incidentally an interesting illustration of the degree of 'outward-lookingness' in the development of the various national economies and cultures.

The ratio for India was 26.1 in 1963. Note that the above figures are on the basis of f = incoming plus outgoing foreign mail, which exaggerates the proportion of foreign mail; the ratios should therefore be reduced by 50 per cent or more to give absolute levels, but may serve here for *relative* comparisons. The differences in circumstances between the countries are obvious, but it is of some interest to note such striking facts as Hong Kong's having almost as large a foreign mail traffic as Japan, the generally rising trend of the ratio in the region, and the increases or decreases in the right-hand column in comparison with those shown in Table 7.13.

Table 8.1. *National budgets: heads of expenditure and receipts*[1]
(in millions of national currency)

1. *Burma* (index 1948=100)

	1948 million Kyat (=100)	1948 (%)	1953 index	1953 (%)	1958 index	1958 (%)	1963 index	1963 (%)	1965 index	1965 (%)
Expenditures:										
Interest on public debt	4.3	(1%)	77	(0.5%)	463	(1.5%)	923	(3%)	1079	(3%)
National defence	48.4	(10%)	588	(34%)	842	(32%)	1005	(32%)	1081	(33%)
Contribution to States	13.9	(3%)	165	(3%)	283	(3%)	371	(3%)		(3%)
Other current expenditure	254.3	(52%)	138	(41%)	203	(40%)	222	(37%)	306	(50%)
Public works and other capital expenditure	45.5	(9%)	230	(12%)	250	(9%)	630	(19%)	703	(20%)
Loans and advances (net)	123.2	(25%)	65	(9%)	146	(14%)	72	(6%)	(minus entry)[a]	
Total expenditure	489.6	(100%)	173	(100%)	261	(100%)	310	(100%)	320	(100%)
Receipts:										
Income Tax	32.4	(6%)	167	(7%)	703	(23%)	1094	(28%)	2679	(44%)
Customs duties	172.5	(31%)	116	(25%)	162	(28%)	189	(26%)	246	(21%)
Other indirect taxes	30.4	(6%)	341	(13%)	747	(23%)	1155	(28%)	1688	(26%)
Civil supplies (net)	38.2	(7%)			56	(10%)	19	(3%)		
From State enterprises	178.7	(32%)	193	(43%)	173	(17%)	181	(14%)	182	(3%)
Other receipts	99.3	(18%)	94	(12%)					182	(9%)
Total receipts[b]	551.5	(100%)	144	(100%)	182	(100%)	226	(100%)	360	(100%)

Notes: [a] Net repayments of 63 million in 1964 and 100 million in 1965.
[b] In addition there were Japanese reparations: 84 million in 1957 (about 6 per cent of internal receipts); 100-110 millions annually since 1958, representing 5-10 per cent of internal receipts.

Chapter 8

NATIONAL BUDGETS

Government budgets display clearly the broad patterns or general lines of development in the respective countries, though detailed analysis is complex and there is no space here for the explanations and qualifications required to sustain any finely focused conclusions. Particulars for nine countries are given in Table 8.1, co-ordinated as far as possible into comparable general headings. This Table confronts the reader with rather a massive amount of indicative evidence, which should, however, appear more digestible when he looks beyond it to the statement of general inferences which follows. Table 8.1 reviews the expenditures and receipts, by main headings; taking a stated base-year (for which the actual amounts are specified) it proceeds to give for subsequent years (a) index numbers of the growth of each head of revenue or expenditure, and (b) for all years the percentage distribution of the totals between these heads. This is to bring out primarily the increase in receipts or

(continued on page 188)

2. *Ceylon* (1951 = 100)

	1951 million Rs (=100)	(%)	1954 index	(%)	1958 index	(%)	1964 index	(%)
Expenditures:								
Interest on public debt	21.4	(2%)	168	(4%)	180	(3%)	519	(5%)
Food subsidies	131.6	(15%)	9	(2%)	85	(8%)	207	(13%)
Current transfers to local governments	18.5	(2%)	123	(3%)	176	(2%)	210	(2%)
Other transfer payments	66.2	(7%)	102	(7%)	246	(11%)	259	(8%)
Current, on goods and services	383.6	(43%)	123	(47%)	178	(47%)	246	(47%)
Gross fixed capital formation	243.5	(27%)	113	(30%)	165	(28%)	246	(30%)
Loans and advances (net)	31.9	(4%)	181	(6%)	40	(1%)	100	(2%)
Total expenditure	896.7	(100%)	105	(100%)	161	(100%)	242	(100%)

	1951 million Rs (=100)	(%)	1954 index	(%)	1958 index	(%)	1964 index	(%)
Expenditures: of which:								
Social services	280.6	(31%)	126	(35%)	184	(36%)	263	(36%)
Economic services	309.2	(34%)	104	(32%)	163	(35%)	137	(21%)
Defence	9.7	(1%)	324	(3%)	661	(4%)	692	(4%)
Receipts:								
Taxes on income and wealth	144.3	(17%)	160	(24%)	93	(26%)	228	(20%)
Export duties	282.7	(34%)	92	(26%)	115	(30%)	109	(19%)
Import duties	245.0	(29%)	100	(24%)	119	(27%)	199	(29%)
Other indirect taxes	84.6	(10%)	119	(11%)	175	(13%)	365	(19%)
Fees and charges	57.7	(7%)	128	(4%)	156	(8%)	234	(6%)
Other receipts	24.1	(3%)	153	(3%)	154	(4%)	359	(3%)
Total receipts	838.4	(100%)	113	(100%)	140	(100%)	197	(100%)

3. *India:* (a) *Central Government*

(Index 1956=100)

	1956 million Rs (=100)	(%)	1960 index	(%)	1965 index	(%)
Expenditures:						
Interest on public debt	837	(8%)	195	(9.5%)	367	(9%)
Subsidies	13[a]	(0%)	1,085[b]	(1%)	2,154[b]	(1%)
Grants to States	875	(9%)	185	(9%)	310	(8%)
Other grants	356	(4%)	215	(5%)	373	(4%)
Current, goods and services	2,852	(28%)	158	(24%)	378	(30%)
Gross capital formation	1,667	(16%)	178	(14%)	364	(18%)
Capital transfers to State and public corporations	322	(3%)	148	(3%)	249	(3%)
Others transfers	138	(1%)	59	(0%)	163	(0%)
Loans for capital formation	2,918	(29%)	168	(24%)	262	(21%)
Loans, other	62	(0%)	594	(2%)	1,548	(3%)
Other capital expenditure	34	(0%)	4,326	(9%)	5,085	(5%)
Total expenditure	10,061	(100%)	188	(100%)	354	(100%)
of which, defence	1,916	(19%)	146	(15%)	446	(24%)

	1956 million Rs (=100)	(%)	1960 index	(%)	1965 index	(%)
Receipts:						
Taxes						
on personal income	762	(12%)	95	(7%)	186	(6%)
Corporate income tax	370	(6%)	288	(10%)	827	(13%)
Other taxes on						
income and wealth	8	(0%)	1,800	(1%)	1,912	(0%)
Export duties	387	(6%)	52	(2%)	24	(0%)
Import duties	1,280	(18%)	106	(13%)	256	(14%)
Other indirect taxes	1,306	(20%)	226	(28%)	498	(28%)
Government						
enterprises	1,109	(17%)	139	(15%)	262	(13%)
Other property, etc.	466	(7%)	266	(11%)	502	(10%)
Fees and misc.	460	(7%)	126	(6%)	130	(3%)
Repayment of loans	341	(5%)	291	(9%)	835	(12%)
Other capital receipts	119	(2%)			22	(0%)
Total receipts	6,608	(100%)	163	(100%)	351	(100%)

Notes: a 1957 (1956: nil). b 1957=100.

India: (b) *State Governments*

	1954 million Rs (=100)	(%)	1960 index	(%)	1965 index	(%)
Expenditures:						
Education	748	(12%)	218	(13%)	411	(15%)
Health	336	(5%)	220	(6%)	380	(5%)
Agriculture						
and Industry	816	(13%)	244	(16%)	458	(18%)
Other current						
expenditure	2,272	(37%)	161	(21%)	283	(32%)
Capital expenditure:						
Multi-purpose river						
valley and						
irrigation schemes	824	(13%)	159	(10%)	223	(9%)
Electricity	203	(3%)	122	(3%)	229	(2%)
Industrial development	45	(1%)	444	(1%)	820	(2%)
Buildings and roads	155	(2%)	603	(7%)	915	(7%)
Other	475	(8%)	153	(6%)	250	(5%)
Loans						
and advances (net)	271	(4%)	378	(9%)	902	(10%)
Total expenditure	6,144	(100%)	203	(100%)	362	(100%)

Note: Not included in the above are the profits and losses made by State trading schemes. These varied very irregularly, as follows (+indicates profit, —indicates loss):

1952: +251	1958: +158	1961: +192	1964: +71
1954: −134	1959: −4	1962: −96	1965: −23
1957: −47	1960: +70	1963: +123	Total: +561

Showing a very small and uncertain profit over the whole thirteen years.

	1954 million Rs (=100)	(%)	1960 index	(%)	1965 index	(%)
Receipts:						
Personal income tax	608	(13%)	145	(10%)	196	(8%)
Land tax	707	(15%)	137	(11%)	168	(11%)
Estate duty	24a	(0%)	113b	(0%)	167b	(0%)
Excise	606	(13%)	200	(14%)	351	(14%)
Turnover tax	583	(12%)	190	(12%)	434	(12%)
Other taxes	798	(17%)	168	(15%)	304	(15%)
Other receipts	1,386	(30%)	241	(38%)	436	(38%)
Total receipts	4,689	(100%)	189	(100%)	332	(100%)

Note: a 1957: previously none.
  b 1957=100.

4. *Indonesia*
Owing to changes in classification and other factors, two periods are distinguished.

(i) 1953-58

	1953 million Rupiah (=100)	(%)	1958e index	(%)
Expenditures:				
Education	858	(6%)	203	(5%)
Health	184	(1%)	339	(2%)
Other social services	204	(1%)	254	(1%)
Economic services	1,579	(10%)	89	(4%)
Communications, public works, power	938	(6%)	138	(4%)
Defence	3,269	(21%)	339	(31%)
Other expenditure	7,914	(51%)	236	(53%)
Total, gross expenditure	15,568	(100%)	227	(100%)
Less: 'revenue directly related to expenditure'	3,383		107	
Total, net expenditure	12,185		260	
Receipts:				
Taxes on personal income	874	(9%)	227	(10%)
Corporation income tax	1,084	(11%)	180	(10%)
Other direct taxes	68	(1%)	406	(4%)
Export duties	1,049	(10%)	18	(1%)
Import duties	1,295	(13%)	127	(8%)
Excise	1,366	(13%)	259	(18%)
Other indirect taxes	736	(7%)	188	(7%)
Foreign exchange levies	1,914	(19%)	347	(34%)
Revenue from public enterprises	205e	(2%)	69	(1%)
Other receipts	1,618	(16%)	118	(10%)
Total receipts	10,208	(100%)	193	(100%)

(i) 1953-59

Receipts:	1953 million B (=100)	(%)	1959 index	(%)
Taxes on income and wealth	266.3	(7%)	161	(7%)
Import duties	1,047.3	(27%)	172	(30%)
Export duties	214.8	(5%)	190	(7%)
Other indirect taxes	1,373.9	(35%)	115	(26%)
Profits of Rice Bureau	322.0	(8%)	235	(12%)
Fiscal monopolies	387.9	(10%)	77	(5%)
Other receipts	317.0	(8%)	242	(13%)
Total receipts	3,929.3	(100%)	154	(100%)

(ii) 1959-65

Taxes on income and wealth	428.0	(7%)	246	(10%)	395
Import duties	1,805.6	(30%)	131	(23%)	226
Export duties	408.6	(7%)	84	(3%)	159
Rice export premium	755.9	(13%)	106	(8%)	..
Fiscal monopolies	319.4	(5%)	150	(5%)	124
Other indirect taxes	1,604.6	(26%)	249	(38%)	291
Fees, sales and other charges	379.6	(6%)	126	(5%)	..
Profits and dividends	209.5	(3%)	177	(4%)	..
Other receipts	125.5	(2%)	465	(5%)	..
Total receipts	6,036.7	(100%)	173	(100%)	266

5. *Korea: South*

Expenditures:	1954 000 million hwan (=100)	(%)	1960e index	(%)	1964a, e index	(%)
Interest on public debt	0.4	(1%)	1,200	(1%)	2,700	(1%)
Price subsidies	..		..b		..b	
Current transfers to :						
Private sector	3.0	(5%)	450	(3%)	1,730	(7%)
Provinces and local bodies	5.3	(9%)	1,343	(17%)	2,198	(15%)
Abroad	—		..c		..c	
Current expenditure on goods and services	41.4	(69%)	515	(52%)	850	(46%)
Capital formation	1.0	(2%)	3,720	(9%)	11,200	(15%)
Capital transfers to :						
Private sector	2.4	(4%)	113	(1%)	150	(0%)
Provinces and local bodies	0.8	(1%)	3,437	(7%)	4,175	(4%)
Direct lending	5.7	(9%)	604	(8%)	1,161	(9%)
Total expenditure	59.9	(100%)	680	(100%)	1,267	(100%)
of which:						
Education	1.4	(2%)	4,157	(4%)	7,929	(15%)
Health	0.4	(1%)	1,175	(1%)	2,175	(1%)
Social security, etc.	1.7	(3%)	1,094	(5%)	2,929	(7%)
Economic services	11.7	(20%)	635	(18%)	1,876	(29%)
National defence	32.6	(54%)	433	(35%)	698	(30%)

Notes: a From 1962 the currency unit became the won (1 won=10 hwan): the 1964 figures are here converted to 'old hwan' i.e. the same basis as the preceding years.

b Disclosed in the following years: 1958, 8.7; 1959, 6.1; 1960e, 1.2; 1960, 2.6; 1961, 2.1; 1962, 2.2; 1963e, 0.9; 1964e, 0.6; price subsidies were thus generally a small and falling percentage of the expenditures.

c Transfers abroad were: 1958, 1.2; 1959, 1.5; 1960, 2.4; 1960, 0.4; 1961, 6.5; 1962, 7.6; 1963e, 4.4; 1964e, 6.7; thus an insignificant percentage (about 1 per cent).

e Estimates.

Receipts:	1954 000 *million hwan* (=100)	(%)	1960e index	(%)	1964a, e index	(%)
Taxes on income and wealth	7.1	(18%)	921	(21%)	1,532	(20%)
Customs duties	3.5	(9%)	1,174	(13%)	2,223	(14%)
Foreign exchange levies	—	—	..d	(15%)	—	
Monopoly profits	4.0	(10%)	638	(8%)	1,528	(11%)
Other indirect taxes	10.4	(26%)	849	(28%)	1,570	(30%)
Net surplus from government enterprises ..	..	..	..f	(2%)	..f	(3%)
Income from property	2.2	(5%)	309	(2%)	977	(4%)
Other current receipts					288	(7%)
and other (net) capital receipts	13.1	(33%)	244	(10%)	215	(7%)
Total domestic receipts	40.3	(100%)	771	(100%)	1,340	(100%)
Foreign grants	2.7	(7%)	1,696	(15%)	8,155	(41%)
Total receipts	43.0		829		1,768	

Notes: d Foreign exchange levies were applied from 1958. In 1958 they yielded 14.3; in 1959, 47.2; in 1960e, 45.6 (in 1960 actual, 50.5); in 1961, only 2.5; in 1962, only 8; 1963 they ceased to be levied. As percentages of the total receipts for the years just cited, they were thus: 1958, 7 per cent; 1959, 18 per cent; 1960e, 15 per cent; 1960 actual, 16 per cent; 1961, 1 per cent; 1962, insignificant.

e Estimates.

f Declared from 1957; forming a small, though generally rising, proportion of total receipts (about 1 per cent in 1957, about 3 per cent in 1964).

6. *Malaysia*

Expenditures:	1953 *million M$* (=100)	(%)	1960 index	(%)	1964e index	(%)
Interest on public debt	13.6	(1.5%)	382	(5%)	649	(6%)
Education	78.2	(8.5%)	211	(16%)	342	(17%)
Health	48.6	(5%)	155	(7%)	210	(7%)
Defence	210.1	(23%)	43	(8.5%)	135	(18.5%)
Other current	364.9	(40%)	117	(40%)	93	(22%)
Capital expenditure	200.4	(22%)	124	(23%)	225	(29%)
Total expenditure	915.8	(100%)	115	(100%)	167	(100%)

	1953		1960		1964e	
	million M$					
	(=100)	(%)	*index*	(%)	*index*	(%)
Receipts:						
Taxes on						
income and wealth	164.2	(25%)	118	(17%)	182	(23%)
Export duties	112.2	(17%)	232	(23%)	370	(32%)
Import duties	198.3	(30%)	178	(31%)	79	(12%)
Other indirect taxes	68.2	(10%)	158	(9%)	277	(15%)
Other recipts	117.1	(18%)	199	(21%)	192	(17%)
Total receipts	660.0	(100%)	174	(100%)	195	(100%)

7. Pakistan: (a) Central Government

	1954		1960		1965e	
	million Rs					
Expenditures:	(=100)	(%)	*index*	(%)	*index*	(%)
Interest on public debt	59.5	(3%)	306	(5%)	612	(5%)
Defence	768.7	(38%)	125	(28%)	142	(16%)
Education and health	17.8	(1%)	324	(2%)	253	(1%)
Transfers to						
Provinces and States:						
Taxes	176.4	(9%)	170	(9%)	541	(14%)
Grants	43.5	(2%)	97	(1%)	86	(1%)
Other						
current expenditure	344.0	(17%)	138	(14%)	375	(18%)
Capital expenditure	223.0	(11%)	433	(28%)	425b	(13%)
Loans and advances to:						
Provinces						
and States (net)	335.9	(17%)	130	(12%)	601	(29%)
Others (net)	23.3	(1%)	267	(2%)	1,212	(4%)
Total expenditurea	1,992.1	(100%)	175	(100%)	353	(100%)

Notes: a The following transactions are not included in the above. 'Currency capital outlays': none in 1954, 1962 and 1965, 62.2 in 1960, 10.6 in 1961, 16.8 in 1963, and 9.8 in 1964, all negligible percentages of total expenditure, except 1960 which was about 3 per cent. And net expenditure on State trading schemes; these realized a *gain* of 310.4 in 1954, offsetting no less than 15 per cent of the total expenditure declared in the budget, and were in balance (no net loss or profit) in 1962 and 1963; but returned the following losses in other years. 33.4 in 1960 and 52.1 in 1961 (i.e. about 1 per cent of the total expenditure in the budget), falling to (estimated) 16.3 in 1964 and 17.6 in 1965, which are much less than 1 per cent of the total budgeted expenditure. See also under State Governments, below.

b This had declined, however, to index 296 in 1961, 350 in 1962, 226 in 1963 and 297 in 1964. The irregularity of capital expenditure was thus extreme, between nearly Rs. 1,000 million in 1960 (28 per cent of all expenditures) and about half that figure in 1963 (10 per cent of all expenditures).

Receipts:	1954 *million Rs* (=100)	(%)	1960 *index*	(%)	1965[e] *index*	(%)
Taxes on income:						
Personal	145.8	(11%)	183	(12%)	323	(13%)
Corporation	61.7	(5%)	153	(4%)	267	(5%)
Customs	440.8	(33%)	127	(26%)	205	(26%)
Excise	169.5	(13%)	200	(16%)	472	(23%)
General turnover tax	157.9	(12%)	197	(14%)	464	(21%)
Other taxes	33.1	(2.5%)	145	(2%)	86	(1%)
Other receipts	309.4	(23%)	171	(25%)	135	(12%)
Total receipts:	1,318.2	(100%)	163	(100%)	267	(100%)

Pakistan: (b) State Governments

Expenditures:	1952 *million Rs* (=100)	(%)	1960 *index*	(%)	1965[e] *index*	(%)
Education	81.9	(10%)	191	(10%)	452	(7%)
Health	37.7	(4%)	122	(3%)	313	(2%)
Other current	453.1	(53%)	188	(53%)	455	(37%)
Capital	254.3	(30%)	144	(23%)	475	(22%)
Loans and advances (net)	29.8	(3%)	919	(12%)	605	(32%)
Total[a]	856.9	(100%)	188	(100%)	649	(100%)

Notes: [a] As in Central budget, this excludes the results of State trading schemes. The part of these relating to the Central budget was noted in the relevant Table immediately above. Here we must add the part relevant to the state budgets; as follows. Overall losses or profits were registered in the following years:

	million *Rs*	*index*	*% of State* *expenditure in budget*
LOSSES			
1952	170.4	100	20%
1963	88.6	52	3%
1965[e]	83.7	49	1%
PROFITS			
1960	27.3	100	2%
1961	207.7	761	10%
1962	68.8	252	4%
1964[e]	259.1	949	6%

[e] Estimates

Receipts:						
Personal income tax	13.7	(2%)	518	(6%)	1,708	(8%)
Corporation tax[b]	..	..	..	..	..	(3%)
Land tax	114.7	(18%)	218	(21%)	268	(11%)
Customs duties	59.2	(9%)	80	(4%)	152	(3%)
Other taxes	192.6	(30%)	210	(35%)	448	(31%)
Other receipts	264.1	(41%)	151	(34%)	460	(43%)
Total receipts[c]	644.3	(100%)	182	(100%)	433	(100%)

Notes: [b] Specified for 1963, 49.5 (2 per cent of total receipts) and 1964, 63.0 (2 per cent). [c] Excludes loans from the Central Government.

8. *Philippines* (index 1961 = 100)

	1954a		1961 million P (=100)		1965e	
	index	(%)		(%)	*index*	(%)
Expenditures:						
Interest on public debt	16	(2%)	29.8	(2%)	241	(3%)
Subsidies	..	..	31.5	(2%)	237	(3%)
Other current transfers	..	..	117.8	(9%)	87	(4%)
Current, on goods and services	..	..	868.8	(63%)	180	(64%)
Gross capital formation	..	..	250.1	(18%)	145	(15%)
Capital transfers	..	..	41.9	(3%)	573	(10%)
Direct lending	..	..	38.8	(3%)	96	(2%)
Total expenditure:	56	(100%)	1,378.0	(100%)	178	(100%)
of which:						
Education	52	(25%)	377.4	(27%)	164	(25%)
Other social services	26	(5%)	143.0	(10%)	116	(7%)
Agriculture and national resources	28	(5%)	127.9	(9%)	337	(18%)
Transport and communication	72	(25%)	265.5	(19%)	138	(15%)
Other economic services	64	(9%)	103.1	(7%)	145	(6%)
National defence	90	(23%)	196.6	(14%)	158	(12%)
Other services	42	(9%)	164.5	(12%)	253	(17%)
		(100%)		(100%)		(100%)

	1954a		1961 million P (=100)		1965e	
	index	(%)		(%)	*index*	(%)
Receipts:						
Taxes on income	39	(16%)	278.2	(22%)	211	(27%)
Import duties	35	(17%)	326.4	(26%)	165	(25%)
Foreign exchange tax	790	(19%)	16.0	(1%)	—b	—
Excise	52	(15%)	190.7	(15%)	189	(16%)
Other taxes	65	(28%)	299.5	(24%)	234	(32%)
Less: tax receipts apportioned to local government	39	(7%)	116.4	(9%)	238	(13%)
Other receipts	31	(12%)	268.2	(21%)	102	(13%)
Total receipts	54	(100%)	1,262.6	(100%)	173	(100%)

Notes: a Expenditure for 1954 not revealed, except interest on public debt and total expenditure.
b Ceased in 1964 and 1965.
e Estimates.

9. *Thailand*

Two bases of classification are available, for two successive periods.

(i) 1953-59

Expenditure:	1953 million B (=100)	(%)	1959 index	(%)
Interest on public debt	74.8	(1%)	357	(4%)
Public health and social welfare	206.7	(4%)	229	(7%)
Education	300.7	(6%)	439	(20%)
National defence	961.0	(19%)	150	(22%)
Economic development	724.3	(14%)	209	(23%)
Government employees' cost of living allowances	1,833.6[a]	(35%)	—	—
Other expenditure	1,064.5	(21%)	646	(24%)
Total expenditure	5,165.6	(100%)	128	(100%)
of which, capital expenditure	1,035.7	(20%)	123	(19%)

Note: [a] This entry reached 2,273.5 in 1956 (24 per cent increase over 1953) but ceased from 1957.

Receipts:				
Taxes on income and wealth	266.3	(7%)	161	(7%)
Import duties	1,047.3	(27%)	172	(30%)
Export duties	214.8	(5%)	190	(7%)
Other indirect taxes	1,373.9	(35%)	116	(26%)
Profits of Rice Bureau	322.0	(8%)	235	(12.5%)
Fiscal monopolies	387.9	(10%)	77	(5%)
Other receipts	317.0	(8%)	242	(13%)
Total receipts:	3,929.2	(100%)	154	(100%)

expenditure under each head, and the changing relative (financial) importance of each type of governmental activity, illustrating the trends of the intentions or performance of governments in each of the respects indicated.

DEFICIT BUDGETING

The first general observation from Table 8.1 may be the prevalence of budget deficits, rapidly and greatly increasing in size. The increase in expenditure tended almost universally to be markedly greater than the rise in recipts (though the latter was also large). The divergence was very pronounced in the developing East Asian countries, causing the index figures for the

(*Thailand, continued*) (ii) 1959-65

Expenditure:

	1959 million B (=100)	(%)	1965e index	(%)
Interest on public debt	281.4	(4%)	213	(5%)
Subsidies	22.0	(0%)	50	(0%)
Current transfers to:				
Households	370.0	(6%)	150	(4%)
Local Government	108.9	(2%)	289	(3%)
Abroad	27.6	(0%)	136	(0%)
Current, goods and services	4,367.7	(68%)	166	(59%)
Gross capital formation	1,169.4	(18%)	275	(26%)
Capital transfers to:				
Local Governments	—b		—b	
Other domestic sectors	3.8	(0%)	266	(0%)
Loans and advances to domestic sectors	2.1c	(0%)	7,142d	(1%)
Purchase of financial assets from:				
Domestic sectors	2.0	(0%)	750	(0%)
Abroad	—e		40f	(0%)
Other gross finance to State trading enterprises	89.0	(1%)	191	(1%)
Total expenditure	6,441.8	(100%)	191	(100%)
of which				
Education	1,290.6	(20%)	168	(18%)
Health	187.0	(3%)	226	(3%)
Other social services	277.4	(4%)	326	(7%)
Agriculture	348.0	(5%)	312	(9%)
Other economic services	1,112.6	(17%)	205	(19%)
Defence	1,420.5	(22%)	135	(16%)
		(71%)		(72%)

Notes: b None in 1959, 1960 and 1965. 10.3 in 1961, 12.6 in 1962, 31.0 in 1963, 17.1 in 1964 (all negligible percentages).
c 1960 (none in 1959).
d Index with 1960=100.
e None in 1959 and 1961. 24.0 in 1960, 10.8 in 1962, 13.6 in 1963, 9.5 in 1965e; all negligible percentages of the totals.
f Index with 1960=100.

Receipts:

Taxes on income and wealth	428.0	(7%)	246	(10%)
Import duties	1,805.6	(30%)	131	(24%)
Export duties	408.6	(7%)	84	(3%)
Rice export premium	755.9	(12.5%)	106	(8%)
Fiscal monopolies	319.4	(5%)	150	(5%)
Other indirect taxes	1,604.6	(27%)	249	(38%)
Fees, sales and other charges	379.6	(6%)	126	(5%)
Profits and dividends	209.5	(3%)	177	(3%)
Other receipts	125.5	(2%)	465	(5%)
Total receipts:	6,036.7	(100%)	173	(100%)

expanding deficits to be high. Burma's deficits in 1958 and 1963 were over five times as large as that of 1953, and represented about 20 per cent of the expenditures; in 1965 a surplus of over 25 per cent of the expenditures was returned. In Ceylon a small surplus in 1954 (0.5 per cent of the expenditures) turned into a deficit of 424 million rupees in 1958 (19 per cent of the expenditures); the deficit was doubled in 1962 and 1964, when it represented 24 per cent of the expenditures. The deficit of the Central Government of India nearly doubled between 1956 and 1958, increased by one-third again by 1963, and further by over a third by 1965; in 1958 it represented over 42 per cent of the expenditures, in 1963 nearly 34 per cent, in 1965 over 36 per cent. The deficit in the budgets of the Indian States meanwhile increased at a greater rate; in 1958 it was 2.3 times the 1952 deficit, in 1963 four times, in 1965 six times, representing 27 per cent of the expenditures in 1958, 26 per cent in 1963 and 30 per cent in 1965.

In Indonesia the deficit in 1953 was 80 per cent larger than that of 1951, and represented less than 13 per cent of the expenditures. In 1958 the deficit balance was reduced to 50 per cent over the 1951 figure, but represented 34 per cent of the expenditures. In 1963 the deficit was three and a half times that of 1951; but this represented a return to the 1951 level of 12 per cent, as a proportion of expenditures. In 1964, however, the estimated deficit was greatly reduced, to near the 1951 level, representing in this case much less than 1 per cent of the expenditures. In South Korea the deficit in 1958 was ten times that of 1954; that of 1963 was fourteen times, but in the following year the proportion fell to eleven times. In 1958 the deficit was over 50 per cent of the expenditure, in 1963 exactly 35 per cent, in 1964 over 27 per cent.

In the case of Malaya the deficits for 1958 and 1964 were lower (by 11 per cent and 3 per cent respectively) than the deficit in 1953, which was a year of political troubles; the 1958 deficit represented less than 12 per cent of the expenditures, that of 1964 nearly 20 per cent. In Pakistan the indices for increasing deficits were particularly high, and they represented large percentages of the expenditures. In the Central Government budget of Pakistan the 1958 deficit was 74 per cent above 1954, that of 1963 was 219 per cent above 1951 and that of 1965 was 421 per cent above. As proportions of the expenditures, they were 39 per cent in 1958, 44 per cent in 1963 and 50 per cent in 1965. In the Pakistan State budgets the deficit in 1958 was more than two and a half times that of 1952, that of 1963 nearly five times and that of 1965 thirteen times. As proportions of the expenditure, they were: 39 per cent in 1958, 37 per cent in 1963 and 50 per cent in 1965. The deficits in the Philippines, as in Malaya, declined from that of the troubled year 1953 (by 29 per cent for 1958 and 17 per cent for 1963); but in 1965 the deficit was three times the 1953 figure. In Thailand the deficits were greatly reduced from 1953 in 1958 (by 65 per cent) and 1963 (by 50 per cent), but the 1965 figure was 51 per cent above 1953; and these figures represent comparatively small proportions of the expenditures: 7 per cent in 1958 and 1963, 15 per cent in 1965.

There was thus apparent improvement in this respect in some of these countries in the last year or two of the period, but their progress is strikingly uneven, with frequent variations on a marked inflationary trend. In strong Regional contrast is Japan, recording *surpluses* of: in 1958 nearly six times that of 1954, in 1963 ten times, in 1965 over eight times; which represented 9 per cent of the expenditures in 1958, 7 per cent in 1963 and 4 per cent in 1965. The developed Western countries also showed large percentage increases in their deficits, it must be noted. With 1954 as 100, the UK Central budget deficit indexed 134 in 1958 and 552 in 1963, the UK Public Sector budget 128 and 152. The US Federal budget deficit in 1958 and 1965 was twelve times that of 1954, that of 1963 seventeen times. The deficit on the US State budgets in 1958 was 173 per cent greater than that of 1955; but in 1963 this turned into a surplus. All these were, however, comparatively small as percentages of the expenditures of the developed Western countries, and very small in proportion to their wealth; UK Central Government 5 per cent of the expenditures in 1958, 14 per cent in 1963, UK Public Sector 9 per cent in 1958, 7 per cent in 1963; US Federal 4 per cent in 1958, $3\frac{1}{2}$ per cent in 1963, $2\frac{1}{2}$ per cent in 1965, US States deficit $2\frac{1}{2}$ per cent in 1958, surplus nearly 4 per cent in 1963.

Table 8.2 summarizes some evidence on the trend of governmental budget-balances. It must be stressed that these figures are partial (in short series) and approximate (with elements of estimation, attempting to adjust for comparabilities, etc.) and are offered only as a rough indication of certain trends: namely, that in the Asian countries expenditures have in most cases tended to rise markedly more than receipts, and deficits to rise more than either (with significant exceptions – and with an improvement in many cases in the last years cited). The deterioration in this respect, from the 'old-fashioned' criteria of soundness in the governmental budgets, and the generally observed increase in 'deficit financing' (of development and welfare policies and defence) are serious matters for the poorer countries.

THE PUBLIC DEBT

The growth of the national debt in many countries may be referred to in this connection. The gross governmental indebtedness of Thailand roughly doubled in seventeen years, that of Malaysia quadrupled in ten years, Indonesia's domestic short-

Table 8.2. National budgets: growth of expenditures, revenues and deficits[a]

(Indices: base year specified = 100)

	Base year (=100)	1954	1958	1963	1964	1965
Burma	(1953)					
Expenditure		..	134	180	..	185
Receipts		..	126	157	..	250
Deficit		..	529	535	..	(surplus)
Ceylon	(1951)					
Expenditure		105	161	220	242	..
Receipts		113	140	175	197	..
Deficit		..[a]	424	824[b]	884	..

Notes: [a] small surplus. [b] 1962.

		1954	1958	1963	1964	1965
India						
(a) Central Government (1956)						
Expenditures		..	160	261	..	356
Receipts		..	140	262	..	351
Deficit		..	197	256	..	359
(b) State Governments (1956)						
Expenditures		..	186	335	..	430
Receipts		..	174	317	..	383
Deficit		..	230	401	..	598
Indonesia	(1951)					
Expenditures		152	254	300	385	..
Receipts		100	194	270	387	..
Deficit		180	152	353	110	..

	Base year (=100)	1954	1958	1963	1964	1965
Japan	(1954)					
Expenditures		(100)	122	288	..	386
Receipts		(100)	132	307	..	402
Surplus		(100)	584	1,000	..	821
Korea: S.	(1954)					
Expenditures		(100)	605	1,334	1,267	..
Receipts		(100)	494	1,304	1,340	..
Deficit		(100)	1,052	1,433	1,117	..
Malaya:						
Federation	(1953)					
Expenditure		..	114	163	149[n]	..
Receipts		..	124	165	161	..
Deficit		..	89	..	97	..
Pakistan						
(a) *Central*						
Government	(1954)					
Expenditures		..	171	349	..	649
Receipts		..	171	309	..	433
Deficit		..	266	473	..	1,303
Philippines	(1953)					
Expenditures		..	132	227	..	301
Receipts		..	140	245	..	301
Deficit		..	71	83	..	304
Thailand	(1953)					
Expenditures		..	116	178	..	239
Receipts		..	142	219	..	266
Deficit		..	35	50	..	151
cf. *United Kingdom*						
(a) *Central*						
Government	(1954)					
Expenditure		(100)	125	183	..	..
Receipts		(100)	125	165	..	..
Deficit		(100)	134	552	..	..
(b) *Public*						
sector	(1954)					
Expenditures		(100)	125	176	..	..
Receipts		(100)	124	178	..	..
Deficit		(100)	128	152	..	..
United States						
(a) *Federal*						
Government	(1954)					
Expenditures		(100)	100	158	..	171
Receipts		(100)	96	153	..	268
Deficit		(100)	1,215	1,728	..	1,271

G

term liabilities quadrupled in seven years, India's total public indebtedness almost quadrupled in eleven years, Ceylon's quintupled in thirteen years, the Philippines' multiplied by six in seventeen years.

In Ceylon, the Philippines and Thailand the increase was strongly in the internal debt, but in Malaysia and India there was predominantly an increase in the foreign debt. In the case of India the foreign debt in 1965 was some twenty times what it had been in 1954; in Malaysia it multiplied over four times, in Ceylon and India rather less than four times, in the periods specified (see Table 8.2).

The distinction between long-term and short-term indebtedness can be drawn in a few cases, and only for the domestic debt; in Ceylon short-term internal indebtedness was very small in 1951 but vastly increased by 1964, in India the long-term and short-term portions increased less unevenly but with the latter strongly leading.

Table 8.3 gives the available information on the public debt of developing Asian countries. It shows great increases in the total indebtedness in the given periods, varying greatly between the countries: in the order of fivefold in Ceylon, fourfold in India and Malaysia, sixfold in the Philippines and twofold in Thailand. The increase in the foreign debt is one marked feature. In Ceylon, it increased over three and a half times, though as a proportion of the total debt it fell from 17 per cent to 12 per cent. In India it multiplied by no less than twenty, rising from only 4 per cent of the total indebtedness in 1954 to 26 per cent in 1965. In Malaysia it more than quadrupled, although as a proportion of the total debt it remained at about one-fifth. In the Philippines the proportion of the debt owed abroad fell greatly, from about 40 per cent in 1948 to about 10 per cent in 1965, but its amount increased by more than two-thirds. In Thailand total foreign debts have remained a smaller proportion of the total indebtedness (in the order of 10 per cent) but have doubled in amount, increasing more than the internal debt.

Fiscal domestic indebtedness increased in the order of fivefold in Ceylon, threefold in India, fourfold in Malaya, tenfold in the Philippines and twofold in Thailand. The evidence (where available) suggests a strong increase in internal short-term borrowing, as against long-term. In Ceylon the long-term domestic debt increased threefold, but fell from 95 per cent of the domestic debt in 1957 to only 56 per cent in 1964; while short-term internal debt, which was only 5 per cent of the domestic debt in 1951, correspondingly rose to 44 per cent in 1964, having increased nearly fifty times. In India, within the domestic debt, long-term debts increased two and one-third times, short-term nearly fourfold; the latter represented 42 per cent of the internal debt in 1954 already, but 54 per cent in 1965. Indonesia's domestic short-term indebtedness increased in no less a proportion than about thirty times.

The solvency position is illustrated in the case of Ceylon by the statement of the sinking fund covering over 20 per cent of the gross indebtedness in 1961, only 10 per cent in 1964.

The burden of debt-servicing is therefore an increasing concern of these countries, though still not a large proportion of their budget expenditures, as appears in Table 8.1. Burma

Table 8.3. *Public debt, East Asian countries*[3]

	Year taken as base: amount ($=100$)		Latest year: amount:		index
1. *Ceylon* (m. Rs)	1951:		1964[e]:		
Domestic debt:					
Long term	582	(79%)	1,839	(49%):	316
Short term	30	(4%)	1,437	(39%):	4,790
Total, domestic	612	(83%)	3,276	(88%):	535
Foreign debt:	125	(17%)	446	(12%):	357
Total debt (gross)	737	(100%)	3,722	(100%):	505
Sinking fund, total	163		390		
(as% of gross debt:		22%		10%)	
2. *India* (m. Rs)	1954[e]:		1965[e]:		
Domestic:					
Long term	13,748	(55%)	32,222	(34%):	234
Short term	10,159	(41%)	37,540	(40%):	370
Total domestic	23,907	(96%)	69,762	(74%):	292
Foreign:	1,129	(4%)	24,181	(26%):	2,142
Total debt	25,036	(100%)	93,943	(100%):	375

3. *Indonesia* (m. Rupiah): only the following available:
Domestic short term 1951: 844   1958: 27,589: index 3,269

4. *Malaysia* (m. M$)		1953:		1963:	
Domestic:					
Long term	261	(52%)	..		
Short term	138	(27%)	..		
Total, domestic	399	(79%)	1,588	(78%):	398
Foreign	103	(21%)	443	(22%):	430
Total debt	502	(100%)	2,031	(100%):	405

5. *Philippines* (m. P)		1948:		1965ᵉ:	
Domestic	337	(59%)	3,086	(89%):	916
Foreign	232	(41%)	391	(11%):	168
Total	569	(100%)	3,477	(100%):	611

6. *Thailand*		1953:	1964ᵉ:	
Domestic:				
Payable in:				
Baht (m. B)	4,151		8,107:	195
Sterling (m. £)ᵃ	—		—:	—
US $ (m.)ᵇ	—		23:	—
Foreign:				
Sterling (m. £)ᶜ	5.3		—:	—
US $ (m.)	21.2		45.4:	214
Deutsche Mark (m.)ᵈ	—		28.1:	—

Notes: a Only a transient entry, £0.1 million in 1959.
b 59.9 in 1959.
c This was regularly reduced, usually at £0.1 million per year, from £1.2 million in 1954 to nil in 1964.
d Began 1963, with 3.2. e Estimates.

devoted about 1 per cent of its expenditures to interest on public debts in 1948, 3 per cent in 1965; the figures for the other countries were Ceylon 2 per cent rising to 5 per cent (1951-64); India an exceptionally large proportion, 8-9 per cent; Indonesia also a more marked proportion, 4-5 per cent (1959-65); Malaysia 1½-6 per cent (1953-64); Pakistan 3-5 per cent (1954-65); the Philippines 2-3 per cent (1954-65); and Thailand 1-4 per cent (1953-9) rising to 5 per cent in 1965.

THE BURDEN OF ARMAMENTS

A far greater burden in these countries – ominously rising, in many cases – is that of national defences. As shown in Table 8.1 Burma devoted one-third of its government expenditures to this heading; India one-fifth in 1956, rising to a quarter in 1965; Indonesia 21-31 per cent (1953-8, not disclosed thereafter); Korea 54 per cent in 1954, 30 per cent in 1964; Malaysia 23 per cent in the 'troubles' of 1953, falling to $8\frac{1}{2}$ per cent in 1960, but rising again to nearly one-fifth in 1964 during the 'confrontation' episode; Pakistan no less than a third in 1954, falling to 16 per cent in 1965; the Philippines 23 per cent in 1954, falling to 12 per cent in 1965; and Thailand 19 per cent in 1953; 22 per cent in 1959, 16 per cent in 1965. The index numbers against the defence expenditures should, however, be noted also; though this item has in many cases declined as a percentage of total expenditure, the absolute amounts have greatly increased, in the following proportions in the designated periods: Burma over ten times, Ceylon nearly seven times, India more than four times, Indonesia three times between 1953 and 1958, Malaysia by one-third, Pakistan by 40 per cent, the Philippines by 58 per cent and Thailand by 50 per cent.

WELFARE ITEMS

In comparison with the disturbing increase in military outlays, the allocations for education and other social services make a very poor showing in many cases. Ceylon and the Philippines have – it must immediately be stressed – a creditable allocation of one third of all expenditure to social services, but the Indian States show only 12 per cent, rising to 15 per cent; Indonesia 6 per cent, falling to 5 per cent; Malaysia, $8\frac{1}{2}$ per cent rising to 17 per cent; Pakistan's Central Government only 1 per cent on education and health; Pakistan's State Governments 10 per cent for education and 4 per cent for health, falling to 7 per cent and 2 per cent respectively; while Thailand had only 6 per cent for education and 4 per cent for other services in 1953, but raised this to 20 per cent and 7 per cent in 1959 and 18 per cent and 3 per cent in 1965.

ECONOMIC DEVELOPMENT HEADS

Allocations for the promotion of national development have generally risen strongly, but in some cases appear to have varied inversely with the requirements of 'defence' and the vagaries of the general financial situation. Burma devoted 9 per cent of

national expenditures to public works and capital outlays in
1948, 20 per cent in 1965. Ceylon's entry for gross fixed capital
formation on government account was 27 per cent in 1957, 30
per cent in 1964; economic services more generally represented,
however, 34 per cent and 21 per cent of total expenditures in
those years. India's Central budget has 16 per cent for gross
capital formation in 1956, 18 per cent in 1965; and the other
significant items which follow this entry in Table 8.1 should also
be noted in the same connection. India's State Governments,
moreover, devoted 13-18 per cent to agriculture and industry,
13-9 per cent to multi-purpose schemes, 3 per cent to electric
power, 1-2 per cent to industrial development, and other inputs
seen in the Table.

Indonesia's allocation for economic services declined from 10
per cent of all government expenditure in 1953 to 4 per cent in
1959, but agriculture is recorded as 5 per cent in 1959, 9 per
cent in 1965, and 'other economic services' as 17 per cent and
19 per cent in 1959 and 1965 respectively. Malaysia's governmental capital expenditure rose from 22 per cent to 29 per cent
between 1953 and 1964. Pakistan's State Governments return
30 per cent for capital expenditure in 1952, 22 per cent in 1965;
and some large part of the great increase in the share of net
loans and advances (3 per cent to 32 per cent) was devoted to
economic-development purposes.

The Philippines devoted 5 per cent of its expenditure total to
agriculture and natural resources in 1954, 18 per cent in 1965,
25 per cent to transport and communications in 1954, falling to
15 per cent in 1965, and 9 per cent and 6 per cent in the respective years to other economic services. Thailand's budget entry
for economic development was 14 per cent in 1953, 23 per cent
in 1959; for gross capital formation 18 per cent in 1959, 26 per
cent in 1965, for agriculture 5 per cent and 9 per cent, and for
other economic services 17 per cent and 19 per cent in the same
two years.

The foregoing presents, however, only the perspectives of the
respective percentages of these items in the expenditure totals.
The index numbers in Table 8.1 show how all these developmental expenditures increased in absolute amounts; for example
the Indian Union Government's gross capital formation more
than $3\frac{1}{2}$ times, loans for capital formation more than $2\frac{1}{2}$ times;
the Indian States' industrial development outlays nearly nine

times; Indonesia's agricultural expenditure trebled, other economic services doubled; Malaysia's capital expenditure more than doubled; Thailand's allocations for economic development doubled; and similarly for other relevant items.

Thus far the headings of expenditure have been considered. An examination of the headings of revenue is equally revealing.

TAXATION

The increases in *direct taxation* are notable. Burma collected nearly twenty-seven times as much in income tax in 1965 as in 1948; which represented 6 per cent of all revenue in 1948, 44 per cent in 1965. Ceylon more than doubled the receipts from taxes on income and wealth in 1951-64, but this was only a little more than the proportion in which total receipts doubled, and this heading represented between 17 per cent and 20 per cent of total revenue. In India the perspective was different; the increases in taxes on personal income was only in the order of half the rate of increase in total revenue; and taxes on personal income declined, as a proportion of total receipts, from 12 per cent to 6 per cent in the Central Government accounts and from 13 per cent to 8 per cent in the State Governments' accounts. India has thus not pressed personal income taxation as hard as other countries have. In Indonesia also, this type of taxation has been pressed much less than many outside observers suppose : the indices for its increase were not greatly higher than the indices in the increase in total receipts, and it has continued to represent 10 per cent or less of all receipts.

In South Korea taxes on incomes and wealth have similarly increased at a rate only slightly higher than total domestic receipts, but have represented a higher proportion of the revenue (18-20 per cent). In Malaysia taxes in this category increased slightly less than overall revenue, but represent a still higher proportion – up to 25 per cent – throughout. In the Pakistan Central budget taxes on income roughly trebled (as did total receipts); they represented 11-13 per cent of total receipts. In the Pakistan States' budgets personal income tax was relatively an extremely small item in 1952, representing only 2 per cent of all receipts. Revenue under this item increased seventeen times by 1965, but still represented only 8 per cent of total revenue; in this case also, the use of this fiscal weapon appears surprisingly slight. In the Philippines the percentage increase in the yield from income taxes, which more than doubled, was higher than the increase in total revenue, and it rose from 16 per cent of the total revenue to 27 per cent. In Thailand total receipts increased by 73 per cent in 1953-9 and by 54 per cent in 1959-65. Taxes on income and wealth increased 146 per cent in 1953-9 and 61 per cent in 1959-65; but they represented only about 7 per cent of total receipts.

In short, the East Asian countries take a relatively small part of their revenue in the form of taxes on income and wealth. In the United Kingdom, for example, taxes on income and wealth were 40 per cent of the Central Government revenue in 1954 and 38 per cent in 1963; the yield from such taxes increased 58 per cent between those years.

In addition to personal income tax, however, the Indian Central budget shows large receipts from income tax on corporations; in 1956 these were only about half the receipts from personal income tax but in 1965 the corporation tax brought in very much more than the personal tax, having increased more than four times as much. The proportions of these two taxes in total receipts were thus reversed; personal income tax was 12 per cent of the whole revenue in 1956 and 6 per cent in 1965, corporation tax 6 per cent in 1956 and 13 per cent in 1965.

The land tax in the Indian State budgets must also be considered. Proceeds from it increased 68 per cent in 1954-65; in 1954 it represented 15 per cent of the States' revenue, 11 per cent in 1965. Corporation tax increased somewhat similarly in Indonesia, at least in the earlier part of the period, Small amounts of this tax were also levied in Pakistan and elsewhere. The land tax was also a substantial item in the Pakistan State budgets – increasing 168 per cent in 1952-65 and ranging between 11 per cent and 21 per cent of total State revenues. Broadly speaking the *tranche* of direct taxation altogether in these countries in their total revenues was in the order of 20 per cent. That was about half its percentage in Western developed countries.

Evidently the fiscal stress in these countries has generally been on *indirect taxation*. The extent of this, and its marked rise, are perturbing features; the financial burdens are widely placed on the poor people of the developing Asian countries.

Customs duties represented 31 per cent of Burma's revenue

in 1948; this proportion was reduced to 21 per cent in 1965, but the amount collected had increased 146 per cent. Other indirect taxes multiplied nearly seventeen times in Burma in the same period, rising from 6 per cent of the total receipts to 26 per cent. In Ceylon export duties yielded only 9 per cent more revenue in 1964 than in 1951, and had fallen from one-third to one-fifth of the total receipts. In general export duties are a declining and unreliable source of revenue for these countries; as are import duties also, though to a less marked extent. Other indirect taxes increased 265 per cent in Ceylon, and rose from 10 per cent to 19 per cent of the total revenue.

In the Indian Central budget the proceeds of *export duties* declined from 6 per cent of total receipts in 1956 to a negligible amount in 1965. *Import duties*, however, yielded 150 per cent more in 1965 than in 1956 (varying from 18 per cent down to 14 per cent of all revenue); while five times as much was collected in other indirect taxes in 1965 as in 1956, their share in total receipts rising from 20 per cent to 28 per cent. The Indian States levied three and a half times as much in excise duties in 1965 as in 1954 (14 per cent of total receipts). Moreover, they levied over four times as much in turnover tax (12 per cent of total receipts) and three times as much in other taxes (15-17 per cent of total receipts). Critics point with some bitterness at the policy of an underdeveloped country with some 40 per cent of its revenue coming from regressive taxation, severely affecting the huge numbers of poor people.

In Indonesia also, the poor performance of export levies is exemplified; they declined from 10 per cent of all receipts in 1953 to insignificance in 1958. Import duties contributed more significantly, at a quarter or more of total receipts. Fiscal monopolies represented another 5 per cent; but the major incidence was that of other indirect taxes, at between 25 per cent and 40 per cent of all receipts. Finally there were miscellaneous fees, at about 5 per cent. (The category 'foreign exchange levies,' 19 per cent to 34 per cent of total receipts, cannot be accurately disentangled from some of the other classifications.) The extent of indirect taxation is quite evident in the Indonesian accounts.

In Korea, customs duties rose from 9 per cent of total revenue in 1954 to 14 per cent in 1964, State-monopoly profits were 10-11 per cent and other indirect taxes 26-30 per cent. In Malaysia the yield from import duties declined 21 per cent in 1953-64: from 30 per cent of total revenue to 12 per cent. In the case of this country, unlike others, the proceeds of export duties increased nearly four times in the same period, and rose from 17 per cent of total receipts to 32 per cent. The irregularity of these sources of revenue is also exemplified by the figures. Meanwhile other indirect taxation nearly tripled in Malaysia, rising from 10 per cent to 15 per cent of the total receipts. In the Philippines the foreign exchange tax disappeared, but import duties rose from 17 per cent to 25 per cent of total revenue in 1954-65, excise took a further 15 per cent and other taxes rose from 28 per cent to 32 per cent.

State enterprises have made a declining or unimportant contribution to the national finances of the countries concerned – and an extremely variable and uncertain one, as Table 8.2 shows.

The public accounts of the developing East Asian countries do not for the most part – despite some distinct improvements in their balances in the last years of the period considered – show positions likely to inspire excessive confidence, or to make them especially attractive to foreign investment.

Chapter 9

ECONOMIC PLANNING

Almost all the East Asian countries have made economic planning in some form a main feature of their development efforts. The various countries' plans have, however, differed so much in their purposes, nature and results that no full description or analysis can easily be made.

PARTIAL PLANNING

Concerning some of the smaller countries, a summary account may suffice; planning has been *ad hoc* on an occasional project basis, or rather ineffective, not dominating the economy as a whole or shaping its development.[1] The witticism was offered at one Regional conference that some Asians have invented a new logical fallacy: '*ante hoc ergo propter hoc.*'

Cambodia had a First Five-Year Plan, 1960-4; but none of the substantial industrial, social or 'infrastructural' development which occurred was related to it. The determinant was rather foreign aid. Substantial aid was extended by the United States – until 1963, when any further American aid was rejected – but also by Communist China, the USSR and France, in each case on a project-basis. A Second Five-Year Plan was announced for 1965-9, under Russian influence. The headings of projected expenditure under the Plan were (percentages of a total of 8,000 million rials).

Production	40%
Infrastructure	28%
Social	24.5%
Administrative	7.5%

South Vietnam recorded some infrastructural and industrial progress under its First Five-Year Plan (1957-61), but these were unco-ordinated Departmental efforts. The period of the Second Five-Year Plan, 1962-6, saw the complete disruption of all such efforts, in conditions of civil war. The planning office reportedly had, in 1965, a staff of one; this may be an exaggeration, but its existence was certainly nominal. At the same time, however, political and organizational moves were made throughout these years in such spheres as resettlement, rehabilitation and restoration of civic functions, which have not been given full credit in the world at large, as they do involve and imply cogent efforts at planful development.

Indonesia produced some 'paper plans' without very effective means of formulating or implementing them. An Economic Emergency Programme (1951-5) was adopted which was rather a statement of priorities – to increase industrial output and equip small factories with more machinery. Some plants were constructed, most of which never manufactured anything; only about 25 per cent of the designated plants received any machinery, and about half of these did not use it.[2]

The Five-Year Development Plan (1956-61) came from the Cabinet to the Parliament; it had been drafted by economists and specified cogent requirements such as long-term growth targets, capital formation and sources of finance, but in conditions of inflation with economic and political disorder it was inoperative. The funds allocated for investment were spent on current expenses.

The present Eight-Year Development Plan (1961-8) related to the public sector only. It tabled a list of 335 development projects (including admixtures of military and other purposes), and a list of sources of internal and external financing for these projects. The claimed 'balance' between these lists was vague; export, cost- and import- projections were optimistic, the strong trend of inflation was ignored, priorities were weakly assessed.

This Plan was the work of a National Planning Council, which was a large and complicated organization established in 1959. It had, however, no economists in its membership; President Sukarno and other leaders took a nominal but highly personal interest in it. It was soon replaced by a National Development Planning organization, more specifically a government body, and this in its turn by a Ministry for Co-ordinating Development; both of these were, however, largely ineffectual, against the background of continuing inflation, in the period of Confrontation against Malaya and subsequently.

A leading regional journal reported as follows at the end of 1964. Economic development in Indonesia has been slight in recent years; the conditions are rather those of stagnation, dilapidation and organizational weakening. The first four years of the Eight-Year Development Plan (1961-4) showed very poor results, and little possibility of improvement was foreshadowed for the second four years (1965-8). By December 1964, 135 out of 335 category 'A' projects (food, clothing, finance and industry) had not been implemented at all. None of the category 'B' projects had been realized; they were to gain, in the whole eight years, some Rupiahs 111 bn. (111,000 million) in foreign exchange, and 120 bn. in Rupiahs. The official (IMF) rate for the Rupiah was 882 to the pound, or say 300 to the dollar.

About half these foreign exchange earnings were to be from exports of oil and oil products, of which Government takes 60 per cent of the profits; but exports in this category declined from Rupiahs 11.7 bn. in 1961 to 9.7 in 1962, recovered to about 12 in 1963, and fell again in the first half of 1964. Other (lesser) planned sources of increased foreign exchange earnings were to be exports of rubber, copra and tin (largely by checking smuggling; which was not, however, achieved), also aluminium, and earnings from tourists (who were, however, deterred by disorderly conditions, etc.). But the operational costs and outlays against these projected earnings amounted to about Rupiahs 100 bn. Leaving only 11 bn. net gain, at best (over the whole eight years); which in fact has so far apparently been a deficit.

The Rupiah revenue from 'B' projects was to be from Government sales, profits of State enterprises, savings, and bond sales; these also have not been realized. The State Railways, for example, are subsidized; as is the State shipping concern (Pelni), which has made no profits since its establishment in 1952. The State Construction Bank receives 55 per cent of the profits of State enterprises; in 1961 it received Rs. 509 million only (millions only – the figures in the preceding paragraph are in billions) in 1962 a mere 12 million, 122 million in 1963, and about 111 million in 1964. Meanwhile (1961-3) it had laid out nearly 89,600 million to finance the projects; less than half the projects had even furnished this Bank with progress reports, and hardly more than half with financial reports (by March 1964). Planned economic development is in a weak and dangerous condition in Indonesia.[3]

In the Philippines also, planning has been a 'verbal' matter. Professor Benjamin Higgins – himself closely involved in economic policy in that country in the period in question – could write in 1959 that

'there is little evidence that the preparation of development plans by the government has accelerated economic growth in the Philippines . . . even if carried out, they would not have accelerated economic growth very much, because they have been too modest . . . the plans remain paper plans for the most part.'[4]

Mr Roxas, who was principally responsible for the Plan launched in 1962, resigned in 1964, declaring that

'it is meaningless at this stage to talk of national planning. Neither the Philippine Government nor any of its agencies is in any position to draw up a meaningful plan. The whole public administration system militates not only against implementing a meaningful plan, but even against formulating one. The 'five year plans' we have had were . . . merely statements of general aspirations.'[5]

Burma was early in the movement towards planning. The Two-Year Economic Development Plan (1949) was, however, only a list of quantified aims; and the country was completely disrupted by political disturbances. From 1951, American consultants were called in and the Eight-Year Plan (1953-60) was the result. It was to double the real GDP in 1959-60 as compared to 1950-1; this would make it 30 per cent above pre-war, but only 4 per cent in *per capita* terms, owing to the rise in population. Total investment was to have been 7,500 million kyat, largely on infrastructure development, over 50 per cent of this being in the public sector. This was based on optimistic assumptions about the price and export-earning prospects of rice. This Plan was abandoned in 1955, and succeeded by the First Four-Year Plan (1956/7-1959/60). In the public sector this gave a higher share of investment than the preceding Plan to agriculture (including irrigation, 11 per cent against 8 per cent), power (16 per cent against 10 per cent), and transport (including communications, 28 per cent instead of 21 per cent) and slightly more to industry (9.7 per cent instead of 9.3 per cent), but reduced social services (from 22 per cent to 10 per cent) and mining (from 0.8 per cent to 0.4 per cent). This was somewhat more successful than the Eight-Year Plan.

The Second Four-Year Plan (1961/2-1964/5) envisaged more than double the investment of the First (about 4,500 million kyat), half of it in the public sector, but raising the share of transport and communications to nearly 30 per cent, and agriculture to 12 per cent, while reducing that of power to less than 8 per cent. The new military Government dropped the Plan in 1962. Planning staffs were inadequate, and poorly paid. The administrative structure was frequently changed. Political uncertainties were great. The account of planning in Burma must therefore be largely negative.

In Ceylon there were two Six-Year Plans, a Ten-Year Plan and a three-year Programme, which were all largely on paper.[6]

LARGE-SCALE NATIONAL-DEMOCRATIC PLANS

India's First-Year Plan was launched in 1951. One of its major aims was to double *per capita* income in twenty-five years, by increasing it 3 per cent a year. This still represented a modest level of aspiration: it would bring the *per capita* income up to only $110 in 1976. A growth rate of 3 per cent a year does not seem ambitious; nevertheless this would require a prodigious effort in India's case, since total income would have to rise at almost double the 3 per cent rate, to offset population growth. In the subsequent fifteen years total national income (in terms of constant prices) grew by less than 4 per cent a year; in bad periods, by hardly more than 2 per cent. Meanwhile the rate of population growth roughly doubled; from about 1.25 per cent in 1951 to 2.5 per cent in 1966.

The required prodigious effort has not been made, or has been unsuccessful. The scale and the technical ambitions certainly increased, in the successive plans. The First Five-Year Plan (1951) involved an outlay of Rs. 33,000 million – about 7 per cent of the national income for the five years. The Second Plan (1956-60) more than doubled the outlay in the First, with Rs. 68,310 million – some 9 per cent of the national income in that period. The Third Plan (1961-5) represented an outlay of Rs. 104,000 million – some 14 per cent of the national income in the quinquennium. The Fourth Plan (1966-71) envisages an outlay of over Rs. 200,000 million, double that of the Third and equal to the total of all the first three Plans together – which may well represent over 20 per cent of the national income in that period.

This has involved largely deficit financing. Money supply in India increased about 110 per cent in 1951-65; while national product, the flow of goods and services, increased about half as much (56 per cent). During the Third Plan, prices rose 37.5 per cent. Public sector enterprises generally showed losses. For example the Government Audit for 1964 reported that in 1961-2 there were forty-six companies with two subsidiaries in this sector, which recorded a loss of Rs. 106 million: about 1 per cent of their capital stock. In 1962-3, with the same number of companies, the loss had increased about 20 per cent and the total capital of these public companies had increased in the same proportion. In 1963-4 there were six more State companies, their overall loss had increased four and a half times since the preceding year (to Rs. 551.5 million) while their capitalization had increased by over 20 per cent. The total increase in the money supply during the Third Plan period (by over Rs. 100,000 million) very closely matched the total outlay on the Plan.

The public sector has grown more than twice as much as the private sector; and in many respects the former dominates the economy, having the heavy-industrial and other 'key' activities in its hands. Nevertheless private enterprise has also expanded. In terms of total paid-up capital, non-Government companies in India represented Rs. 7,750 in 1950-1 (about eight times the figure for 1917-18). In 1956, at the end of the First Plan, their total capitalization had increased 23 per cent; in 1961, at the end of the Second Plan, it had increased by a further 25 per cent. In the capital available to them, the two sectors are roughly equal.[7]

Table 9.1 analyses the investment-patterns in the Second and Third Plans of India. The scheduled investment in the Third Plan was over 50 per cent greater than in the Second; and the increase was much larger for the public sector (over 70 per cent) than for the private sector (over 30 per cent) so that the former increased its share of the total from 54 per cent to 61 per cent. Taking the increases by items, from the Second Plan to the Third, the trends become apparent. The total investment in agriculture was raised 75 per cent; but that of the public sector increased much more than that of the private sector, moving from equality with the latter to preponderance over it. Power development was heavily in the hands of the Government, which invested ten times as much in it as the private sector in the Second Plan, twenty times as much in the Third; the total investment in power doubling in the Third Plan, the Government's more than doubling while the private sector's rose only 28 per cent and only 1 per cent of the private investment being in power (c.f. 12-16 per cent of the Government's).

Table 9.1. Investments in India's Second and Third Five-Year Plans (million Rs. Index = % of corresponding entry in Second Plan)

	SECOND PLAN						THIRD PLAN								
	Public	%	Private	%	Total	%	Public	%	(index)	Private	%	(index)	Total	%	(index)
Agriculture and community development	2,100	6%	6,250	20%	8,350	12%	6,600	10%	(314)	8,000	20%	(128)	14,600	14%	(175)
Major and medium irrigation works	4,200	11%	(a)	..	4,200	6%	6,500	10%	(155)	(a)	..	..	6,500	6%	(155)
Power	4,450	12%	400	1%	4,850	7%	10,120	16%	(227)	500	1%	(125)	10,620	10%	(219)
Village and small industries	900	2%	1,750	6%	2,650	4%	1,500	2%	(167)	2,750	7%	(157)	4,250	4%	(160)
Organized industry and mining	8,700	24%	6,750	21%	15,450	23%	15,200	24%	(175)	10,500	26%	(156)	25,700	25%	(166)
Transport and communications	12,750	35%	1,350	4%	14,100	21%	14,860	24%	(117)	2,500	6%	(185)	17,360	17%	(123)
Social services and miscellaneous	3,400	9%	9,500	31%	12,900	19%	6,220	10%	(183)	10,750	26%	(113)	16,970	16%	(132)
Inventories	..	..	5,000	16%	5,000	8%	2,000	3%	(−)	6,000	15%	(120)	8,000	8%	(160)
Total	36,500	100%	31,000	100%	67,500	100%	63,000	100%	(173)	41,000	100%	(132)	104,000	100%	(154)
	(54%)		(46%)				(61%)			(39%)					

Note: (a) included in Agriculture: but small compared to the public sector.

In village industries and small industries the sectors' movements were more even, and the Government's part remained at about one-third. In 'organized' industry and mining also, the sectors moved rather evenly in the aggregates; this category represented about 24 per cent of the total investment in both Plans, 24 per cent of the Government's in each case; of the private sector's, 21 per cent in the First Plan and 26 per cent in the Second. In the absolute amounts involved, however, there was a 75 per cent increase in the Government's case and only 56 per cent in that of the private sector; while the Government investment under this heading exceeded the private sector's by 29 per cent in the First Plan, 45 per cent in the Second Plan. Moreover, the aggregation here conceals the extent to which the heavy industries and 'key points' in the developing economy were concentrated in the public sector.

The largest item in the public investment in the First Plan had been in transport and communications (35 per cent of the public investment in this field). The Government maintained this interest, increasing the public investment in this category by 17 per cent in the Second Plan; but reduced the percentage of public investment in this account from 35 per cent to 24 per cent, while the private investment increased 85 per cent and represented about one-fifth of the public (c.f. about one-tenth in the First Plan).

For 'social services and miscellaneous' items the First Plan scheduled 31 per cent of the private investment, 9 per cent of the public. In the Third Plan the Government's allocation, as a percentage of its total investment, remained the same; but the amount involved was 83 per cent greater. The amount invested on this account by the private sector increased only 13 per cent, and it represented only 26 per cent of the total private investment in the Third Plan, against 31 per cent in the Second.

There was no explicit allocation for inventories in the public sector in the Second Plan, but 3 per cent of public investment in the Third Plan was for this entry; placing it at one-third (in value) of the investment in inventories by the private sector during the Third Plan (which was scheduled to be 20 per cent greater than in the Second Plan).

Such was the Plan framework during this decade. The advance of the public sector – the progress towards Socialism, which is embodied in the Constitution of India – is clearly delineated by this analysis. That trend is evident; but how far were the specific targets of the Plans realized?

The answer is as complex as the planning process itself, and can only be summarily attempted here.

Industrial production increased 39 per cent during the Second Plan. This was a very substantial gain; but the overall statement conceals various crucial shortfalls and 'bottlenecks'. The inflationary trend created general alarm and stress. The consumer price index for the working class population (1949 = 100) moved from 96 in the last year of the First Plan to 124 in the last year of the Second. The First Plan period thus saw a slight fall in prices for the masses, the Second an increase of nearly 30 per cent. Shortfalls in the production of food grains in several years were a major factor: large food imports were made. In some years industrial crops also failed. Speculation was very heavy. The price of gold in India fluctuated around double the world-market price. At the end of the Second Plan, border tensions with China were acute, and fighting ensued in the latter part of 1962. At the end of the Third Plan there was war with Pakistan. The wholesale price index rose from 123 in mid-1960 (1952-3 = 100) to 166 in mid-1965 – a 35 per cent rise during the Third Plan, c.f. 30 per cent during the Second Plan. Industrial production increased just over 4 per cent per annum during the Third Plan, i.e. by less than 20 per cent in the quinquennium. National

Table 9.2. Investments in India's proposed Fourth Five-Year Plan (Rs. million. Index = % of corresponding entry in Third Plan)

	Public sector		Private sector			Total	
	Amount	% (index)	Amount	%	(index)	Amount	% (index)
Agriculture	15,140	13% (229)	7,000	10%	(87)	22,140	12% (152)
Irrigation	9,240	8% (142)	—	—	—	9,240	5% (142)
Power	18,280	15% (181)	500	1%	(100)	18,780	10% (177)
Small industry	2,500	2% (167)	4,000	6%	(145)	6,500	3% (153)
Organized industry	28,660	24% (188)	24,000	34%	(229)	52,660	28% (205)
Transport and communications	27,680	23% (186)	6,500	9%	(260)	34,180	18% (197)
Education, welfare and miscellaneous	18,840	15% (303)	15,800	23%	(147)	34,640	18% (204)
Inventories	—	—	12,000	17%	(200)	12,000	6% (150)
Total	120,340	100% (191)	69,800	100%	(170)	190,140	100% (183)

income per head increased by less than 2 per cent per year, in real terms.

Following the conflict with Pakistan in 1965 the Fourth Five-Year Plan which had been elaborated for 1966-70 was postponed; an Emergency Programme was applied for 1966-7. The outlays proposed for the Fourth Plan are summarized in Table 9.2.

SOME PLANNING DIFFICULTIES EXEMPLIFIED BY THE CASE OF INDIA

Large-scale planned and controlled economies have generated an amount of paper-work unprecedented in history, and a prodigious expansion of office staffs. Full analysis would be complicated and wearisome.

The matter may be illustrated by the case of India. Table 9.3 notes the expansion of staffs – at the top Central Government ('Secretariat') levels only – from the Partition to 1965.

Table 9.3. Numbers of senior officials, India[8]

	1947	1965	*Increase*
Secretaries of Departments	18	46	156%
Additional Secretaries	10	20	100%
Joint Secretaries	34	115	238%
Deputy Secretaries	70	235	236%
Under-secretaries	167	429	157%
Total	299	845	183%

Rising costs seriously affect the validity of plans. For example, the first phase of the great Bokaro steel plant in India (to reach a capacity of 1.7 million metric ingot tons) was originally costed by the Russian experts at Rs. 5,500 million, and the second phase (completion at a capacity of 4 million tons) Rs. 2,200 million. By March 1966 the estimate for the first phase had been raised 14 per cent, for the second 35 per cent, or for the whole project 20 per cent.[9]

The targets of Pakistan's First Five-Year Plan (1955-60) were only '60 per cent achieved', but it did lay down a substantial 'infrastructure'. Exogenous or uncontrolled factors which affected the outcome were: bad weather in three of the years, a serious deterioration of the terms of trade, and upward revision of the costs of projects owing to the rise in world prices. Endogenous variables which should theoretically have been better controlled, but were not, were: unexpectedly large increases in consumption, inefficient resource-utilization, and insufficient public co-operation.

The plan aimed at an increase in national income by 15 per cent. The actual increase was 10 per cent, owing chiefly to agricultural production increasing only 6 per cent instead of the 13 per cent aimed at by the Plan. Food grains production was especially deficient, large imports were required, though the Plan had hoped for self-sufficiency in food by 1960. The actual increase in population proved to be 1.6 per cent *per annum* instead of the expected 1.4 per cent. The other aims which were partly achieved were: irrigation or formation of 1.8 million acres of new land, desalination or reclamation of 5.1 million acres of old land, an increase in industrial production by 75 per cent, and attainment of a small surplus in the balance of payments. The industrial results were considerable but hard to evaluate; the production increase was over 50 per cent, though much of the new plant capacity created was not utilized. The total outlay was about Rs. 11,000 million – roughly 9 per cent of the national income in the period.

Pakistan's Second Plan (1960-5) aimed at: increasing national income by 20 per cent, production of food grains by over 20 per cent, industrial production by 50 per cent, a large improvement in the balance of payments, the creation of new employment for 4 million persons, and raising standards in depressed districts of the country, in addition to such general aims as education, control of disease, cultural facilities, etc. The projected outlay for the Second Plan was Rs. 19,000 million (75 per cent more than the First, and about 11 per cent of the national income in the period). Of this total outlay 60 per cent would be financed by the Government, 58 per cent from internal resources and 42 per cent through foreign aid, loans and investments, 51 per cent was for the public sector, 17 per cent for the 'semi-public sector' and 32 per cent for the private sector.

The Second Plan gave distinct priority to agriculture: 22 per per cent of the total outlay going to direct benefits to agriculture, including formation of 2.5 million acres of new land, improvement of 7 million acres of old land, and many other facilities. The aim of self-sufficiency in food grains by the end of the Plan was repeated.

The results were distinctly good; Pakistan made much greater progress in this period. Agricultural production increased by over 3 per cent per annum (c.f. 1 per cent p.a. in the First Plan period), industrial production at over 8 per cent p.a. (c.f. 7 per cent). The increase in g.n.p. was a few percentage points above the 24 per cent aimed at in the Plan. There was much progress in education, including technical education. The exogenous and endogenous factors mentioned above as hampering the First Plan were very much less in evidence. The Government expenditure on the Second Plan was as projected, but private investment exceeded the target by about 17 per cent. Total investment as a percentage of g.n.p. rose from about 11 per cent in 1960 to about 15 per cent in 1964, domestic saving from about 6 per cent to over 9 per cent. The share of foreign investment in total investment decreased, from about 44 per cent to about 6 per cent. The money supply rose (particularly in 1962-4; by some 14 per cent in each of those years) yet prices were rather stable. Foreign exchange earnings increased at almost double the rate planned (3 per cent *per annum*). 62 per cent of the imports were capital goods and materials for the same.

Developmentally, Pakistan was thus in a promising and stimulating posture at the end of the Second Plan. An emergency then supervened : the outbreak of (undeclared) war with India imposed a brief halting of economic progress. The Third Five-Year Plan (1965-70) came into operation nevertheless. Its aims were optimistic – envisaging in fact the attainment of the 'take-off stage in economic development'. The development programme for the first year had, however, to be cut by about 25 per cent. The main objectives of the Third Plan (at the outset) were a 30 per cent increase in g.n.p., additional employment openings for 4.5 million persons and increase of exports by nearly 40 per cent. Industry would receive nearly 30 per cent of the total outlay (a slightly higher proportion than in the Second Plan) but some 40 per cent of the outlay would directly benefit agriculture.

The Third Plan was presented also as the first phase of a Twenty-year 'Perspective Plan' (1965-85), including such objectives as doubling *per capita* income, securing full employment and universal education, eliminating regional differences and dispensing altogether with foreign aid. The verbal 'take-off' into the latest economic parlance has clearly already occurred. The material take-off still lies far ahead, though Pakistan's recent progress has been marked and inspiriting. Advocates of private enterprise stress the part of the latter in this success. In the Second Plan the private sector exceeded its 'targets' and in the Third it was allocated an outlay of Rs. 18,000 million – almost equal to the *total* outlay in the Second Plan, three times the part the private sector had in the Second Plan, and representing 35 per cent of the total outlay in the Third Plan (c.f. 32 per cent in the Second Plan). Critics would also stress the continued dependence on foreign aid – which would be required to provide some 16 per cent of the outlay in the Third Plan. Though this level of aid represents a much smaller percentage than in the Second Plan (in which it was 42 per cent) it represents a larger absolute sum (by some 4 per cent).

PLANNING IN A DEVELOPED CAPITALIST COUNTRY

In Japan, post-war planning grew out of the systematic programming of reconstruction under SCAP (the Allied Occupation authority). The Economic Stabilization Board established in 1946 produced, in particular, the Economic Rehabilitation Plan (1949-53). When the Occupation ended (1952) there was some reaction against this. The Stabilization Board was converted into an Economic Counsel Board, with reduced functions of an advisory kind; but it was promptly seen that the longer-term adjustment and development of the Japanese economy in the new post-war era required 'planful' foresight. In 1955 the Economic Counsel Board became the Economic Planning Board, and produced a Five-Year Plan, which, however, was little more than an indication (like the British National Plan of 1965) of the theoretical requirement of a growth rate to meet the immediate needs. In this case it was, however, a question of securing a viable economy by 1960, envisaging the cessation of 'special' dollar receipts by that time. A growth in g.n.p. by 5 per cent a year was postulated; but this was doubled in the first two years and the whole basis had to be reconsidered.

The result was a Long-Range Plan for 1958-62, setting investment, saving, employment, production and export targets, and an annual increase in g.n.p. by 6½ per cent, distinguishing a 'planned' public sector and a 'guided' private sector. This was, however, entirely an indicative Plan, without any prescriptive powers. All the aims were over-fulfilled by 1960 – with an annual growth-rate of over 10 per cent. The terms of trade had improved in a way that could not have been anticipated, the rate of capital formation was 35 per cent (gross) against 28.5 per cent in the Plan, and engineering standards were sharply raised.

A new Ten-Year Plan (1961-70) was therefore produced in 1960 by the Economic Planning Agency (the former Board had been so renamed in 1957) assisted by panels of industrialists and professionals. This came to be known, by its main aim, as the Plan to Double National Income. It proposed a larger public-sector investment than previously (over half the total, instead of over one third) and concentrated heavily on capital equipment, social (housing, etc.) as well as entrepreneurial. The policy is that of a mature industrial nation, reducing the proportion (but not the absolute amount) of capital investment in manufacturing and devoting relatively more to infrastructural facilities raising social standards and amenities. This Plan also was distinctly exceeded in the first half of its currency and Japan's standard of living, as well as its output, ranks in the category of the developed countries.[10]

COMMUNIST PLANNING

In Communist China, the First Five-Year Plan (1953-7) set the course strongly towards 'Socialist Industrialization', with powerful emphasis on heavy industries. The initial vagueness may be realized, however, when it is known that no details were announced until 1955, in the third year of the Plan's currency. Cost calculations were partial or unsophisticated, only labour costs being fully considered. The quantitative aims of the Plan were not excessively high – they represented large percentage rises, but from a low war's-end base, by a country achieving a return to more normal levels.

The main aims, Socialization and heavy industrialization, were significantly achieved. The share of producer goods in the gross product rose (1952-7) from 43 per cent to 57 per cent; that of food and textiles fell from 63.5 per cent to 49.1 per cent. The share of modern industry (as compared to handicraft production) rose, but was still a very minor share – from a little under 2 per cent to nearly $2\frac{1}{2}$ per cent. Full nationalization was, however, immediately completed (in 1956). There was some stress on the decentralization of industry into the interior of the country – partly from strategic considerations (very soon to become out of date) and partly from Marxist reasonings about reducing the industrial 'monopoly' of Shanghai, Manchuria and other centres, and reversing their 'colonial' basis of bringing the raw materials to the industrial regions, by bringing industries to the primary-producing areas.

The Second Five-Year Plan (1958-62) more boldly and clearly proposed a doubling of the industrial output – also the long-term aim of overtaking the (total) industrial output of the United Kingdom. This proceeded strongly, though not altogether evenly, at first. The period opened, however, with the swift completion of collectivization, placing all activities under Communes, and the 'Great Leap Forward' was attempted in 1958-9; the pace of production was precipitately accelerated, with much emphasis on the making of iron and steel (and other items) in 'backyard' (small-scale local) units. The results were catastrophic, in terms of a flood of low grade output which was largely unusable but clogged the transport system and created much confusion. Experience was certainly gained, but at very high cost. The upshot of the Second Plan was far from clear.

Moreover, both the First and the Second Plans had depended very largely on Soviet aid, including wide provision of complete plants, as well as all forms of technical assistance and training. From 1960 – closely following the downfall of the Great Leap – the acute ideological dispute between Russia developed, the Russians withdrew and took even their blueprints away with them. A period of uncertainty, reconsideration and readjustment necessarily followed. The Third Five-Year Plan, due in 1962, may start in 1967, but by the end of 1966 there were still no very full or fully confirmed details available about it. Though the resumption of comprehensive and confident planning appeared likely, grave political turmoil, centring on the problem of the succession to Chairman Mao and on the current activities of young Red Guards, made the prospects very uncertain.[11]

NO PLANNING

At the other extreme to Mainland China – 'odd man out' indeed, in this respect and in its political system – is the British Crown

Colony of Hong Kong, which holds strongly to essential *laissez-faire* and private enterprise with minimal Government intervention, in close consonance with the precepts of Adam Smith.

A VARIED PATTERN

Planning in East Asia thus presents an extremely variegated pattern; to classify by aims or forms and methods, as well as by results of the criteria of success, would necessitate at least as many categories as there are countries. For the most part Western observers to some extent overestimate the scope, effectiveness, and realism of these various Plans – and even the firmness of their motivation, in the economic sphere at least. In most cases the Plans sweepingly reflect political and general motivations, rather than fully analysed and studied *a priori* economic calculations. In this respect as in others the Asian countries are so heterogeneous and their patterns and directions of progress so varied, that any over-generalization or oversimplification of statement obscures the essential fact that Asia is still in a fluid stage of experiment and transition. The present situations are far less crystallized, the further prospects far less studied and definitive than is widely supposed.

Chapter 10

INTERNATIONAL AID

The nature and extent of foreign aid to East Asia are difficult to assess. Only a brief account can be attempted here. What constitutes economic aid – within a flow of assistance of various kinds, on widely differing terms, involving political, military and other considerations and motivations as well as the desire to contribute to economic development *per se* – is in itself a complicated question. Even if the factor of aid is identified, the assessment of its effects involves many further difficulties and complications.

Asia has not received any specially large share of aid – even in total, and certainly not per head of the population (see Table 1.1 above). The aid going to Asia has been largely concentrated on a few countries. Even in those countries, foreign aid can certainly not be said to have been the main factor in the development which has occurred. However – in combination with other factors – it has been of key importance in certain respects, at some times and places. Very large sums have been given and lent; they appear inadequate only in relation to the still more gigantic and prodigious problems, needs and difficulties. Foreign aid has filled some gaps which, in a qualitative sense at least if not quantitatively, have been decisive. Indications have been given above of the numbers of people who have been kept alive in Asia by foreign aid, the key projects which it has supported, and the extent to which national development plans have in many cases depended upon it.

AMERICAN AND WESTERN AID

The United Nations Organization uses the widest definition of economic aid, including all grants and loans significant to economic development; even in the case of military aid it excludes only items directly and specifically for military purposes. Its Statistical Year Book has, however, given particulars only for the non-Communist countries and for a limited number of years (1958-60). The details for the underdeveloped countries of the

Region are summarized in Table 10.1; which immediately shows the salient features. The total of bilateral grants was five times that of bilateral loans. 85 per cent of the bilateral grants and 72 per cent of the bilateral loans came from the United States.

This aid went preponderantly to the countries most directly and strongly supported, politically and militarily, by the United States. South Korea received 37 per cent of the US grants, South Vietnam 22 per cent, Taiwan 10 per cent – the largest *per capita* amounts for the populations concerned – Pakistan 12 per cent, India 6 per cent, Cambodia, the Philippines and Thailand 3 per cent each. Thus South Korea alone received from the US a much larger sum in grants than all the other countries received altogether from countries other than the US. The same applies to Vietnam; and Taiwan, whose aid was almost solely from the US, received almost as much as 'the rest from the rest'. (Later, in the 1960s, Taiwan's economic progress brought it much nearer to being able to dispense with American aid.)

Political and military considerations also explain the concentration of the UK aid on Malaysia. The UK did, however, extend loans much more than grants, particularly to India – which, it must be noted, is the only country to be helped in this period by loans much more than by grants. It may be surprising that Japan extended nearly five times as much in grants in the Region as did the United Kingdom; but Japan's grant to Indonesia may be considered in effect as a war-reparations payment.

The whole multilateral account – the aid channelled internationally through the UN agencies – is strikingly small, at about one twenty-seventh of the bilateral total. Within this smaller total large percentages went again to Korea, also in this case to India, Pakistan, Burma, Ceylon and Thailand, but not to Taiwan and Vietnam. Some essential features of the aid pattern are thus exemplified in this period. The Region's share of worldwide aid, it must again be emphasized, has been distinctly small in *per capita* terms and its share has gone chiefly to certain countries, while the motives of the donor countries have largely been not solely or purely 'economic' or disinterested.

The total sums involved (1954–60) are summarized in Table 10.1.

In *per capita* terms this aid represents very low sums; even in the countries receiving the largest assistance, the amount per inhabitant was small. The UN figures are as follows. (Table 10.2.)

Table 10.1. *International aid received by East Asian countries, 1954-60,*
from Western countries and UN agencies (amounts in US$ million)

	1954-6	1958-9	1960	Total
Burma	16.7	21.8	8.4	46.9
Cambodia	49.0	..	..	..
Ceylon	17.7	42.4	14.8	74.9
China: Taiwan	218.3	173.6	104.6	501.5
India	245.2	622.7	447.8	1,315.7
Indonesia	41.9	210.6	17.5	270.0
Korea: S.	675.4	643.5	255.2	1,574.1
Malaya: Fed.	..	..	13.6	..
Pakistan	309.4	322.9	207.0	839.3
Philippines	43.1	80.9	30.1	154.1
Vietnam: S.	325.6	..	..	..

Table 10.2. *International aid received by East Asian countries, per*
head of population, 1954-60

(Figures in Table 10.1 divided by the population of each country)

	(US $) 1954-6 (annual average)	1958-9 (annual average)	1960
Burma	0.30	0.55	0.40
Cambodia	3.70	..	..
Ceylon	0.70	2.25	0.75
China: Taiwan	8.50	8.75	9.90
India	0.20	0.53	1.00
Indonesia	0.17	0.80	0.20
Korea: S.	10.46	14.30	10.30
Malaya: Fed.	..	..	2.00
Pakistan	1.26	1.90	2.20
Philippines	0.65	1.15	1.10
Vietnam: S.	4.45	..	..

In the years 1958-60, the total assistance was as shown in
Table 10.3.

Thus, in the bilateral aid, the grants were more than three
times the loans. The United States was the only universal donor
and lender, helping all countries, accounting for 87 per cent of
the grants and 71 per cent of the loans. The political alignments
are very clear: 32 per cent of the US grants in East Asia went to
South Korea, 20 per cent to South Vietnam, 12 per cent to
Pakistan, 8 per cent to Indonesia, 6 per cent to Taiwan, 63 per
cent of the loans to India and 20 per cent to Pakistan. Britain's
very limited largesse (of a direct kind) in East Asia (less than one
half of one per cent of the United States') went almost entirely
to India and Malaysia.

Table 10.3. International aid to East Asian countries, 1958-60³
(million $) (excluding Communist states)

By:	Australia	Canada	Japan	New Zealand	UK	US	Others	Total
Burma	1.1 (5%)	0.4 (0%)	—	0.4	—	2.9 (0%)	—	4.8 (0%)
Cambodia	1.4 (6%)	0.2 (0%)	—	—	—	62.6 (3%)	—	64.2 (2%)
Ceylon	1.7 (8%)	9.2 (11%)	0.1	0.4	0.9 (2%)	29.1 (1%)	—	41.4 (2%)
China: Taiwan	—	—	—	—	—	240.1 (10%)	—	240.1 (9%)
Hong Kong	—	—	—	—	0.3 (0%)	10.4 (0%)	—	10.7 (0%)
India	3.6 (16%)	26.9 (31%)	—	2.8	1.6 (4%)	140.6 (6%)	1.7ᵃ	177.2 (6%)
Indonesia	3.1 (14%)	1.5 (2%)	176.9ᵇ	0.6	—	31.6 (0%)	—	213.7 (8%)
Korea: S.	—	0.8 (1%)	—	—	—	870.9 (37%)	0.6ᵇ	872.3 (32%)
Malaysia	1.8 (8%)	0.7 (1%)	—	1.0	32.2 (87%)	4.3 (0%)	—	40.0 (1%)
Pakistan	5.3 (24%)	46.2 (53%)	—	1.5	1.7 (4%)	274.7 (12%)	—	329.4 (12%)
Philippines	0.9 (4%)	0.1 (0%)	0.1	0.3	0.2 (0%)	72.3 (3%)	—	73.8 (3%)
Thailand	1.5 (7%)	0.1 (0%)	—	—	—	74.8 (3%)	—	76.5 (3%)
Vietnam: S.	1.6 (7%)	0.7 (1%)	—	—	—	519.4 (22%)	—	521.7 (19%)
Total	22.0 (100%)	86.8 (100%)	177.1	7.0	36.9 (100%)	2,333.7 (100%)	2.3	2,665.8 (100%)

Notes: ᵃ By Norway. ᵇ 0.2 by Norway, 0.4 by Sweden.

Loans

	Canada		UK		US		Others	Total	
ma	—		—		9.3	(2%)	—	9.3	(1%)
lon	1.5	(6%)	—		5.9	(1%)	—	7.4	(1%)
ia: Taiwan	—		—		36.2	(6.5%)	—	36.2	(5%)
ig Kong	—		4.4	(3%)	—		—	4.4	(0%)
a	24.2	(94%)	145.5	(96%)	280.2	(50%)	44.5a	494.4	(63%)
nesia	—		—		3.2	(0.5%)	—	3.2	(0%)
ea: S.	—		—		3.2	(0.5%)	—	3.2	(0%)
aysia	—		—		0.8	(0%)	—	0.8	(0%)
stan	—		1.0	(1%)	153.7	(28%)	—	154.7	(20%)
ippines	—		—		20.1	(4%)	—	20.1	(3%)
iland	—		—		19.2	(4%)	—	19.2	(2%)
nam: S.	—		—		25.0	(4%)	—	25.0	(3%)
.l	25.7		150.9		556.8	(100%)	44.5	777.9	(100%)

Note: a 44.0 by Germany, 0.5 by Japan.

(B) *Multilateral*
  (i) *Grants*

By:	UNTA[a]		UNICEF[b]		IBRD[c]	UNHCR[d]	Total	
Burma	2.9	(10%)	2.5	(16%)	—	—	5.4	(8%)
Cambodia	1.8	(6%)	0.0		—	—	1.8	(3%)
Ceylon	1.5	(5%)	0.2	(1%)	—	—	1.7	(3%)
China: Taiwan	1.1	(4%)	0.5	(3%)	—	—	1.6	(2%)
Malaysia	1.0	(4%)	0.0		—	—	1.0	(1%)
Hong Kong	0.0		0.0		—	0.3	0.3	(0%)
India	9.1	(32%)	7.5	(47%)	—	—	16.6	(25%)
Indonesia	2.7	(9%)	1.8	(11%)	—	—	4.5	(7%)
Korea: S.	0.5	(2%)	0.2	(1%)	22.0	—	22.7	(34%)
Pakistan	1.3	(5%)	0.9	(6%)	—	—	2.2	(3%)
Philippines	2.9	(10%)	1.4	(9%)	—	—	4.3	(6%)
Thailand	2.6	(9%)	0.9	(6%)	—	—	3.5	(5%)
Vietnam: S.	1.1	(4%)	0.1	(0%)	—	—	1.2	(2%)
Total	28.5	(100%)	16.0	(100%)	22.0	0.3	66.8	(100%)

  (ii) *Loans*

To:	IBRD only	
Burma	10.0	(28%)
Ceylon	6.8	(19%)
Pakistan	8.2	(23%)
Philippines	1.5	(4%)
Thailand	8.7	(25%)
Total	35.2	(100%)

Notes: a United Nations Technical Assistance.
  b United Nations International Children's Fund.
  c International Bank.
  d United Nations High Commissioner for Refugees.

In the multilateral account – international aid extended to East Asia indirectly, through the UN Agencies – grants were nearly twice as much as loans, but both were on a comparatively small scale. Bilateral relations greatly predominate in this sphere. The only lender, in the multilateral relationship, is the International Bank. Of the multilateral grants nearly one quarter went to the humanly invaluable relief work of UNICEF; three-quarters to the operations of the Technical Assistance organizations and the International Bank, more immediately and directly implementing economic development as such.

The grand total of foreign aid extended to the whole world by the United States from the end of the war in 1945 to the end of 1964 was nearly $100,000 million. Almost exactly one-third of this was military aid ($34,000 million) and two-thirds economic and technical ($62,000 million); 40 per cent of this went, however, to West Europe; and about 25 per cent of the total aid (but over 30 per cent of the military part) to the East Asian Region. Main recipients in East Asia were the following (in $000 million):

South Korea 5.78 (36 per cent of which military)

China: Taiwan (including Mainland China until 1948) 5.48 (62 per cent military)

India 4.30 economic aid; plus an undisclosed amount of military aid.

South Vietnam 2.68 (only 24 per cent military)

Pakistan 2.25 in economic aid; plus an undisclosed amount of military aid.

The above figures total $20,490 million. This sum appears to be about three times the total US aid to Latin America, over eight times the total US aid to Africa and some 80 per cent larger than total US aid to the Middle East and West Asia, but only about half that given to Europe.[4]

If, however, only that portion of the aid which is identified as economic and technical is counted, a world total of some $62,000 million appears. Of which East Asia received about two-thirds, about four times as much as Latin America and ten times as much as Africa, but about 25 per cent less than West Europe.

The figures in these latter comparisons – which comprise the whole period since 1945 – exaggerate the shares of China and Europe, in respect of the large amounts of aid in those areas at the very beginning of that period.

Further it must be strongly emphasized that the distinction between military and other aid is far indeed from absolute. Much of the military expenditure contributes very widely, directly and immediately to economic development in the recipient countries. The wording above, inevitably contrasting the two categories very broadly, should not be allowed to give the false impression that military expenditure is not 'economic' or 'developmental'.

In 1956-64, the fifteen member-countries of the OECD extended a total of about $45,000 million in aid to developing countries – this, however, includes private net long-term investment but excludes credits.[5] Balancing these *per capita* items, the aid component in the above figure would seem to be about $40,000 million. Of this, about 75 per cent was from the United States. The aid of the others (the West European countries and Japan) is interesting but, in East Asia particularly, small compared to that of the US; details will not be pursued here.

COMMUNIST AID

Finally, aid by the Communist countries must be considered. It has been extremely small compared to that of the Western world – some 5 per cent of the latter's total, or 6 per cent of the US'. It amounted altogether to some $6,400 million up to the end of 1964, of which exactly two-thirds was extended by the Soviet Union, just over one-fifth by the East European countries and the remainder (one eighth) by Communist China.

The countries concerned in Asia are those appearing in Table 10.4.

Forty-seven per cent of the total Communist bloc aid has thus been devoted to the Asian Region: the rest going to the Middle East (29 per cent), Africa (19 per cent), and Latin America (5 per cent). Russia apportioned her aid similarly between: Asia 48 per cent, Middle East 32 per cent, Africa 18 per cent and Latin America 2 per cent. The East Europeans' priorities were slightly different: Asia 41 per cent, Middle East 29 per cent, Africa 16 per cent and Latin America 14 per cent. China extended no aid to Latin America, giving 49 per cent of her total aid to Asia, 32 per cent to Africa and 19 per cent to the Middle East – the relatively heavy emphasis by China on areas other than Asia is

H

Table 10.4. *Aid to Asia by the Communist countries*[6]
(Grand total to end of 1964, in $ million)

To:	USSR	East Europe	China	Total
Afghanistan	541	7	—	548
Burma	14	1	84	99
Cambodia	21	5	50	76
Ceylon	30	10	41	81
India	1,022	255	—	1,277
Indonesia	369	260	107	736
Nepal	20	—	43	63
Pakistan	44	28	60	132
Total	2,061	566	385	3,012

noteworthy. 68 per cent of the Communist aid to Asia came from the Soviet Union, 19 per cent from East Europe and only 13 per cent from Communist China. Of Russia's aid to Asia, one half (or nearly one quarter of Russia's worldwide aid) went to India – to which China is hostile, and extends no aid. East Europe also concentrated its aid on India – and on Indonesia, to which China's largest contribution was also directed (but in that quarter, too, China's relations became hostile in 1965). Thanks to the large contribution of the USSR, India received 42 per cent of the total Communist aid to Asia.

In *per capita* terms, however, the ranking is interestingly different. The smaller countries had far greater amounts per head of Communist aid than the more populous ones: and they were the states on the Communist borders. It should be noted that all the percentages in the last two paragraphs exclude Cuba, which received a large but unknown amount of aid from the other Communist states.[7]

Chapter 11

THE RESULTS FOR THE ASIANS

THE WELFARE OF THE INDIVIDUAL

Over the two post-war decades the East Asian countries made extensive, varied and arduous efforts in economic development. In the final assessment, an attempt must be made to measure the gain for the average Asian, the ordinary individual in this Region. The broad answer must be that the large increase in population, on a base already huge, has swallowed most of the material gains. The Asian masses remain in dire poverty: the dangers of this situation are being intensified rather than mitigated. It is advisable to begin by stressing the low levels among these people in respect of some of the most elementary requirements. Health, shelter and security of livelihood are considered below – such aspects as food and clothing having been reviewed in earlier chapters.

MEDICAL FACILITIES

To emphasize the low level of welfare in the Region, the figures of the numbers of persons per physician may be cited. The total of qualified medical practitioners proper (excluding midwives, etc.) was in approximate round numbers in 1962, except where otherwise indicated, as follows. The lowest level in the Region would seem to be in Nepal: 76,000 inhabitants per physician. This is apparently exceeded by only one country in the world – the Upper Volta with 76,100. Another African country came next, the Niger with 72,000. Indonesia had 41,000, South Vietnam 29,000 (similar to the Sudan, and a little better than Somalia or Togo), Cambodia 25,000.

In a better-off group are Pakistan with (1960) 11,000, Thailand (1961) 10,000, Burma 9,600, India (1961) 5,800, the Philippines (1961) 5,000, South Korea and Hong Kong with 2,900 each, and Taiwan with 1,700. Even the lowest of these are rather shocking figures. A high level is reached only in Japan, with 900. This is a better figure than in England and Wales, which had (1960) 960; but less than Scotland (760 in 1960) or the USA (760), while the best ratios in the world are claimed by the USSR (500), West Berlin (440) and Israel (400).[1]

Unfortunately it is not possible to make comparisons with earlier years to show how far the proportion of physicians to the total population may have increased since the war; but the improvement cannot have been very considerable. More probably there was some deterioration; expatriate doctors in the colonial services left, and the annual output of new graduates would be numbered in thousands (some of whom emigrated to the developed countries) while the total population increased by millions. Against this it must certainly be noted that the methods of reducing or controlling disease greatly improved. However, the poor conditions in this aspect must be strongly emphasized. The same applies to the conditions of housing.

HOUSING

Table 11.1 summarizes available indications on this subject. Under this heading also, it is unfortunately not possible to give a time-series indicating what *per capita* improvement there may have been; but it is again unlikely that the improvement has

Table 11.1. Housing (densities)

	Year	Average number of Persons per household	Rooms per dwelling	Per cent of dwellings with 1-2 rooms	3-4 rooms	5 or more rooms
CEYLON	1953					
Urban		5.7	2.5	63%	27%	10%
Rural		4.8	2.2	70%	25%	5%
Total		4.9	2.2	69%	25%	6%
INDIA	1960					
Urban		5.2	1.9	78%	16%	6%
Rural		5.2	2.0	76%	18%	6%
Total		5.2	2.0	76%	17%	6%
JAPAN	1958					
Urban		4.7	3.4	35%	42%	23%
Rural		5.2	4.0	24%	44%	32%
Total		4.9	3.6	31%	43%	26%
KOREA South	1960					
Urban		5.5	1.9	78%	19%	3%
Rural		5.7	2.3	65%	32%	3%
Total		5.6	2.2	69%	28%	3%

	Year	Average number of Persons per household	Rooms per dwelling	Per cent of dwellings with 1-2 rooms	3-4 rooms	5 or more rooms
MALAYSIA	1960					
Brunei:						
urban		4.5	2.3	73%	21%	6%
Sabah:						
urban		5.2	2.3	65%	28%	7%
Sarawak:						
urban		5.9	2.9	61%	31%	8%
PAKISTAN	1960					
Urban		5.6	1.8	81%	14%	5%
Rural		5.4	1.7	83%	15%	3%
Total		5.4	1.7	83%	15%	3%
PHILIPPINES	1956					
Urban		6.0	—	—	—	—
Rural		5.5	—	—	—	—
Total		5.7	—	—	—	—
VIETNAM						
South	1962					
Urban		6.2	—	—	—	—
cf. *UK*						
England and Wales	1961					
Urban		3.0	4.7	5%	38%	58%
Rural		3.1	5.0	2%	36%	62%
Total		3.0	4.8	4%	37%	59%
USA	1960					
Urban		3.2	4.8	7%	33%	60%
Rural		3.6	5.1	4%	30%	66%
Total		3.3	4.9	6%	32%	62%

been considerable, with the increase in population strongly out-pacing the production of more or better living accommodation. Table 11.1 sufficiently emphasizes the disparities – if it is borne in mind also that usually a 'room' and a 'dwelling' in Asia and in Western countries differ so much in size and in quality as to be hardly comparable. The great majority of people in East Asia live in one-roomed or two-roomed dwellings; the majority in the Anglo-Saxon countries live in dwellings with five or more rooms. The average number of persons in a household in East Asia is nearly five, in the Western countries about three. There is more than one room per person in the Western countries, two or more persons per room in Asian countries.

NATIONAL INCOME

It is with these welfare-evaluations in mind that the increases in gross domestic product should be considered: such increases are on an extremely low base, in real terms. Table 11.2 gives figures of the total product for the various Regions in the world.

Table 11.2. *Gross domestic product, at parity rates: total, by Regions*[3]
(At factor cost; index 1953 = 100)

	1953 million $	1953 % of world[e]	1958 million $	1958 % of world	1958 index	1963 million $	1963 % of world[e]	1963 index
Africa:								
South Africa	6,389	0.9%	8,298	0.9%	130	11,421	0.9%	179
Other	18,000[e]	2.5%	22,602	2.4%	126	26,350[e]	2.1%	146
Total	24,389	3.4%	30,900	3.3%	127	37,771[e]	3.0%	155
N. America								
Canada	21,897	3.1%	28,972	3.1%	132	37,280	3.0%	170
USA	333,249	47.2%	406,474	43.5%	122	528,287	42.1%	159
Total	355,146	50.3%	435,446	46.6%	123	565,567	45.0%	159
Central America								
Total	12,664	1.8%	19,154	2.0%	151	24,770[e]	2.0%	196
South America								
Total	24,478[e]	3.5%	34,600	3.7%	141	43,532[e]	3.5%	178
Asia[a]								
Japan	19,478	2.8%	31,020	3.3%	159	60,213	4.8%	309
Others	58,885[e]	8.3%	73,180	7.8%	124	89,356[e]	7.1%	152
Total	78,363	11.1%	104,200	11.1%	133	149,569	11.9%	191
Europe[a]								
Total	210,711[e]	28.6%	292,500	31.3%	139	411,085[e]	32.7%	195
Oceania								
Total	12,944[e]	1.8%	18,100	1.9%	140	23,638[e]	1.9%	183
World[a]	706,031[e]	100%	935,000	100%	132	1,255,932[e]	100%	178

Notes: [a] Excluding Communist states.

[e] Estimated.

The percentage increase for Asia in 1953-8 was thus about the world average and above that of North America; but this result is due to the inclusion of Japan, the rest of Asia showing a percentage which is higher than the United States but lower than all others in the table. For 1958-63, the same considerations for the most part apply still more strongly, though in this period the underdeveloped countries of Asia showed a larger increase than those of Africa and a smaller increase than the United States.

Particulars for the individual countries of East Africa are given in Table 11.3.

Table 11.3. *Index of total and* per capita *product, Asian region*[4]
(Index, GDP at market prices; 1953 = 100)
(*TP* = total product; *PC* = *per capita*)

	1950 TP	1950 PC	1958 TP	1958 PC	1963 TP	1963 PC
Burma	78	82	120	115	163	133
Cambodia	..	..	123	109	..	..
Ceylon	91	97	115	101	132	105
China: Taiwan	..	..	139	116	197	140
India[a]	88	92	116	105	134[b]	111[b]
Japan[c]	..	..	137	130	249	226
Korea, S.	..	..	128	118	156	125
Pakistan[a]	92	98	109	97	127[b]	104[b]
Philippines[d]	83	91	130	112	161	120[b]
Thailand	..	..	118	93	173	118
cf. UK	95	96	110	109	129	123
USA	86	91	109	100	133	113

Notes: [a] NDP at factor cost. [b] 1962. [c] GNP at market prices. [d] NNP at factor cost.

Limited figures are cited by the United Nations for Mainland China. In terms of the Marxian definition of national income ('net material product at market prices') with 1955 as 100, the total product index rose as follows in the next five years: 115 in 1956, 119 in 1957, leaping to 161 in 1958, 197 in 1959 and 218 in 1960. While the *per capita* index rose as follows: to 112 in 1956, the same (no rise) in 1957, 147 in 1958, 175 in 1959 and 191 in 1960. A short run of figures is also given for the Federation of Malaya, with 1955 = 100, whereby the total product index 1956-61 was 103-106-106-111-122-130, but the *per capita* 101-100-97-98-105-108.

These figures epitomize the way in which large population increases heavily offset – in terms of individual welfare, for the average person – the rise in total income. This rise has represented a prodigious and arduous effort on the part of these poor countries. All these Asian nations (except latterly Japan) have been and remain at income levels far below the Western lands. In terms of the *rate* of progress in raising income (national product) even the weakest among them (Pakistan, India, Ceylon) did, however, in this period roughly equal the UK or USA; the rest markedly outstripped them.

In *per capita* terms the same three Asian countries did not progress so fast ('index-number-wise') as the UK and USA, but others did markedly better. The dragging effect is a function both of absolutely high populations and of high demographic growth-rates; affecting both large and small countries, various economic and social systems. Japan is again outstandingly exceptional in Asia, with very high recent rises in the indices – to double the US figure, in the case of the *per capita* index. The spread between the two graph-lines, total product and product per person, is marked; moreover it appears to have increased, as may be immediately visualized by subtracting the figures in each of the year-columns.

The divergence between total and *per capita* GDP is further shown in Table 11.4.

Table 11.4. *Annual growth in total and* per capita *gross domestic product*[5]

| | | Increase in GDP per annum | |
	Period	Total	per capita
Burma	1954-62	5.0	2.7
Cambodia	1953-58[a]	3.8	0.8
Ceylon	1953-61	3.7	1.1
China: Mainland	1953-58	12.6	9.5
China: Taiwan	1954-62	6.9	3.2
India	1953-60[c]	3.5	1.4
Indonesia	1953-58[c]	3.9	1.7
Japan	1954-62[d]	10.1	9.1
Korea: S.	1954-62	4.6	1.9
Malaya	1956-60[a]	4.1	0.8
Pakistan	1953-61[c]	2.7	0.6
Philippines	1954-62[d]	5.1	2.2
Thailand	1954-62	10.1	6.8
cf. UK	1954-62	2.7	2.1
USA	1954-62	2.9	1.2
USSR	1953-61[b]	9.4	7.5

Notes: [a] GDP at constant factor cost.
 [b] Marxian definition (net material product) at constant prices.
 [c] NDP at constant factor cost.
 [d] GNP at constant market prices.

Ostensibly the growth rates in the region may thus appear satisfactory at first sight, both in the total and *per capita*; but the same considerations apply as before, e.g. that a 2 per cent rise in the UK or 1 per cent in the US represents a multiple of the same change in an Asian country. The differences between the trends in the total and the *per capita* are relatively much greater in the underdeveloped than the developed countries and the gaps are increasing.

The difficulties of international income-comparisons are well known. In this connection it must be emphasized that exchange-rate uncertainties are particularly great in the case of the East Asian countries, their non-monetarized sectors large and their patterns of living in many respects peculiar.

INFLATION

Price rises affected the poor Asians heavily; it may be convenient at this point to identify the trends in the region in this respect (Table 11.5).

Table 11.5. Price indices[6]
(1953 = 100)

| | Wholesale | | Consumer | | | |
| | | | All items | | Food | |
	1953	1963	1958	1963	1958	1963
Burma (Rangoon)	..	..	108	107	110	111
Cambodia (Phnompenh)	..	..	135	166	141	172
Ceylon (Colombo)	..	..	103	107	100	95
China: Taiwan	102[a]	146[b]	134[b]	198[b]	138[b]	196[b]
Hong Kong[c]	..	..	96	101	93	100
India	107	127	109	125	109	124
Indonesia (Jakarta)	147[d]	..	..	(1254[f])	258	3292
Japan (Tokyo)	98	101	108[b]	137[b]	106[b]	139[b]
Korea: S. (Seoul)	143[g]	200[g]	339	628	310	552
Malaya: Fed.	..	..	97	100	96	100
Malaya: Singapore	..	..	92	94	92	94
Pakistan (Karachi)	..	(111[h])	110	116	117	120
Philippines (Manila)	103	132	105	114	111	128
Thailand (Bangkok)[c]	126	125	124	130	125	133
Vietnam: S. (Saigon)	124	146	130	155	125	149
cf. UK	111[i]	120[i]	119	123	107	109
USA	108	108	108	114	107	110

Notes: [a] Taipei. [b] Whole country. [c] Clerical and skilled workers. [d] Imported goods. [f] (1958=100). [g] 1955=100. [h] (1957-8=100). [i] Finished goods.

The difficulties of international income-comparisons may be avoided insofar as the effects of inflationary movements are concerned, by using one set of figures published by the United Nations Statistical Office which takes account of variations in the value of both the US dollar (in which the figures are stated) and the national currency of each country compared. This is done by means of 'calculated parity rates' which 'adjust the . . . exchange rates for each country by the relative change in the level of prices from 1938 to the year in question between the United States and the country concerned' (using implicit or explicit national price-indices, as available and appropriate. Such figures may thus be taken broadly as 'net of inflation' on both sides of the exchange rate, or as being in purchasing power parity terms. The parity rates for the Asian region are given in Table 11.6; with indices of their variations, which are of interest as showing the decline in the purchasing power of the national currency units, relative to that of the US dollar. These parity rates have already been used above, in Table 11.2.

Table 11.6. *Parity rates* for international income-comparisons[7]
(Units of national currency per US $) (index 1953 = 100)

	1953	1958	index	1963	index
Burma	5.01	4.41	(88)	4.05[a]	(81)
Ceylon	4.99	4.76	(95)	4.45	(89)
China: Taiwan	29.2	37.0	(127)	48.3	(165)
Hong Kong	..	13.9	(..)	13.8	(99[b])
India	4.51	4.57	(101)	4.90[a]	(109)
Indonesia	17.8	27.6	(155)	..	(..)
Japan	313	303	(97)	338	(108)
Korea: S.	22.1	65.8	(298)	109	(493)
Malaya: Fed.	..	3.57	(..)	3.35[a]	(94[b])
Pakistan	4.57	4.66	(102)	4.64[a]	(102)
Philippines	3.76	3.45	(92)	4.09	(109)
Thailand	18.9	19.4	(103)	18.6	(98)
Vietnam: S.	..	73.5	(..)	78.6[a]	(107[b])
cf. UK	.285	.311	(109)	.325	(114)

Notes: [a] 1962. [b] 1958 = 100.

Using these parity rates, GDP in the countries of the region is found to be as follows (Table 11.7).

On the basis of the parity rates the total incomes of the countries of the region have satisfactorily risen, as shown in Table 11.7. The total for all of them would appear to have risen by

Table 11.7. *Gross domestic product, total, at parity rates*
(Table 11.6)[8]
(At factor cost, in us $ million; index 1953 = 100)

	1953	1958	index	1963	index
Burma	998	1,332	(133)	1,755[a]	(176)
Ceylon	899	1,153	(128)	1,494	(166)
China: Taiwan	645	958	(149)	1,491	(231)
Hong Kong	..	302	..	455	(151[b])
India	24,385	28,737	(118)	33,336[a]	(137)
Indonesia	..	4,866	..	6,518	(134[b])
Japan	19,478	31,020	(159)	60,213	(309)
Korea: S.	1,780	2,560	(144)	3,345	(188)
Malaya: Fed.	..	1,206	..	1,638[a]	(136[b])
Malaya: Singapore	..	488	..	..	..
Pakistan	4,512	5,722	(127)	7,637[a]	(169)
Philippines	2,001	2,908	(145)	3,848	(192)
Thailand	1,607	2,092	(130)	3,221	(200)
Vietnam: S.	..	947	..	1,083	(114[b])
Total	56,305	84,291	(150)	126,014	(224)
Total excluding Japan	36,827	53,271	(145)	65,801	(179)
cf. UK	51,825	64,199	(124)	80,530	(155)
USA	333,249	406,474	(122)	528,287	(159)

Notes: [a] 1962. [b] 1958=100.

perhaps 45 per cent in 1953-8, and roughly doubled by 1963. The total indices compare favourably with those of the United Kingdom and United States. The true perspective is, however, determined by four main considerations.

In the first place, the indices for the individual countries show great disparities between them, ranging from the comparatively low percentage increases in India through the high ones in Taiwan and Thailand to the very high one in Japan. Japan's gross product was about 20 per cent less than India's in 1953; in 1958 it was 8 per cent larger than India's and in 1963 some 80 per cent larger. Japan's figure was about one third of the region's total in 1953, when India's was some 45 per cent; Japan's share rose to 37 per cent in 1958 and 48 per cent in 1963, while India's declined to 34 per cent in 1958 and 26 per cent in 1962. If Japan is excluded the regional index is greatly reduced, especially in the latter half of the decade.

In the second place and more important, all these countries' income bases are small, some extremely small. Japan's GDP was less than 40 per cent of the UK's in 1953, rising to about 75 per cent in 1963. India's was 47 per cent of the UK's in 1953, declining to about 40 per cent in 1962-3. Even Japan's GDP was only 7.6 per cent of the world total in 1958, India's 7.0 per cent and all the other Asian countries in Table 11.7 together only 5.4 per cent.

The third consideration, qualitatively decisive, is the familiar one of the size of the Asian populations and their rapid rates of growth, with drastic implications for the all-important *per capita* results. If the GDPs of India and Japan fluctuated as indicated in the last paragraph between 40 per cent and 75 per cent of that of the UK, it must, of course, be stressed that India's population was over seven times the UK's and increasing greatly; Japan's about double, though comparatively stable.

The exact *per capita* comparisons are given in Table 11.8, on the same basis of the parity rates. The index figures are in all cases very significantly reduced. Roughly speaking, even in the United States 16 per cent of the income-rise was 'taken up' by increased population, in the United Kingdom some 5 per cent; but the corresponding Asian figures were Burma 18 per cent, Ceylon 22 per cent, Taiwan 28 per cent, Hong Kong (1958-63) 21 per cent, India 17 per cent, Japan 10 per cent, Korea 21 per cent, Federation of Malaya (1958-63) 12 per cent, Pakistan 17 per cent, Thailand 31 per cent and South Vietnam (1958-63) 12 per cent.

Even so, all the Asian countries did make notable *per capita* progress. If their populations had been stabilized, output per person would, however, have increased by the percentages indicated in Table 11.7; if their rates of increase had been reduced to that of the UK, their *per capita* increases would have been about 5 per cent less than the indices in Table 11.7 minus 100.

The fourth aspect of concern is the increasing gap – which tends actually to be concealed by the foregoing index and percentage-increase figures – between the income levels of the Asian countries and those of the advanced Western countries. The gap between the *per capita* income of the United States and others has been increasing, for virtually all countries in the world. This has applied even to the United Kingdom in recent years. Percentagewise, the UK's 'gap' as against the US has in fact increased more than that of some countries in the Asian Region (though less than that of others).

Table 11 8. *Gross domestic product,* per capita, *at parity rates*
(*Table* 11.6) *at factor cost* ($)[9]
(Index 1953 = 100)

	1953	1958	(*index*)	1963	(*index*)
Burma	52	66	(127)	75	(144)
Ceylon	108	123	(114)	141	(130)
China : Taiwan	73	92	(126)	121	(166)
Hong Kong	. .	106	. .	127	(120[b])
India	65	70	(108)	74[a]	(114)
Indonesia	60	73	(122)	. .	. .
Japan	225	339	(151)	628	(279)
Korea : S.	83	110	(133)	124	(149)
Malaya : Fed.	. .	186	. .	222[a]	(119[b])
Singapore	. .	322	. .	. .	. .
Pakistan	56[b]	64	(114)	79[a]	(141)
Philippines	90	113	(126)	127	(141)
Thailand	82	84	(102)	112	(137)
Vietnam : S.	. .	73	. .	73	(100[b])
Average of above	90	130		173	
cf. All Asia	. .	112		173	
All Africa	. .	125		. .	
All S. America	. .	257		. .	
All Europe	. .	996		. .	
All Oceania	. .	1,202		. .	
UK	1,019	1,238	(121)	1,497	(147)
USA	2,080	2,324	(112)	2,790	(134)

Notes: [a] 1962. [b] 1958 = 100.

The UK gap is, however, about half that of the Asian countries; this aspect must, of course, also be considered in relation to the respective income levels. The UK gap per person in 1963, for example, could be said to be almost enough to keep another Briton alive at the British standard; but it would have kept nearly twenty Burmese, or ten people in Ceylon, twelve in Taiwan, twenty Indians, two Japanese, and so on, at their current standards. Table 11.9 gives the figures, in which the absolute levels should be pondered, as well as the index-increases.

PRODUCTIVITY

The question of productivity is therefore a vital one. Unfortunately the information on this subject is scanty and generally unreliable. In 1965 ECAFE analysed productivity for some countries on the following lines. (Table 11.10.)

Table 11.9. The per capita income gap: Asian countries and others[10]

Gross domestic product per capita in us $ at parity rates (Table 11.6) at factor cost. (Index 1953=100).'Gap'=difference between each country and the United Kingdom and United States.

	cf. UK					cf. USA				
	1953 gap	1958 gap	1958 (index)	1963 gap	1963 (index)	1953 gap	1958 gap	1958 (index)	1963 gap	1963 (index)
Burma	967	1,172	(121)	1,422	(147)	2,028	2,258	(111)	2,715	(134)
Ceylon	911	1,115	(122)	1,356	(149)	1,972	2,135	(108)	2,649	(134)
China: Taiwan	946	1,146	(121)	1,376	(145)	2,007	2,166	(108)	2,669	(133)
Hong Kong	..	1,132	..	1,370	(121b)	..	2,152	..	2,663	(124b)
India	954	1,168	(122)	1,423	(149)	2,015	2,254	..	2,716	(135)
Indonesia	959	1,165	(121)	..	..	2,020	2,251	(111)	..	..
Japan	794	899	(113)	869	(109)	1,855	1,985	(107)	2,162	(116)
Korea: S.	936	1,128	(121)	1,373	(147)	1,997	2,214	(111)	2,666	(134)
Malaya: Fed.	..	1,052	..	1,275	(121b)	..	2,138	..	2,568	(120)
Malaya: Singapore	..	916	..	..	..	..	2,002	..	..	..
Pakistan	963	1,174	(122)	1,418	(147)	2,024	2,260	(112)	2,711	(134)
Philippines	929	1,125	(121)	1,370	(134)	1,990	2,211	(111)	2,663	(134)
Thailand	937	1,154	(123)	1,385	(148)	1,998	2,240	(112)	2,678	(134)
Vietnam: S.	..	1,165	..	1,424	(122b)	..	2,251	..	2,171	(121b)
cf. UK	—	—	—	—	—	1,061	1,086	(102)	1,311	(124)

Note: b 1958=100.

Table 11.10. *Value of output per worker in certain industries*[11]
(*per capita* of employed population in all industries, in current US $)

		$	(*index*)
Japan[b]	1950	264	(100)
	1960	734	(278)
Philippines[b]	1948	403	(100)
	1960	600	(149)
China: Taiwan[a]	1956	416	
Ceylon[a]	1953	315	
India[b]	1951	149	(100)
	1961	166	(111)
Pakistan[b]	1954-56	165	
cf. Australia[a]	1954	2,643	(100)
	1961	3,461	(131)
New Zealand[a]	1954	3,059	

Notes: [a] GDP at factor cost.
[b] NDP.

Unfortunately this analysis cannot be extended to other countries. For the countries in Table 11.10 it is interesting to note the following indications. There has been some rise in output per head in money terms, almost trebling in Japan, very satisfactory also in the Philippines, but only slight in such countries as India. In India – to exemplify the contrast very roughly – there was only an 11 per cent rise in ten years, compared to a 30 per cent rise in Australia in seven years; and the output per worker in Australia in 1954 was valued at over seventeen times that per worker in India in 1951, while in 1961 the figure for Australia was over twenty times the figure for India.

It must be noted, however, that the gains in the money value of output were much greater in the non-agricultural employments than in agriculture; in some countries manufacturing showed the largest increase, in others service trades and the like. Japan is again the exception.

In the Asian countries except in Ceylon (where a relatively high-value plantation agriculture is mainly in question) the *per capita* output is about three times as high in manufacturing and tertiary occupations as it is in agriculture; and (except in Japan) the non-agricultural pursuits appear more distinctly to offer increasing returns. In such countries as India the increase in the

Table 11.11. *Value of output per worker, in sectors — agricultural and other*[12]
(*Per capita* of employed population, in current US $)

		Agriculture $	(index)	All non-agricultural $	(index)	Manufacturing $	(index)
Ceylon[a]	1953	322	—	307	—	150	—
China: Taiwan[a]	1956	245	—	630	—	629	—
India[b]	1951	104	(100)	268	(100)	261	(100)
	1961	105	(101)	349	(130)	314	(120)
Japan[b]	1950	142	(100)	379	(100)	413	(100)
	1960	344	(242)	925	(244)	1,013	(245)
Pakistan[b]	1954-6	139	—	212	—	177	—
Philippines[b]	1948	244	(100)	794	(100)	486	(100)
	1960	327	(134)	1,023	(129)	849	(175)
cf. Australia[a]	1954	3,221	(100)	2,554	(100)	2,625	(100)
	1961	4,003	(124)	3,394	(133)	3,618	(138)

Notes: [a] GDP at factor cost.
[b] NDP.

agricultural sector is almost imperceptible. In agriculture the Australian worker's output is valued at over ten times the highest of the Asian levels, or forty times the lowest; in industry it is 'only' about three and a half times Japan's, and twelve times the lowest Asian figure, but it is notable that all the Asian countries have improved their ratios in this comparison.

INDUSTRIALIZATION: A CONCLUSION

The enthusiasm of the Asian countries for industrialization is thus very understandable. Recently they have realized that a balanced development, with substantial investment also in agriculture, is essential. Their difficulties and their achievements have been broadly surveyed in this book. Since their overriding ambition continues to be the attainment of the 'take off' mainly through industrialization, the concluding comment must refer especially to the criteria of success in that respect.

One of the 'yardsticks' for measuring roughly the degree of progress in industrialization was applied above in the chapter in industrialization: namely, the *per capita* consumption of steel. Another may be cited here, in further illustration: the *per capita* use of power. The industrial revolution depends most directly on the application of power, which is the most certain measure of industrialization.

The growth in industrial power in Asia is quantitatively substantial, yet still on an extremely low base, much below world levels, and showing the relatively limited basis of industrialization. Table 11.12 summarizes overall results.

Table 11.12. Per capita *consumption of energy*[13]
(Kilograms of coal equivalent per annum)[a] (Index in brackets)

	1937		1950		1960	
World	900	(100)	1,054	(117)	1,405	(176)
USA	5,890	(100)	7,740	(131)	8,013	(136)
UK	4,280	(100)	4,420	(103)	4,920	(115)
USSR	1,000[b]	(100)	2,000[b]	(200)	2,847	(285)
China: Mainland	70	(100)	70[b]	(100)	600	(857)
India ⎱	90	(..)	170	(100)	250	(147)
Pakistan ⎰		(..)	100	(100)	140	(140)
Indonesia	50	(100)	60	(120)	134	(168)
Japan	930	(100)	780	(84)	1,164	(125)
Non-communist Asia	180	(100)	170	(94)	250	(139)
Africa	150	(100)	210	(140)	270	(180)
Australia	2,140[b]	(100)	2,600[b]	(121)	2,947	(138)

(*Notes:* a Technical progress is very marked and makes the statistical handling intricate. The accepted conversion-ratios of hydroelectric power to coal equivalent have been reduced, owing to technical changes, by more than 50 per cent; but the efficiency of conversion of coal into electricity has been raised, to a possibly offsetting extent. The comparability of various mineral resources, in terms of energy content, is rather uncertain. The data on the underdeveloped countries is certainly less adequate than that on the industrialized countries; the quantity of their mineral resources may have been underestimated, but their quality overestimated.
b Estimated.)

It must be strongly emphasized that the international disparities in this field are in fact very much greater than those in food and nutrition: 'the range of disparities in energy consumption among different countries are of the order of 100 to 1, whereas in food values they are only of the order of 6 to 1, and in calories less than 2 to 1.'

Communist China has certainly expanded greatly, on a very low base, but its figures are received with varying degrees of scepticism. The industrial performance of Japan (which really has 'caught up with the United Kingdom' in so many industrial respects – as China has aspired to do) is especially remarkable for efficiency of use of a restricted resource endowment. It strongly illustrates what can be achieved on a relatively low power-consumption base.

In the underdeveloped countries rapid industrialization requires at least a doubling of *per capita* power-use in each decade. This was perhaps half-way achieved, in East Asian developing countries, in the 1950s. The *per capita* power-use in Asia would have to be tripled or quadrupled in the Development Decade of the 1960s or the following decade, to establish the geometrical progression required for a real 'take off' into industrialization. Such a prospect appears extremely unlikely, though substantial improvement has been achieved, and will continue. The needs are, however, enormous, the dangers acute. To meet them even half-way, all efforts to assist the progress of Asia, by aid, trade, investment – and, it may be pleaded, support also in terms of study, thought and understanding, in terms of an informed and intelligent human sympathy – must not merely be maintained but must be very greatly multiplied and intensified. On this depends the future of the world.

LIST OF ABBREVIATIONS

EB = (ECAFE) *Economic Bulletin for Asia and the Far East* (quarterly, 1955–)

ECAFE = United Nations Economic Commission for Asia and the Far East

ES = (ECAFE) *Economic Survey of Asia and the Far East*, 1947—(UN Dept of Economic Affairs) (Sales No. II. F) (annual)

FAO = Food and Agriculture Organization of the United Nations

FEER = *Far Eastern Economic Review*, Hong Kong (weekly, 1946–)

UN(O) = United Nations (Organization)

UNDYB = *Demographic Year Book* of the UN, annual

UNFAYB = UN *Food and Agriculture Year Book* (annual)

UNSYB = *Statistical Year Book* of the UN, annual

YBNAS = (UN) *Year Book of National Accounts Statistics*

NOTES

INTRODUCTION

[1] ECAFE Press Releases. Wightman, D., *Towards Economic Co-operation in Asia*, London, 1963. [2] E.g. Kirby, E. S. (ed.), *Contemporary China*, Hong Kong, 1955–; Hsia, R. (ed.), *China Mainland Review*, Hong Kong, 1965–; *China Quarterly*, London. [3] Ginsburg, N. S., in *Asia in the Modern World*, New York, 1963, pp. 60 *seq.* [4] ES, EB, FEER, *passim.*

CHAPTER 1

[1] ES, 1947. [2] *Oxford Economic Atlas of the World*, 1954, pp. 108–9; 1965, pp. 18–19. [3] UNSYB, relevant years.

CHAPTER 2

[1] UNSYB, 1950, 1965, T.1. [2] ES, 1948–65. [3] UNDYB, 1965. [4] *Ibid.* [5] *Ibid.*, Belshaw, H., *Population Growth and Levels of Consumption*, London, 1956. [6] *Economist Diary*, London, 1964 *seq.* [7] See Introduction note [2], above.

CHAPTER 3

[1] UNFAYB, 1964. [2] *Ibid.* [3] ES, 1964, Brown, L. R., in *World Population and Food Supplies*, London, 1965. [4] ES, 1964, 1965. [5] ES, 1950–65. [6] *Ibid.* [7] FAO, Fisheries Year Book, 1964. [8] *Ibid.* [9] *Ibid.* [10] ES, 1964. [11] *Ibid.* [12] *Ibid.* [13] *Ibid.* [14] *Ibid.* [15] *Ibid.* (p. 117).

CHAPTER 4

[1] UNSYB and ES, relevant years. [2-7] *Ibid.* [8] From the above Tables. [9] *Ibid.* [10] *Ibid.* [11] *Loc. cit.*, [1-7] above. [12] From the preceding Tables. [13] *Ibid.* [14] *Ibid.*

[15] See note [1].   [16-20] *Ibid.*   [18a] Fadiman, C., *The Road to Huddersfield*, New York, 1963.   [21] From Table 4.19.   [22] From preceding Tables.   [23] UNSYB and ES, relevant years.   [24] *Ibid.*

CHAPTER 5

[1] UNSYB, 1964, T.47.   [2-5] *Ibid.*   [6] *Oxford Economic Atlas*, 1954, p. 80; 1965, p. 78.   [7] UNSYB, 1964, T.51.   [8] *Ibid.*, T.58.   [9] *Ibid.*, T.60, T.63.   [10] *Ibid.*, T.59.   [11] *Ibid.*, T.56.   [12] Rowe, J. F. W., *Primary Commodities in World Trade*, Cambridge, 1965.   [13] *Barclay's Bank Review*, London, xl–xli, 1965–66.   [14-16] *Ibid.*   [17] UNSYB, 1964, T.62.   [18] *Ibid.*, T.61.   [19] *Ibid.*, T.53.   [20] *Ibid.* (T.53).   [21] *Ibid.*, T.54.   [22] *Ibid.*, T.64.   [23] *Ibid.*, T.65.   [24] *Ibid.*, T.57.   [25] *Ibid.*, T.74.   [26] *Ibid.*, T.69.   [27] *Ibid.*, T.71.   [28] *Ibid.*, T.72. 73.   [29] *Ibid.*, T.70.   [30] *Ibid.*, T.68.   [31] *Ibid.*, T.66.   [32] *Ibid.*, T.67.

CHAPTER 6

[1] UNSYB, 1964, T.11.   [2] *Ibid.*, T.17.   [3] *Ibid.*   [4] *Ibid.*   [5] *Ibid.*, T.141.   [6] Census data.   [7] *Oxford Economic Atlas*, 1954, p. 81; 1965, p. 79.   [8] *Ibid.*   [9] *Ibid.*, 1954, p. 78; 1965, p 76.   [10] *Ibid.*, 1954, p. 83; 1965, p. 81.   [11] *Ibid.*, 1954, pp. 100–1; 1965, pp. 102–3.   [12] *Ibid.*, 1954, p. 102; 1965, p. 104.   [13] ES, relevant years.   [14] UNSYB, 1960, T.120; 1964, T.130.   [15] *Ibid.*, 1960, T.121; 1964, T.131.   [16] *Ibid.*, 1960, T.123; 1964, T.133.   [17] *Loc. cit.*, note [15].   [18] *Ibid.*   [19] *Ibid.*, 1960, T.80; 1964, T.89.   [20] *Ibid.*, 1960, T.82; 1964, T.91.   [21] *Ibid.*, 1960, T.81; 1964, T.90.   [22] *Ibid.*, 1960, T.83; 1964, T.92.   [23] *Ibid.*, 1960, T.84; 1964, T.93.   [24] *Ibid.*, 1960, T.85; 1964, T.94.   [25] *Ibid.*, 1960, T.87; 1964, T.97.   [26] *Ibid.*, 1960, T.88; 1964, T.98.   [27] *Ibid.*, 1960, T.89; 1964, T.99.   [28] *Ibid.*, 1960, T.102; 1964, T.116.   [29] *Ibid.*, 1960, T.107; 1964, T.116.   [30] *Ibid.*, 1960, T.108; 1964, T.117.   [31] *Loc. cit.*, notes [29] and [30], *ibid.*, 1960, T.105; 1964, T.114.   [32] *Ibid.*, 1960, T.91; 1964, T.100.   [33] *Ibid.*, 1960, T.92; 1964, T.101.   [34] *Ibid.*, 1960, T.93; 1964, T.102.   [35] *Ibid.*, 1960, T.94; 1964, T.103.   [36] 1960, Ts. 98–101, 104, 114–17; 1964, Ts. 107–10, 113, 124–6.   [37] *Ibid.*, 1960, T.11; 1964, T.13.   [38] *Ibid.*, 1960, T.10; 1964, T.11.   [39-40] *Ibid.*   [41] *Ibid.*, 1960, Ts. 5, 6; 1964, Ts. 7, 8.

CHAPTER 7

[1] UNSYB, 1960, T.139; 1964, T.149.   [2] *Ibid.*, 1960, T.141; 1964, T.151.   [3] *Ibid.*, 1960, T.140A; 1964, T.150A.   [4] *Ibid.*, 1964, T.150B.   [5] *Loc. cit.*, note [2] above.   [6] UNSYB, 1960, T.136; 1964, T.146.   [7] *Ibid.*, 1960, T.137; 1964, T.147.   [8] *Ibid.*, 1960, T.138; 1964, T.148.   [9] *Ibid.*, 1960, p. 376; 1964, p. 453.   [10] *Ibid.*, 1960, T.146; 1964, T.158.   [11] *Ibid.*, 1960, T.145; 1964, T.157.   [12] *Loc. cit.*, note [11].   [13] UNSYB, 1960, T.144; 1964, T.156.   [14] *Loc. cit.*, note [13].   [15] From the preceding Tables.

CHAPTER 8

[1] UNSYB, 1960, T.174; 1964, T.183.   [2] From the preceding Table.   [3] *Ibid.*

CHAPTER 9

[1] Wilcox, C., 'The Planning and Execution of Economic Development in South-East Asia', Harvard University Center for International Affairs, *Occasional Papers*, No. 10, 1965.   [2] Paauw, D. S., *Development Planning in Asia*, National Planning Association, Washington, 1965.   [3] FEER, January 7, 1965.   [4] Higgins, B., *Economic Development*, New York, 1959, p. 747.   [5] Roxas, S. K., *Organising the Government for Economic Development Administration. A Report to (the) President*, Manila, 1964, p. 1.   [6] Onslow, C. (ed.), *Asian Economic Development*,

London, 1965 ⁷ *Ibid.* and official publications, India and Pakistan. ⁸ Debates in the Lok Sabha, February 1966. ⁹ *Ibid.*, April 1966. ¹⁰ Allen, G. C., *Japan's Economic Expansion*, London 1965. ¹¹ Wu, Y-L., *The Economy of Communist China*, New York, 1965; Kang Chao, *The Rate and Pattern of Industrial Growth in Communist China*, Ann Arbor, 1965; Liu, T. C., and Yeh, K. C., *The Economy of the Chinese Mainland*, Princeton, 1965.

CHAPTER 10

¹ UNSYB, 1960, Ts. 155–8; 1961, Ts. 156–9. ² *Ibid.* ³ *Ibid.* ⁴ Arnold, H. J. P., *Aid for Development*, London, 1966, Appendix B. ⁵ *Ibid.*, Appendix D. ⁶ *Ibid.*, Appendix F. ⁷ Little, I. M. D., and Clifford, J. M., *International Aid*, London, 1965.

CHAPTER 11

¹ UNSYB, 1960, T.176; 1964, T.184. ² *Ibid.*, 1964, T.185. ³ YBNAS, relevant years. ⁴ UNSYB, 1964, T.172. ⁵ UNSYB, 1960–64, Ts. on National Accounts; YBNAS, relevant years; ES, 1964, pp. 233–4. ⁶ UNSYB, 1960, Ts. 160, 161; *ibid.*, 1964, Ts. 168–9. ⁷ UNSYB, 1960, T.167; 1964, T.176. ⁸ From preceding Tables. ⁹ *Ibid.* ¹⁰ *Ibid.* ¹¹ ES, 1965, p. 11; *ibid.*, 1964, p. 10. ¹² ES, 1964, T.1–5. ¹³ UNSYB, 1960, T.120–1; 1964, T.130–1.

abbreviations, 243
Afghanistan, 16
Africa, 24, 31; aid, 224-5; cement, 133; chemicals, 132; energy, 134f, 241; industrial, 155; iron, 102; medical, 227-8; national incomes, 230; population, 33f; railways, 166; shipping, 162f; telephones, 169; (UN)ECA, 15
agriculture, 30, 42f, 87f, 239
aid, international, Ch. 10; 24, 40, 46; Cambodia, 203; Pakistan, 215
alloys, 103f, 148f
aluminium, 106, 154; bauxite, 154
Annam, 15
antimony, 112
apartheid, 23-4
apathy, 25
Arabs, 22
arable areas, 51
areas of countries, 24-5
armaments, 28, 196f
asbestos, 113
Asia, concepts of; Asianism, 19, 21
Australia, 16, 54f; aid, 222; cement, 133; chemicals, 131f; copper, 110; energy, 241; iron, 102; labour, 126-7; lead, 111-12; meat, 55; nutrition, 56f; population, 34; productivity, 239f; tin, 107; trade, 68
Austria, 153

balance of payments, 123
balance of trade, 66, 71, 79-84
balanced growth, 30, 52
Bandung group, 18
bauxite, v. aluminium
Belgium, 107
beverages, 120
birth control, v. family planning
Bolivia, 107-8
Borneo, British North, 15-16; energy, 138; population, 33f
brain drain, 228
Brazil, 102
budgets, Ch.8
Burma, 15, 16, 19, 21, 26; aid 24, 220f; area, 24; budget 178f; cement, 133; cereals, 58; copper,

110; customs duties, 200; defence, 196-7; development budget, 197-8; energy, 134f; exports, 24; food, 42f; imports, 24; industrial, 155; inflation 233f; irrigation, 51; lead, 112; lumber, 152; mail, 173f; manganese, 104; meat, 55; medical, 227; motor vehicles, 168; national income, 24, 133, 231f; nickel, 109; petroleum, 100, 154; planning, 206-7; population, 24, 33, 36; railways, 167; salt, 114; shipping, 162; silver, 115; taxes, 199f; telegraphs, 170f; telephones, 169-70; tin, 105; trade, 62f; tungsten, 109; zinc, 111-2
Brunei, 16; energy, 138; petroleum, 100.

calories, 56-7
Cambodia, 15, 16; aid, 24, 203, 220f; area, 24; dairy products, 55; energy, 135f; exports, 24; food, 49; imports, 24; inflation, 233f; lumber, 152; mail, 173f; medical, 227; motor vehicles, 168; national income, 24, 231f; planning, 203; population, 24, 33f; railways, 167; salt, 114; steel, 125; telegraphs, 170f; telephones, 169-70
Canada, aid, 222; cotton, 140; industrial, 119; iron, 102; lumber, 151; national income, 230; nickel, 108; population, 34; rubber, 148; silver, 115; steel, 125; tin, 107; trade, 68; wood pulp, 152
capital: output ratio, 34
capital goods, 88f
capitalism, 29, 125
cassava, 26, 46f
Catholicism, Roman, 40
caustic soda, 153
cement, 132-3
census, 36-7, 39
cereals, Ch. 3; 58; production, 59; trade, 45
Ceylon, 15, 16, 19; agriculture, 239; aid, 24, 26, 220f; area, 24; budget, 179f; cement, 133; cereals, 58f; cotton, 139f; debt, 194f; development

budget, 198; duties, 200; energy, 135f; exports, 24; food, 43f; gas, 138; housing, 228; imports, 24; industrial, 155; inflation, 232f; irrigation, 51; labour, 126, 157-8; lumber, 152; mail, 173f; meat, 55; motor vehicles, 168; national income, 24, 133, 231f; nutrition, 56; planning, 207; population, 24, 33f; productivity, 239f; railways, 167; salt, 114; shipping, 162; steel, 125; taxes, 199f; telegraphs, 170f; telephones, 169-70; trade, 62f; welfare, 197

chemicals, 113-14, 120, 129f

Chile, 104, 115

China: Mainland, 15, 17, 26; aid, 22, 203, 217, 224-6; aluminium, 113, 154; antimony, 112; area, 23; caustic soda, 153; cement, 132-3; chemicals, 131f; coal, 99; coke, 151; Communism, 28-30; copper, 110; cotton, 139f; energy, 241; fibres, 146f; family planning, 37; fish, 53f; food, 43; Great Leap Forward, 126, 149, 217; industrial, 18-19, 216-17, 241; instability, 126; iron, 101-2, 127f, 148-51, 217; lead, 111-12; manganese, 104; molybdenum, 104-5; national income, 231f; paper, 152; petroleum, 100; planning, 216-17; population, 33f; railways, 167; and Russia, 217; salt, 114; shipping, 160f; soda ash, 153; steel, 127f, 149-51, 217; tin, 104f; trade, 61f, 69; transport, 217; tungsten, 109; zinc, 111

China: Taiwan, 15, 16, 19; aid, 24, 26, 29, 220-4; aluminium, 154; asbestos, 113; area, 24; caustic soda, 153; cement, 132-3; cereals, 58f; chemicals, 131f; coal, 99; coke, 151; copper, 110; cotton, 139f; energy, 135f; exports, 24; fertilizers, 153; fibres, 145f; fish, 53f; food, 43f; gas, 138-9; gold, 115; imports, 24; industry, 155; iron, 148-50; irrigation, 51; labour, 126f; mail, 173f; meat, 55; medical, 227; motor vehicles, 168; national income, 24, 133, 231f; natural gas, 100; nutrition, 56; paper, 153; petroleum, 100, 154; population, 24, 33f; productivity, 239f; rail-

ways, 167; salt, 114; shipping, 154, 160f; soda ash, 153; steel, 125, 148-50; sulphur, 113; superphosphates, 153; telephones, 169-70; trade, 62f; wool, 144

chrome, 104

coal, 30, 96, 98-9, 120, 123f, 241

cobalt, 104

Cochin China, 15

coke (metallurgical), 150f

Cold War, v. confrontation

Colombia, 115

colonialism, 18, 23, 25, 27, 29, 98, 124, 126, 163f, 228

communications, Ch. 7

Communism, Communists, 17, 28, 125

Communist China, v. China: Mainland

Communist countries, aid, 225-6; trade, 69f

confrontation, 29, 108, 197

Congo, lead, 111-12; tin, 105-8

consumption goods, 88f

copper, 106, 109-10

cotton, 96, 139f

Cuba, aid, 226; iron, 102

customs duties, 200f

Czechoslovakia, 127

dairy products, 54f

debt (public, national), 192f

defence expenditure, 196-7

deficit budgeting, 188f

demonstration effect, 29, 91

Denmark, tin, 107; wool, 144

developed countries, 17-18, 22-4, 35; trade, 68; Japan one, 17

developing countries, 17-18, 24, 29, 35; trade, 68f

development budgets, 197-9

Development Decade, the, 37, 51, 46, 242

diamonds, 114

diet, v. nutrition

ECAFE (United Nations Economic Commission for Asia and the Far East), establishment, definition, 15; scope and membership, 15-17; work of, 19, 34, 36-7, 56, 243

electricity, 51, 121-3, 134f, 241; v. energy, hydro-

emigration, 33-5

energy, industrial, 134f, 241-2
Europe, aid, 224; area, 23; cement, 132-3; chemicals, 130f; cultural contrast with Asia, 21; ECE, 15; energy, 134f; industrial, Ch. 6, 155; iron, 102; national incomes, 230; railways, 166; shipping, 162f; steel, 127f; telephones, 169; trade, 68, 74; war effects, 26
exports, 63-4

family planning, 38, 40
famine, 44-5
fatalism, 25
fertilizers, 153
fibres, artificial, 29, 145f
Finland, gas, 139; gold, 115; paper, 152
fish(eries), 26, 52f, 96
food, 26-7; Ch. 3; aid, 45-6; farm-food balance, 57; imports, 58; India, 211; production, 120; trade, 86f; wartime, 26
foreign exchange, 46, 84-5
Formosa, v. China: Taiwan
France, 16, 17; aid, 203; cement, 132; iron, 102, 127f; tin, 106-7; wheat, 44
fuels, 86; 98f; v. coal, petroleum

gas, coal, 138-9
Germany, aid, 222; cement, 132-3; medical, 228; Nazi, 26; rubber, 148; silver, 115; steel, 127f; tin, 106; zinc, 111
Goa, v. Portuguese India (former)
gold, 114-5; India, 211
Governments, China, 216-17; Hong Kong, 218; India, 212-13; Indonesia, 204f; role, 27; state enterprises, 202
Gourou, P., 54
Greater East Asia Coprosperity Sphere, 26

health, 35-6, 40, 228
hemp, 96
hides and skins, 96
Higgins, B., 205-6
Hong Kong, 15-17, 29; aid, 24; area, 24; cement, 133; cotton, 139f; energy, 135f; exports, 24; fish, 53f; gas, 139; imports, 24; inflation, 233; iron, 101; labour, 126, 158; mail, 173f; medical, 227; motor vehicles, 168; national income, 24, 234f; population, 24, 33f; railway, 167; shipping, 160; steel, 125-6; telephones, 169-70; trade, 62f; tungsten, 109; unplanned economy, 217-18; wool, 144
housing, 228f
hydroelectricity, 135

imports, 62f
India, 15-16, 19, 21, 23; agriculture, 211, 239-40; aid, 24, 26, 28, 220f; aluminium, 113, 154; area, 24; asbestos, 113; budget, 180f; bureaucracy, 212; caustic soda, 153; cement, 132-3; cereals, 58f; chemicals, 131f; chrome, 104; coal, 99; copper, 110; cotton, 139f; customs duties, 201; development budget, 198; dairy products, 55; diamonds, 114; debt, 194f; energy, 135f, 211, 241; exports, 24; famine, 44; fertilizers, 153; fish, 53f; food, 43f, 211; gold, 115; housing, 228; imports, 24; industrial, 118f, 155, 157, 211; inflation, 231f; iron, 101-2, 148, 150-1; irrigation, 51, 211; labour, 126; lead, 111-12; lumber, 152; magnesite, 113; manganese, 103-4; medical, 227; motor vehicles, 154, 168; national income, 24, 133-4, 231f; nutrition, 56; paper, 153; petroleum, 99-100, 154; planning, 207-13; population, 24, 33f; productivity, 239f; radio, 154; railways, 167; salt, 114; shipping, 154, 160; soda ash, 153; steel, 125f, 150-1, 212; superphosphates, 153; taxes, 199f; telegraphs 170f; telephones, 169-70; tin, 107; trade, 61f, 97; transport, 211; tungsten, 109; TV, 154; welfare, 197, 211; wool, 144-5; zinc, 111
Indochina, 15-16, 19, 21, 26; steel, 125; trade, 62-3, 74
Indonesia, 15, 19; aid, 24, 26, 28; aluminium, 113; area, 24; budget, 182f; cement, 133; cereals, 58f; chemicals, 131f; coal, 99; cotton, 139f; customs duties, 201; debt, 192f; defence, 197; development budget, 198-9; energy, 135f, 241; exports, 24; fish, 53f; gas, 139;

gold, 115; imports, 24; industrial, 155; inflation, 232f; irrigation, 51; labour, 158; lumber, 152; mail, 173f; manganese, 104; medical, 227; motor vehicles, 168; national income, 24, 133-49, 232f; natural gas, 100; petroleum, 99-100, 154; planning, 204-5; population, 24, 33f; railways, 167; salt, 114; shipping, 160; taxes, 199f; telegraphs, 170f; telephones, 169-70; tin, 105, 107-8; trade, 62f; welfare, 197
Industrial Revolution; 23, 30, 148
industrialization, Ch. 6; 26-30, 88, 101, 155f, 242
industry, heavy and light, 28, 30, 117f; Japan, 155
inflation, 233f
infrastructure, 34, 203
Iran, 16
iron, 28, 30, 96, 101f, 127f, 129, 148f
irrigation, 50f
Israel, 228
Italy, 26; cement, 132; mercury, 112; tin, 107; zinc, 111

Japan, 15-17, 22, 25-7, 29, 37, 159; aid 220f; aluminium, 154; antimony, 112; asbestos, 113; budget, 191f; caustic soda, 153; cement, 132-3; cereals, 58f; chemicals, 130f; chrome, 104; coal, 99, 155; coke, 150-1; copper, 110; cotton, 139f; dairy products, 55f; energy, 135f, 241; fertilizers, 153; fibres, 145f; fish, 52f; food, 43f; gas, 138; gold, 115; housing, 228; industrial, 116f, 155, 157, 241f; inflation, 232f; iron, 148; labour, 126-7, 158; lead, 111-12; lumber, 152; mail, 173f; manganese, 104; manufactures, 155; meat, 54; medical, 227; mercury, 112; metals, 155; mining, 155; motor vehicles, 154, 168; national income, 133-4, 230f; natural gas, 100; nickel, 109; nutrition, 56; paper, 152-3; petroleum, 100, 154; planning, 215-16; population, 33f; postwar recovery, 30; productivity, 239f; radio, 154; railways, 167; rubber, 147-8; salt, 114; silver, 115; soda ash, 153; shipping, 154, 159f; steel, 125, 127f, 148, 150; superphosphates, 153; 'take-off', 122;

telegraphs, 170f; telephones, 169-70; tin, 105-7; trade, 61f; tungsten, 109; TV, 154; wood pulp, 152-3; wool, 144-5; zinc, 111
jute, 96

Kalimantan, v. Indonesia (n Borneo)
Keynesian economics, 92
Korea, North, 21, 26; chemicals, 131f; copper, 110; iron, 148, 150; lead, 112; lignite, 99; steel, 149f; trade, 69; zinc, 111
Korea, South, 15, 16; aid, 24-8, 220f; area, 24; budget, 183f; cereals, 58f; chemicals, 131f; coal, 99; copper, 110; cotton, 139f; customs duties, 201; defence, 197; energy, 135f; exports, 24; fertilizers, 153; fibres, 146f; fish, 53f; gold, 115; housing, 228; imports, 24; industrial, 155; inflation, 232f; iron, 101, 148, 150; irrigation, 51; labour, 126; lead, 112; mail, 173f; manganese 104; meat, 55; medical, 227; molybdenum, 105; motor vehicles, 168; national income, 24, 133, 231f; nickel, 109; paper 153; population, 24, 33f; railways, 167; salt, 114; shipping, 162; steel, 148-50; taxes, 199f; telephones, 169-70; tin, 107; trade, 62f; tungsten, 109; wool, 144; zinc, 111
Korean war boom, 80, 87, 105, 122-3

labour, 35, 126, 157-8
Laos, 15, 16, 105
Latin America, 24, 31, 32; aid, 224-5; cement, 133; chemicals, 131f; energy, 134; industrial, Ch. 6, 155; national incomes, 230; railways, 166; shipping, 162f; telephones, 169; trade, 69; v. UNECLA
lead, 111-12
lumber, 151-2; v. wood
Luxembourg, 139

Ma Yin-chü, 40
Macao, 17
magnesite, 113
mail, domestic, 173f; foreign, 174f
maize, 44f
Malaya (n Federation), Malaysia, 15, 16, 19, 21; aid, 24, 26, 220f; area, 24; aluminium, 113; budget, 184f;

cement, 133; chemicals, 131f; cereals, 58f; customs duties, 201-2; defence, 197; development budget, 198-9; energy, 135f; exports, 24; fish, 53f; food, 43f; gas, 139; gold, 115; housing, 229; imports, 24; industrial, 155; inflation, 232f; iron, 101; irrigation, 51; labour, 126-7; lignite, 99; lumber, 152; mail, 173f; motor vehicles, 168; national income, 24, 133, 231f; petroleum, 154; population, 24, 33f; railways, 167; steel, 125; taxes, 199f; telegraphs, 170f; telephones, 169-70; tin, 105-8; trade, 62-4, 97; welfare, 197

Manchuria, 26, 121
manganese, 96, 103-4
manufactures, 87, 117-18, 121f
Mao Tse-tung, Maoism, 28-30, 217
markets, 23
Marx(ism), 23, 28, 40
materialism, 25
meat, 54f
medical facilities, 36, 227-8
Mekong river, 21
mercury, 112-13
metals, 101f, 120f
Mexico, 99-100; cement, 133; chemicals, 131f; silver, 115; tin, 107
millet, 46f
minerals, mining, 23, 96-9, 120f
modernization, 25, 28, 37, 52
molybdenum, 104
Mongolia, Mongols, 16-17, 21
motor vehicles, 154, 168

national finances, Ch. 8
national incomes, 24-5, 37, 133, 230, 238
nationalism, 27, 29, 40
natural gas, 99-100, 120, 135
Near East, 24; aid, 224-5; chemicals, 132-3; energy, 134; industrial, 155, 159
Nepal, 16, 227
Netherlands, 16-17, 100; tin, 107
neutrality, 27
New Zealand, 16; aid, 222; cement, 133; chemicals, 132f; food, 54f; labour, 126-7; meat, 55; nutrition, 56f; productivity, 239f; trade, 68
Nicaragua, gold, 115
nickel, 108-9

Nigeria, tin, 105, 107-8
North America, 32; cement, 132; chemicals, 130f; energy, 134f; industrial, Ch. 6, 155; railways, 166; telephones, 169-70; trade, 68
North Borneo, v. Borneo, British
Norway, aid, 222
nutrition, 26, 42f, 48, 52, 55f, 60, 241

obsolescence, 27, 30
Oceania, 16, 31; energy, 134; industrial, 155; national incomes, 230; railways, 166; shipping, 162f; telephones, 169; trade, 68
OECD, aid, 222; Japan, 17
oilseeds, 96
organization, 27, 30, 37
output, 30

Pakistan, 15-16, 19, 23, 26; agriculture, 213, 220f; aid, 24, 215, 220f; aluminium, 113; antimony, 112; area, 24; budget, 185f, 198; cement, 133; cereals, 58f; chemicals, 131f; chrome, 104; coal, 99; cotton, 139f; defence, 197; energy, 135f, 241; exports, 24; fish, 53f; food, 43f, 213; housing, 229; imports, 24; industrial, 155; inflation, 232f; iron, 101; irrigation, 51, 213; labour, 126-7; mail, 173f; meat, 55; medical, 227; motor vehicles, 168; national income, 24, 133, 231f; natural gas, 100; paper, 153; petroleum, 100, 154; planning, 212-13; population, 24, 33f; productivity, 239f; railways, 167; shipping, 160; taxes, 199f; telegraphs, 170f; telephones, 169-70; trade, 61f; welfare, 197
paper, 120f, 152-3
Peru, chemicals, 132; fish, 53
petroleum, 84-5, 96, 99-100, 120, 123, 135, 154, 164
Philippines, 15-16, 19; aid, 24, 220f; area, 24; asbestos, 113; budget, 187f; cereals, 58f; cement, 133; chemicals, 131f; chrome, 104; copper, 110; cotton, 139f; customs duties, 202; debt, 194f; defence, 197; development budget, 198; energy, 135f; exports, 24; fertilizers, 153; fibres, 146f; fish, 53f;

food, 43f; gas, 139; gold, 115; housing, 229; imports, 24; industrial, 155; inflation, 232f; iron, 101; labour, 126, 157-8; lead, 112; lumber, 152; manganese, 104; meat, 55; medical, 227; mercury, 112; molybdenum, 105; motor vehicles, 168; national income, 24, 133, 231f; nutrition, 56f; petroleum, 154; planning, 205-6; population, 24, 33f; productivity, 239f; radio, 154; railways, 167; salt, 114; shipping, 160; taxes, 199f; telegraphs, 170f; telephones, 169-70; trade, 62f; TV, 154; wool, 144

phosphate, 113
planning, Ch. 9
plantations, 23, 49, 239
Poland, cement, 132; iron, 127; lead, 111-12; paper, 153
population, 19, 21, 24-5, 47, 51; Ch. 2; birth and death rates, 36f; occupational distribution, 126-7
Portuguese India (former), iron, 101; manganese, 104; salt, 114
Portuguese Timor, 17
potash, 113
potatoes, 28, 46f
poverty, 25, 27, 125, 227, 238; Maoist ethos, 28
power (industrial), v. energy
prices, 65, 87, 233f
primary products, v. raw materials
productivity, 237f
proteins, 56-7

quietism, 25

radio, 154
railways, 166f
rationing, 27
raw materials, 23, 29, 86, 96, Ch. 5, 122, 163
rayon, v. fibres
refugees, v. emigration
Region(s), defined, 15, 17-19; characteristics, 21-2; Regionalism, 26, 32
resources, Ch. 5; 28, 241
rice, 43f, 96
roads, 166
Roxas, S. K., 206
rubber, products, 120; synthetic, 29, 96, 147

Rumania, 99-100; wool, 144
rural areas, 30, 37, 40, 52; industries, 30

Sabah (North Borneo), energy, 138
salt, 113-14
Samoa, Western, 16
Sarawak (North Borneo), energy, 138; petroleum, 100
Scandinavia, wood pulp, 152
self-sufficiency, 26, 29, 213
shipping, 22, 26-7, 154, 159f
Siberia, 19, 159
silver, 115
Singapore, 15, 16, 29; energy, 135f; labour, 126-7, 157-8; meat, 55; population, 32f; shipping, 162; telephones, 169-70; trade, 67
social problems, 17, 24
soda ash, 153
sorghum, 46f
South Africa, 101-2; chemicals, 131f; gold, 115; national income, 230; trade, 68
South America, v. Latin America
Soviet, v. USSR
Spain, copper, 110
speculation, 211
spices, 96
standards of living, 29, 37, 40-1, 54-6, 59-60
steel, 28, 148f; consumption, 125; prices, 129; production, 127f
Sterling area, trade, Ch. 4
substitute materials, 29
sugar, 96
sulphur, 113
sulphuric acid, 129f
superphosphates, 153
Sweden, aid, 222; gold, 115; iron, 102
Switzerland, paper, 153

Taiwan (Formosa), v. China, Taiwan
taxation, 199f
tea, 96
technical assistance, 17
technology, technique(s), 28f, 30, 147, 241; nuclear, 28, 40; space, 28; technological gap, 29-31, 147f
telegraphs, 170f
telephones, 168-70
television, 153
terms of trade, 122, 129

textiles, 120f, 139f
Thailand, 15-16, 19, 21; aid, 24, 26, 220f; antimony, 112; area, 24; budget, 188f; cereals, 58f; chemicals, 131f; cotton, 139; debt, 192f; defence, 197; development budget, 198-9; energy, 135f; exports, 24; fish, 53f; food, 42f; imports, 24; industrial, 155; inflation, 232f; iron, 101; irrigation, 51; labour, 126; lead, 112; lignite, 99; lumber, 152; motor vehicles, 168; national income, 24, 133-4, 231f; population, 24, 33f; railways, 167; salt, 114; shipping, 162; steel, 125; taxes, 199f; telegraphs, 170f; telephones, 169-70; tin, 105-8; tungsten, 109; trade, 62f; welfare, 197
Tibet, 21
tin, 96, 104f; Agreements, 107; consumption, 106; price, 107-8
tobacco, 120
trade, international, Ch. 4; 22, 24-5; terms of, 87f; war effects, 26
transport, Ch. 7; 22, 34, 52; wartime, 26-7
tungsten, 109
Tunisia, gas, 139; lead, 111
Turkey, mercury, 113

underdeveloped countries, v. developing countries
Union of Soviet Socialist Republics (USSR), 16-19; aid, 203, 217; cement, 132-3; Central Asian, 19; chemicals, 130f; and China, 217; energy, 136f, 241; influence, 28-9, 32; iron, 102, 127; lumber, 151; manganese, 103; medical, 228; mercury, 112-13; nickel, 108; population, 32; salt, 114; Siberia, 19; tin, 107; trade, 70; wood pulp, 152
United Kingdom (UK), 16-17, 30; aid, 220f; budget, 191f; cement, 132; energy, 136f, 241; fertilizers, 153; fibres, 145f; housing, 229; iron, 101, 148; mail, 173f; medical, 227; motor vehicles, 168; paper, 152; petroleum, 100; radio, 154; railways, 167; rubber, 147; shipping, 160f; steel, 125, 127f, 149f; superphosphates, 153; taxes, 200; telegraphs, 170f; tin, 106; TV, 154; wood pulp, 152

United Nations (Organization) (UN), 37; aid, 223-4; Economic Commission for Africa (ECA), 15; Economic Commission for Asia and the Far East v. ECAFE; Economic Commission for Europe (ECE), 15; Economic Commission for Latin America (ECLA), 15; ECOSOC (Economic and Social Council), 15, 17; Food and Agricultural Organization (FAO), 42; Regional Commissions, 15; UNRRA (post-war relief agency), 22
urbanization, 38-9; v. housing
United States of America (USA), 16-17; aid, 203, 218f; area, 23; budget, 191f; caustic soda, 153; copper, 110; crop yields, 44; energy, 136f, 241; exports, 24; fertilizers, 153; fibres, 145f; gas, 138; housing, 229; iron, 102, 148; lead, 112; lumber, 151; mail, 173f; manganese, 103; medical, 227; mercury, 112; molybdenum, 104; motor vehicles, 168; natural gas, 100; petroleum, 100; radio, 154; railways, 167; salt, 114; shipping, 160f; silver, 115; soda ash, 153; steel, 125, 127f, 149f; sulphur, 113; superphosphates, 153; tin, 106-7; telegraphs, 170f; trade, 68f; TV, 154; wood pulp, 152
upland cultivation, 54

vanadium, 104
vegetables, 26, 50
Vietnam, North, cement, 133; chemicals, 131f; salt, 114; steel, 125; trade, 69
Vietnam, South, 15-16; aid, 24, 220f; area, 24; cereals, 58; chemicals, 131f; coal, 99; cotton, 139f; energy, 135f; exports, 24; food, 42f; housing, 229; imports, 24; inflation, 233f; lumber, 152; mail, 173f; meat, 55; medical, 227-8; national income, 24, 133-4; planning, 203; population, 24, 33f; railways, 167; salt, 114; shipping, 162; steel, 125; telegraphs, 170f; telephones, 169-70; trade, 67

war, effects of, 25f, 196-7, 211; Germany, 121; industrial, 116f, 120f; Japan, 159; North Korea, 99; trade, 65

welfare, 197; Ch. 11
Western World, Asia's dependence on, 22, 159f; relations with, 30
whaling, 54
wheat, 44f
wood, 96; v. lumber
wood pulp, 152-3
wool, 144-5
world economy, 25

xenophobia, 35

yams, v. potatoes
yields, crop, Ch. 3
Yugoslavia, 100-1; mercury, 113; wool, 144

zinc, 110

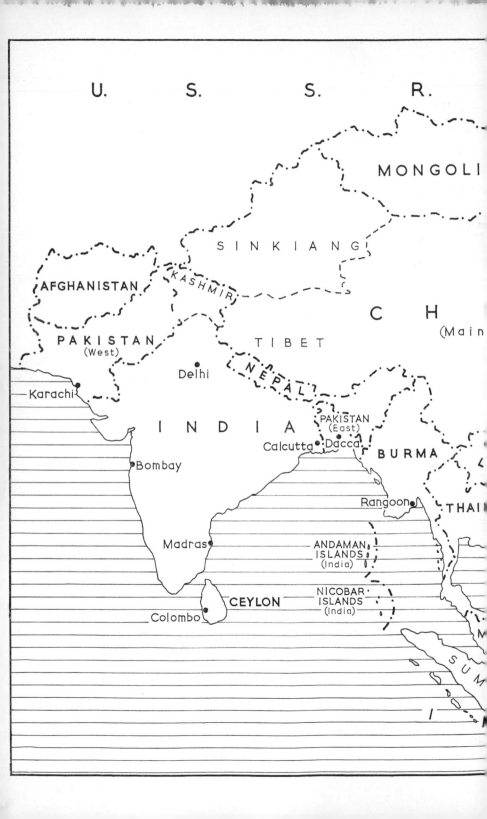